second skins

Gender and Culture Series
Edited by Carolyn G. Heilbrun
and Nancy K. Miller

second skins

The Body Narratives of Transsexuality

Jay Prosser

Columbia University Press
New York

Columbia University Press
Publishers Since 1893
New York   Chichester, West Sussex
Copyright © 1998 Columbia University Press
All rights reserved
Library of Congress Cataloging-in-Publication Data
Prosser, Jay.
    Second skins : the body narratives of transsexuality / Jay
  Prosser.
        p.   cm. — (Gender and culture)
    Includes bibliographical references and index.
    ISBN 978-0-231-10934-5 — ISBN 978-0-231-10935-2 (pbk.)
    1. Transsexualism. I. Title. II. Series.
  HQ77.9.P76   1998
  306.77—dc21   97-32529

Casebound editions of Columbia University Press books are
printed on permanent and durable acid-free paper.
Printed in the United States of America

For my parents

contents

Acknowledgments	ix
Introduction: On Transitions—Changing Bodies, Changing Narratives	1

Part 1: Bodies

1. Judith Butler: Queer Feminism, Transgender, and the Transubstantiation of Sex	21
2. A Skin of One's Own: Toward a Theory of Transsexual Embodiment	61

Part 2: Narratives

3. Mirror Images: Transsexuality and Autobiography	99
4. "Some Primitive Thing Conceived in a Turbulent Age of Transition": The Invert, *The Well of Loneliness*, and the Narrative Origins of Transsexuality	135
5. No Place Like Home: Transgender and Trans-Genre in Leslie Feinberg's *Stone Butch Blues*	171
Epilogue: Transsexuality in Photography—Fielding the Referent	207
Notes	237
Index	261

acknowledgments

This book took shape as a dissertation under the direction of Nancy K. Miller. Her unwavering support, her astute readings, and, of course, the example of her own work, have been indispensable to every step of my project's progress. I thank her here for her intellectual and professional guidance, for her personal generosity, and for providing me with a profound, pleasurable, and ongoing learning experience.

Others' interventions have been invaluable at various stages of the process. Joan Nestle was the first to read transsexual autobiographies with me as part of a field for my doctoral qualifying exams; her enthusiasm for their narratives and her question about home served as a crucial spur to the emergence of this project. Tom Hayes and Gerhard Joseph as members of my defense committee read the manuscript in dissertation form. I thank them for their incisive feedback on what was then very much a tome. My dissertation writing group helped me formulate ideas in the early stages; other readers to fine-tune those ideas in the all-important final stages. Of particular help en route have been friends and colleagues, Deirdre Day McLeod, Clare Hemmings, Deborah Nelson, and Victoria P. Rosner; my readers at Columbia University Press; and my editor there, Susan Heath. I thank Professor Constance Jordan, the Center for Lesbian and Gay Studies, and the City University of New York Graduate School English Department for awarding me fellowships that allowed me to focus on the writing, and faculty and colleagues throughout CUNY for their continued support of my work and welfare.

This book would not have been possible without the transsexual authors whose work is its subject. In addition to those who have allowed their photographs to be reproduced here, I thank especially those transgendered and transsexual authors, artists, autobiographers, and activists who have given time to discuss their work and my engagement with it; Leslie Feinberg, Zachary I. Nataf, Raymond Thompson, and Del LaGrace have been particularly treasured interlocutors, inspirations in themselves. For her generous interest in my work and the continuing provocation of her own take on transgender, Judith Halberstam has been a precious recent addition to this list; I have already benefited greatly from her direction and her camaraderie. I should also mention in this category my dear friend Katie Wasserman, since she has enabled me to make vital connections of all kinds—professional and personal. I trust that our transitions will continue to unfold together in rewarding ways.

Finally, I am grateful to my family—to my brother and his wife for their insider medical understanding—but especially to my parents; for it is their undeviating love, above all, that has made this narrative (the life as much as the book) followable.

second skins

> It is a matter of transitions, you see; the changing, the becoming, must be cared for closely.
> —Leslie Marmon Silko, *Ceremony*

introduction

On Transitions—Changing Bodies, Changing Narratives

Personal

I spent the bulk of the first month of my transsexual transition from female to male teaching an undergraduate course on the contemporary American novel. Scheduled over an intensive summer session, the class met for almost four hours a day, four days a week. My hormone treatment, beginning the week before the course, was comparably intensive. My endocrinologist believed in shocking my body into transition, starting me up on massive dosages of testosterone and leveling these off once my body had adjusted. Under this program not only did I experience rapid dramatic somatic changes, some of these became immediately apparent. My face squared off and my neck thickened; accumulating facial "fuzz" required shaving every few days; and, while it didn't crack, my voice deepened enough to get me an invariable "sir" over the phone. Within two weeks of the course ending, after just over a month of treatment, I was thus able to begin living full-time as a man, documents all changed to reflect a new, unambivalent status.

Although the minutiae of these somatic changes might have bypassed my students, I have no doubt that I failed to cut a clearly gendered figure in the class. In the world outside academia I was already passing as male almost consistently. Yet my profile at college would have led students to expect a female teacher. For the entire month my poor students remarkably, collectively, assiduously, and awkwardly avoided referring to me with a pronoun or a gendered title. The two exceptions occurred not in speech but in writing—in the absence of my body—in the logs students handed in weekly: one "Miss," which I circled viscerally; one "he," which I left unmarked. Students seemed to sex me individually (how not to make this most fundamental of identity assignments?), so their careful avoidance must have stemmed from their failure to reach consensus as a group—perhaps even a collective sense that I was going through some kind of significant transition.

The group's uncertainty on how to read me earned my immediate sympathy. Yet in no way did I seek to resolve its predicament. I felt unable, too caught up in my own predicament, the circumstances of teaching at this most transitional point in my transition. I did not feel I could present as a man in a department in which I had been known as a butch woman for five years and that I was anyway leaving that semester. At the same time I was so relieved to be moving away from femaleness that nothing could have persuaded me to anchor myself back to it, even provisionally. The obvious alternative—to have come out as a transsexual—I thought would have rooted rather than alleviated my students' confusion and discomfort. For, in common perception, to name oneself transsexual is to own precisely to being gender displaced, to being a subject in transition, moving beyond or in between sexual difference. So I left them uncomfortably (all of us horribly uncomfortable) leaving me to my ambivalence; and as the class progressed, this not attributing me with a gender, in my experience, became more and more glaring—a kind of deafening unspoken. In this gendered nonzone, I felt too embodied (only body) yet also disembodied: for what on earth did I embody? Not surprisingly, I was massively relieved once the course was over, and I sensed students felt similarly.

Some breathing space did open up toward the end of the course, however. One student gave a dazzling presentation on Leslie Marmon Silko's *Ceremony*, tracing the theme—of all things—of transition.[1] Of the novels assigned, *Ceremony* clearly frustrated students. It made them feel unconfident, uncertain of how to read. They couldn't place it: its hybrid characters; its plot that mixes and yet refuses to merge realistic historical moment and mythic quest; the novel's genre, its shifting affiliation to a modern psychological novel and a traditional Native ceremony. Staking its value to the course topics and to her own reading pleasure precisely on its treatment of transition, the presenting student mounted an inspiring defense of the novel. She argued that it was *Ceremony*'s layered investment in the theme of transition that the class was making its stumbling block, even as the importance of understanding and pursuing transition was the novel's very point. An intermediate nonzone, transition represents the movement in between that threatens to dislocate our ties to identity places we conceive of as essentially (in every sense) secure. Transition provokes discomfort, anxiety—both for the subject in transition and for the other in the encounter; it pushes up against the very feasibility of identity. Yet transition is also necessary for identity's continuity; it is that which moves us on.

Does it even need saying how I heard her presentation as a poignant metacommentary on my own dislocation in the course? With uncanny precision she appeared to cut through (and reveal in cross-section) the thick layers of anxiety that had coated our discussions. Even when she added an autobiographical postscript to her presentation, I found it impossible to disown or disembody transition. Revealing her entanglement in her interpretation of the novel and the class reading, the student described *her own* status as transitional: in her identity, consciously and complexly in between Native, Spanish, and Irish cultural heritages; and at this period of her life. My course marked her transition from college to beginning graduate school the following semester; it was part of her transition to making this kind of reading and thinking her career.

Instead of moving me away from my personal through hers, my student's revelation brought into relief (again, in my perspective) my own silence. My body had brought transition to the surface, embodied it as transsexual bodies in a disconcertingly literal way not unlike bodies "in between" racial difference do. Unlike my articulate student, however, I had remained unable to remark on, to reassure, or to confront others over my in-betweenness. In part I felt as though my experience of transition, my very movement in between, obturated any expression of my transsexuality, exceeded the grounds of its own speakability. But the difference between us—the fact of my student's "coming out" and my not— was also informed by the relation our respective bodies found to the narratives we were reading: by what we, as a class, had set up as speakable material. Her autobiographical voicing was patently prompted and supported by our reading of narratives of cultural crossing. If in contrast my body remained as unspeakable for me as it was unreadable for students, it was in part because narratives of sexual crossing lay outside our designated subject matter. Indeed, such narratives had yet to be formed into any kind of equivalent critical tradition.

Reading the narratives that follow here into the beginnings of such a tradition, this book works as a deferred return in writing to that absent act of articulation: so much easier with the body framed in narrative; so much easier now this body has a clearer gendered location. The question of how to represent the transitions of transsexuality, of how to put into narrative its remarkable bodily trajectories, is the preoccupation of the transsexual narratives examined in the chapters that follow here—and thus of the theoretical narrative of this project—as much as it was mine in my summer class. Without doubt, my turning as critic to write on transsexual narratives represents a displaced autobiographical act: "I chose to work, academically, *on* autobiography, because in a parallel direction I wanted to work *on* my own autobiography."[2] But articulating the transitions in these texts is not only an oblique means of articulating mine; it has also been quite profoundly a way of working on mine. For transsexuality is always narrative work, a transformation of the body that requires the remolding of the life into a particular narrative shape.

Material
Transsexuality consists in entering into a lengthy, formalized, and normally substantive transition: a correlated set of corporeal, psychic, and social changes. As the insider joke goes, transitioning is what transsexuals *do* (our occupation, as consuming as a career). While thoroughly interwoven in the body of my text, five senses of transition in application to the transsexual trajectory and its inscription in narrative may be separated here as a means of specifying the task of each chapter and of locking together the crucial terms of this book—body and narrative—in their relation to transsexuality.

My primary purpose in reading transsexual narratives is to introduce into cultural theory a trajectory that foregrounds the bodily matter of gender crossings. While theory is grappling with various forms of gendered and sexual transitions, transsexual narratives, stories of bodies in sex transition, have not yet been substantially read. Conceiving of transition first in a conceptual sense, I contend that we must make changes to our theoretical paradigms if we are to make room for the materiality of transsexual narratives. In the second and most substantial sense, I use transition to denote this ontological condition of transsexuality: the term transsexuals use to describe the physical, social, and psychic transformations that constitute transsexuality. In this sense I seek to substantiate transsexual identity, to reveal the materiality of the figure of transition. Third, I enlist transition in its narratological sense: transition as the definitive property of narrative, the progression and development that drives narrative and coheres its form. Reading transsexuality through narrative, I suggest that the resexing of the transsexual body is made possible through narrativization, the transitions of sex enabled by those of narrative. Fourth, in documenting the origins of transsexuality, I use transition in a historical sense: to describe the developments that take place in and between discourses of gender that allowed the transsexual to emerge as a classifiable subject. The specific circumstances of this historical emergence underline the investment of transsexual identity mutually in soma and narrative. Finally, I consider how transition as a geographic trope applies to transsexual narratives: that is, transsexuality as a passage through space, a journey from one location to another. In this sense transition serves as a key means by which transsexuals represent their relations not only to gendered belonging but to sexual communities and politics (lesbian, gay, straight, queer, and, most recently, transgendered). These different meanings of transition—conceptual, somatic, narrative, historico-discursive, and political—provide the theoretical scaffold for my critical reading of transsexual narratives and a frame for each chapter in turn.

First, then, conceptual transitions. This book begins with the argument that queer studies has made the transgendered subject, the subject who crosses gender boundaries, a key queer trope: the means by which not only to challenge sex, gender, and sexuality binaries but to institutionalize homosexuality as queer. With the focus on the gender-ambivalent subject, transition has become the lever for the queer movement to loosen the fixity of gender identities enough to enable affiliation and identification between gay men and lesbians. My project takes off from queer theory's investment in transgender—both sprung by it and beginning with it. Chapter 1 attends to the place of transgender in the early canon of queer theory—in particular in the writings of Judith Butler, for nowhere is the pivotal function of transgender in queer studies more evident or more intricate. Butler's interest in transgender undergoes its own transition moreover, her work moving from using the transgendered subject to "trouble" the naturalization of heterosexuality and sex to using the transsexual subject, the subject who crosses the bounds of sex, to mark the limits of the trouble the subject in transition can effect. While queer theory's and in particular Butler's focus on transgender makes my reading of transsexual narratives possible—transgender wouldn't be of the moment if not for the queer moment—this association of transsexuality with limits, and queer theory's limitations around transsexuality, make my project necessary. As Butler exemplifies, queer theory has written of transitions as discursive but it has not explored the bodiliness of gendered crossings. The concomitant of this elision of embodiment is that the transgendered subject has typically had center stage over the transsexual: whether s/he is transvestite, drag queen, or butch woman, queer theory's approbation has been directed toward the subject who crosses the lines of gender, not those of sex. Epitomizing the bodiliness of gender transition—the matter of sex the cross-dresser has been applauded for putatively defying—the transsexual reveals queer theory's own limits: what lies beyond or beneath its favored terrain of gender performativity.

Second Skins reviews and begins the task of redressing queer theory's elision of the experience of "trans" embodiment by focusing on transsexual narratives. It is imperative to read transsexual accounts now in order to flesh out the transgendered figure that queer theory has made prominent. If, for queer theory, transition is to be explored in terms of its deconstructive effects on the body and identity (transition as a symptom of the constructedness of the sex/gender system and a figure for the impossibility of this system's achievement of identity), I read transsexual narratives to consider how transition may be the very route to identity and bodily integrity. In transsexual accounts transition does not shift the subject away from the embodiment of sexual difference but more fully into it.

The first part of this book thus concerns bodies. From queer theory's deployment of transgender to disembody sex in chapter 1, I move in chapter 2 to my theory of the transsexual body: an examination of the ontological sense of transition, the actual somatic, psychic, and social shifts entailed in transsexuality. How do material reconfigurations enable the transsexual to feel sex-changed? How do transsexuals represent their experience of their bodies? Is there a substance to gendered body image that it can motivate somatic transition? Transsexuality reveals the extent to which embodiment forms an essential base to subjectivity; but it also reveals that embodiment is as much about feeling one inhabits material flesh as the flesh itself. In representing the subject's initial absence of and subsequent striving for this feeling, transsexual narratives contribute significantly to discussions of what constitutes the "matter" of the body in cultural theory, suggesting ways in which this matter may not be commensurable with the cultural construction of identity. Documenting the claims made by transsexual autobiographers about gendered embodiment before, during, and after transition, this chapter is my attempt to read individual corporeal experience back into theories of "the" body. As such, it is my most tentative chapter; for the task of addressing how the material flesh may resist its cultural inscription, because it goes against the flow of theory's insistence on the cultural constructedness of the body, can only be carried out at first, as Lynne Segal suggests, "with humbling tentativeness."[3]

Notions of the body's constructedness have a distinctively literal edge in the context of transsexuality. The overwhelming tendency in work that does address transsexual bodies is to isolate medical discourses to the exclusion of subjective accounts and to emphasize the transsexual's construction by the medical establishment. The transsexual appears as medicine's passive effect, a kind of unwitting technological product: transsexual subject only because subject to medical technology. Janice Raymond's lesbian feminist *The Transsexual Empire: The Making of the She-Male* set the precedent by arguing that the transsexual is the gender-stereotypical construct (and support) of a patriarchal medical establishment.[4] Dwight Billings and Thomas Urban's sociological critique likewise insisted on transsexuality as medicine's invention: "a socially constructed reality which only exists in and through medical practice." Combining theories of the social construction of illness and constructionism in postmodern culture with the transsexual's sexed reconstruction, Billings and Urban argued that not only does the medical establishment reify the gender-disturbed into transsexuals, it commodifies gender, creating the transsexual as consumer of simulated sex who buys into "an alluring world of artificial vaginas and penises."[5] Most recently, Bernice L. Hausman's *Changing Sex: Transsexuality, Technology and the Idea of Gender*—which represents itself as supplanting Raymond's book-length study only to replicate its key points—has added the Foucauldian ingredient to this stew of constructionist theories of transsexuality.[6]

Hausman argues that the transsexual is an historically engineered subject. Her thesis is that the transsexual was produced by endocrinology from the twenties and thirties and plastic surgery after the second world war when these developments in medical technology were brought together with the notion of authentic or true gender arrived at in the treatment of intersexuality. All of these readings represent the transsexual as archetypal constructed subject *because of* his or her medical construction. The literal somatic constructions of sex reassignment have been shunted all too automatically into the transsexual's culturo-technological construction.

Constructionist theories of transsexuality overwhelmingly fail to examine how transsexuals are constructing subjects: participants and actors who have shaped medical practices as much as they have been shaped by them. Even though in one of its chapters *Changing Sex* offers the first focus on transsexual autobiography, like Raymond and Billings and Urban before her, Hausman attributes unequivocal ideological power to medical practitioners, imaging transsexuals as the "dupes of gender" (taking literally the invented category of gender identity) and duplicitous (attempting to convince everyone else that gender identity is inherent). Consistently, approaches to the transsexual as a constructed effect—whether figuring her or him as the pawn, victim, or dupe of medical technology—preclude a discussion of transsexual agency: that is, the subject's capacity not only to initiate and effect his/her own somatic transition but to inform and redefine the medical narrative of transsexuality. While Hausman mentions transsexual agency (how could she read transsexual autobiography and not do so?), it is always only in conjunction with its being "not unproblematic."[7] Since she never commits really to outlining this agency, her gesture remains specious, lip service to the transsexual as prodigious object of her study. Indeed, beyond the reaches of the poststructuralist valorization (its essentialization) of construction, construction in fact connotes nothing positive. Construction in a more mainstream sense is overtly a means of devaluing and discriminating against what's "not natural," precisely to desubjectivizing the subject and—in the context of transsexuality—to invalidating the subject's claims to speak from legitimate feelings of gendered difference. "Transphobia" (literally, the fear of the subject in transition), the stigmatization of transsexuals as not "real men" and "real women," turns on this conception of transsexuals as constructed in some more literal way than nontranssexuals—the

Frankensteins of modern technology's experiments with sexual difference. Since their arguments merely recycle this popular stereotype into theory, what feminist Carroll Riddell writes with wonderful directness of *The Transsexual Empire* may be said of all of these theoretical narratives equally: "My living space is threatened by this book."[8]

Second Skins attempts to recreate the "living space" of transsexuals in cultural theory by reading the transsexual as authorial subject. Prioritizing transsexuals' own accounts over the medicodiscursive texts, I suggest that transsexual narratives place us in a stronger position to understand how dynamic and complex are the relations of authorship and authorization between clinicians and transsexuals and to reexamine the whole problematic of the subject's construction in postmodern theory. The second half of this book attends to narrative, to the ways in which transsexuals have authored their plots in dialogue with medical discourse. In the third sense of transition as narrative, chapter 3 considers how transsexuality is a matter of constructing a transsexual narrative *before* being constructed through technology. The transsexual's capacity to narrativize the embodiment of his/her condition, to tell a coherent story of transsexual experience, is required by the doctors before their authorization of the subject's transition. As they remain invested in the therapeutic/analytic origins of the transsexual story, published transsexual autobiographies underline the continuing importance of narrative for transsexual subjectivity: where transsexuality would heal the gendered split of transsexuality, the form of autobiography would heal the rupture in gendered plots. Narrative is not only the bridge to embodiment but a way of making sense of transition, the link between locations: the transition itself.

The transsexual was not officially "invented" until 1949 when David Cauldwell diagnosed as a "psychopathic transexual" a female who identified as a man and wrote to Cauldwell seeking treatment with hormones and surgery.[9] In 1953 Harry Benjamin began to outline what would become in the psychiatric and medical arena the foundational theory of "transsexualism." His first formulations emphasize its distinctiveness from transvestism on the one hand (transsexuality is concerned more severely with body not dress)[10] and homosexuality on the other (transsexuality is concerned with sex and gender and not sexuality, in spite of that misleading suffix).[11] Yet was transsexual subjectivity simultaneous with its discursive naming, as absolutist constructionist theories would have it? Arguing that it was not, that this naming of transsexuality was rather a response to preexistent transsexual identity patterns and indeed embodiments, chapter 4 examines the historical transitions around the body, gender, and sexuality that made possible the official emergence of transsexual subjectivity. The discourse of inversion in turn-of-the-century sexology, its medicalization of transgender in the body, provided the significant threshold under which the transsexual as a sex-changeable and indeed sex-changed subject could make his/her first appearance. Sexology's case histories reveal subjects seeking out (and sometimes achieving) somatic transitions before the invention of the transsexual as a discursive subject, before sex hormones and plastic surgery had been decided by clinicians as treatment for the condition—indeed, before the condition had even been recognized as such. The first transsexual to effect a full somatic transition (surgery and hormones) did so several years before the medical diagnosis was written. Female-to-male Michael Dillon convinced a doctor to prescribe testosterone pills in 1939; underwent a double mastectomy in 1942; and began in 1945 a series of operations to construct the first female-to-male phalloplasty, effectively harnessing this technology for transsexuality and shaping the female-to-male narrative. Like other personal accounts, Dillon's story is significant for demonstrating how transsexuality constitutes an active subjectivity that cannot be reduced to either technological or discursive effect.[12]

Lesbian and gay historians have read sexology's cross-gender taxonomies as the medicalization of homosexuality. In so doing, they have dismissed as heterocentric constructs for homosexuality both its transgendered paradigms and its rendering of identity as embodied and diagnosable. However, individual case histories validate both the sexologists' prioritization of the categories of cross-gender identification over those of same-sex desire and their sense of the embodiment of this transgender condition; among the case histories of sexual inverts, we find our first transsexual narratives. If sexology's medicalization represents the bogy in the modern history of homosexuality, I argue that for transsexuals sexology in fact represents the crucial medicalization of transgender, the transitional discourse necessary for enabling the transsexual to bring about a somatic transition. Chapter 4 drives home the transsexual significance of inversion by recasting the famous invert novel, Radclyffe Hall's *The Well of Loneliness*, from canonical lesbian text to foundational transsexual narrative.[13] Situating *The Well* alongside the contemporaneous sexological case histories, I read the novel to elucidate the problematics of inversion in the text and the surrounding literary critical debates as transsexual.

In the new discourse of transgender in our own fin de siècle, homosexuality and transgender, lesbian and transsexual become significantly reentangled. Another shake of the discursive kaleidoscope and new relations between sex, gender, and sexuality, some frictional, some interconstitutive, allow for yet new identities to be named. Chapter 5 reads Leslie Feinberg's *Stone Butch Blues: A Novel* to examine, through the figure of the transgendered stone butch, the difference of contemporary transgendered narratives, the way in which this difference refolds those between transsexual and queer.[14] In my fifth sense of transition I ask: to what "home" does the trajectory of transition lead the transitioning subject? The female protagonist of *Stone Butch Blues* moves away from a lesbian origin though somatic transition but without finding refuge in transsexual man. Refusing to close on a transsexual transition, she makes of transition itself a transgendered subjectivity—of the movement in between a destination. Feinberg's departure from conventions is symptomatic of a larger political transition underway: the creation precisely of a transgender *movement*—a politics and culture of transition. If transsexual has been conceived conventionally as a transitional phase to pass through once the transsexual can pass and assimilate as nontranssexual—one begins as female, one becomes a transsexual, one is a man—under the aegis of transgender, transsexuals, now refusing to pass *through* transsexuality, are speaking en masse as transsexuals, forming activist groups, academic networks, transgender "nations." No longer typically ending transition, transsexuals are overtly rewriting the narrative of transsexuality—and transsexual narratives—as open-ended.

Ultimately, I understand this refusal to disappear as strategic, its purpose to produce transgendered and transsexual as specific and, importantly, allied subjectivities. Transgendered narratives as much as transsexual ones continue to attest to the valences of cultural belonging that the categories of man and woman still carry in our world: what I term "gendered realness." That is, transsexual and transgendered narratives alike produce not the revelation of the fictionality of gender categories but the sobering realization of their ongoing foundational power; and why hand over gendered realness when it holds so much sway? While coming out is necessary for establishing subjectivity, for transsexuals the act is intrinsically ambivalent. For in coming out and staking a claim to representation, the transsexual undoes the realness that is the conventional goal of this transition. These narratives return us to the complexities and difficulties that inevitably accompany real-life experiences of gender crossing and to the personal costs of not simply being a man or a woman. In accounts of individual lives, outside its current theoretical figuration transition often proves a barely livable zone.

In closing this book, I read a selection of photographs of transsexuals that capture the contradictions entailed in transsexual (self-)representation in poignantly material ways. Photographs of transsexuals seek to represent the transsexual's transition, to expose in the photographic image the difference of transsexuality. Yet at the same time they also work to conceal this difference, their very purpose to show that, posttransition, we look just the same as you. The transsexual's doubled bid to the referentiality of sex and to representation as a transsexual, to bodily realness and to telling the narrative of this route to realness, is caught graphically in the photographic medium's own peculiar situation between referentiality and representation.

Categorical

If its critical purpose is to introduce transsexual narratives as a set of texts with shared concerns about transition, the theoretical purpose of this book is to call for and initiate transitions in our paradigms for writing bodily subjects. My compound "body narrative" is intended to spin out the broader implications of transsexuality for contemporary theory, to allow transsexuality through its narratives to bring into view the materiality of the body. Many theorists have recently expressed discontent with contemporary discussions of the body—in particular, with their tendency to elide bodily materiality. Elizabeth Grosz contends that the "[t]he body has remained a conceptual blind spot in both Western philosophical thought and contemporary feminist theory."[15] Her "corporeal feminism" is one attempt to angle the mirror so as to bring this blind spot into view. A glance at any number of new titles shows bodies are everywhere in contemporary cultural theory; yet the paradox of theory's expatiation upon bodies is that it works not to fill in that blind spot so much as to enlarge it. That the human body has become centralized in our theory is a sure sign, as Cécile Lindsay astutely observes, that "our postmodern sensibility desires to make contact with some ground, with the physical stripped of metaphysical pretensions. This physical ground would be the body."[16] The irony is that the focus on bodies as effects or products of discourse re-metaphysicalizes bodies, placing their fleshy materiality even further out of our conceptual reach.

Is this paradox about the body—the body's materiality slips our grasp even as we attempt to narrate it—our inevitable poststructuralist legacy? Certainly, in Foucault and Lacan, our key legators, materiality figures only in reference to discourse and signification: in Foucault, to institutions, technologies, ideologies; in Lacan, to language and the signifier. In neither does materiality refer to the flesh. Materiality is our subject, but the body is not our object. The body is rather our route to analyzing power, technology, discourse, language. As Somer Brodribb remarks in her materialist feminist critique of postmodernism (of which she conceives Foucault and Lacan along with Derrida as founding fathers: disembodying matter for her is a repudiation of the feminine, mat(t)er, the mother), "[w]ith the modern alchemists, the flesh is made word." We have signification without referents, and "genders without sexes."[17] Tracing the "contemporary fetishization of 'discourse'" specifically to Lacan's return to Freud, Marcia Ian argues similarly of Lacanian psychoanalysis that it has effected "the conflation of *soma* and *seme* typical of fetishism": "The body itself, reduced to being an idea—and somebody else's idea at that—joins the ranks of the unknowable."[18] The materiality of language in contemporary thought has taken the place of the materiality of the body—as in Freud's scene of fetishism the boy mistakes his projection for the referential mother. If sexual difference is where the body's materiality is most displaced as these feminist analyses suggest, transsexuality, the attempt to materialize this difference in the body, may be the matter to recall theory to the residue of referentiality in the body.

The importance of making transitions in our conceptual paradigms for thinking bodies becomes particularly clear when we examine how transsexuals have been represented in cultural theory thus far. Since the body is conceived as a discursive effect, in terms of signification, the transsexual is read as either a literalization of discourse—in particular the discourse of gender and sexuality—or its deliteralization. In operation has been a binary pivoting on the literal—surely the most repudiated category in postmodernism and poststructuralism, whether in its association with the body, experience or language. When figured as literalizing gender and sexuality, the transsexual is condemned for reinscribing as referential the primary categories of ontology and the natural that poststructuralism seeks to deconstruct: "Transsexualism literalizes the loss patriarchy tropes as woman," writes Carole-Anne Tyler. Lacanian Catherine Millot sees a similar conflation at work: "In their requirement of truth . . . transsexuals are the victims of error. They confuse the organ and the signifier." Marjorie Garber condemns the identical collapse of signifier into referent in the language of poststructuralist theory: transsexuals "*essentialize* their genitalia." And June L. Reich dismisses transsexuality as retrogressively conformist for these reasons: "A word about transsexuality: it works to stabilize the old sex\gender system by insisting on the dominant correspondence between gender desire and biological sex."[19] If the transsexual is conceived as literalizing in accounts that seek to deliteralize the body, it is not surprising that his/her experience has been deemed worth little more than "a word" in cultural theory, that the narratives of transsexuality have yet to be carefully read.

Yet contrarily, contemporary theory has also located the transsexual on the other side of its literalism binary, reading him/her antithetically as deliteralizing the gendered body. If in the first mode of reading the transsexual is condemned for positing a sexed body before language, in the second mode the transsexual is celebrated for pushing sex as a linguistic signifier beyond the body. "[W]hat is more *postmodern* than transsexualism?" ask Julia Epstein and Kristina Straub. Their rhetorical question assumes that what is postmodern about transsexuality is self-evident: a *petitio principi*. Likewise, for Arthur and Marilouise Kroker transsexuality creates sex as it should be in our postmodern age, sex free from the body: "sex [that] has fled its roots in the consanguinity of nature, refused its imprisonment in the phallocentric orbit of gender." And for Judith Halberstam the transsexual is the apogee of postmodern identity, transition illustrating that the sex/gender system is a fiction: "We are all transsexuals except that the referent of the *trans* becomes less and less clear (and more and more queer). We are all cross-dressers but where are we crossing from or to what? There is no 'other' side, no 'opposite' sex, no natural divide to be spanned by surgery, by disguise, by passing. We all pass or we don't. . . . There are no transsexuals."[20] We are all transsexuals and there are no transsexuals. Transsexuals 'r' us, full of postmodern liberatory promise, their very constructedness encapsulating the essential inessentiality, what we take for granted as the unnaturalness of the body. In readings that embrace the transsexual as deliteralizing as much as those that condemn the transsexual as literalizing, the referential transsexual subject can frighteningly disappear in his/her very invocation. Like the materiality of the body, the transsexual is the very blind spot of these writings on transsexuality. Juxtaposing both sets of readings, it becomes clear that neatly superimposed on the literalizing/deliteralizing binary is another binary, that of the reinscriptive versus the transgressive. In so much contemporary theory this "fear of the literal"[21] (what we might term referential panic: the enormous pressure to disown, to abrogate the referent) encodes all literalizing as hegemonic ("bad") and all deliteralizing as subversive ("good"). It's become an unfortunately formulaic way of reading in a body of thought that otherwise purports to value multiplicity, difference, and the deconstruction of binaries. Indeed, it's become a way of not attending to the specificity of narratives.

Both of these binaries (literalizing/deliteralizing; reinscriptive/transgressive), and in particular the way in which they shore up the "current thinking routines of 'theory,' " come in for critique in an essay that represents an extraordinary moment in poststructuralist theory, Eve Kosofsky Sedgwick and Adam Frank's, "Shame in the Cybernetic Fold: Reading Silvan Tomkins."[22] Sedgwick and Frank argue that structuring contemporary theory is a mechanical antiessentialism, operative especially in discourse on bodies. So foundational is this "automatic" (512) or "reflexive antibiologism" (513), so much are we accustomed to awarding value proportionately according to the "distance of any such account from a biological basis," they suggest, that " 'theory' has become almost simply coextensive with the claim (you can't say it often enough), *it's not natural*"(513). What has become most routine in theory is the evaluation of all representations on the basis of whether they reveal ("good": antiessentialist) or conceal ("bad": essentialist) their constructedness. And, as all routines are restrictive, this practice limits interpretative frameworks, effectively imposing a constraint on the variety of narratives: we are stuck with an "impoverishing reliance on a bipolar analytic framework that can all too adequately be summarized as 'kinda subversive, kinda hegemonic' " (500). The binary of textual effect (subversive/hegemonic) is calcified onto the binary of the subject's relations to referentiality (literalizing/deliteralizing).

Admittedly, poststructuralist theory has always produced self-reflexive critiques of its own routines (indeed, this self-reflexive self-subversion might be thought characteristically poststructuralist); and the pervasive antiessentialism on which Sedgwick and Frank fix has been this type of work's most recurrent concern, surely because "essence" (under the aegis of the literal) has been poststructuralism's most targeted category.[23] But Sedgwick and Frank's intervention is startling and exceptional in two ways: first, for the enchanting and quite essentialist affectivity that characterizes their reading of the affect narratives of psychologist Silvan Tomkins, an essentiality that manifests itself in talk of the experience of sheer joy felt in the rhythms of Tomkins's prose; and second, for the essay's specific authorial circumstances. As Sedgwick's own work has been (as the essay acknowledges) significantly "responsible for [the] popularization [of theory's trends]," her critique of these trends marks an exquisite folding back of her thinking in on itself, a startling circumscription of its own former achievements (512, n. 14). For both reasons the effect of reading "Shame in the Cybernetic Fold" on those of us steeped in the practices of poststructuralist theory is precisely that of the *gestalt* Sedgwick and Frank wish it to be. And this is especially true for those of us turning our dissertations into first books, a category in which I am included. For the dissertation/first book, as Sedgwick and Frank remark in singling out a scholar's dissertation-revised-as-first-book for their critique of theory's routines, is the "rite of passage whose conventions can best dramatize the economy of transmission" that leads precisely to such institutional routinizing of critical practices (512, n.14). The dissertation/first book functions in part as a sign that we recognize and can practice our discipline's "routines."

If it is within these theory routines that the transsexual has been caught up and rigidly binarized, I want to use this "disciplinary routine" to break with some of those routines. It seems clear that it cannot be adequate to reduce the complex body of work—sometimes essentialist and biologistic—that transsexual narratives represent to these two operative binaries: literal/deliteralizing; subversive/hegemonic. But so thoroughly do these frameworks imbue our current critical methods that it is impossible simply to move "beyond" them. Sedgwick and Frank's essay suggests that, as we need to resist herding our readings into the enclosure of these binaries ("binary homogenization"), we also need to refrain from reading as if they didn't matter, as if they held no sway ("infinitizing trivialization") (512). Perhaps we might begin our conceptual transitions by reading transsexual narratives to rupture the identity between the binaries, opening up a transitional space between them. This task is both required and enabled by transsexual narratives precisely as they are body narratives: texts that engage with the feelings of embodiment; stories that not only represent but allow changes to somatic materiality. Along the way the category that we will need to reevaluate most is that of the literal, of what's essential. To the extent that transsexual narratives cannot be read without our accounting for the subjective experience of being transgendered, reading them necessitates our taking at every step what Sedgwick and Frank term—it's a phrase that's been much circulated recently—"the risk of essentialism" (513). That is, to the extent that they are written out of experience, the body, sex, feeling, belief in an immanent self, reading transsexual body narratives necessitates our using these categories that we have come to believe require deconstructing a priori. Transsexuality might then be valued for providing the recalcitrance of bodily matter—what Sedgwick and Frank term the "inertial friction of a biologism" (512)—that reopens the space between the strictures of binaries and the meaninglessness of infinity, the wedge that drives specificity back into our reading of texts. The transitions of transsexuality are densely layered, unpredictable, so that, indeed, "the changing, the becoming, must be cared for closely." And in the context of that reading the anxiety that transitions bring with them might well prove what is most constructive: the very braking mechanism for slowing our critical trajectory to ensure that we read these—and from these, other—narratives of sex and gender closely and articulate their transitions carefully.

part one **bodies**

> There is little time for grief in the *Phenomenology [of Spirit]* because renewal is always close at hand. What seems like tragic blindness turns out to be more like the comic myopia of Mr. Magoo whose automobile careening through the neighbor's chicken coop always seems to land on all four wheels. Like such miraculously resilient characters of the Saturday morning cartoon, Hegel's protagonists always reassemble themselves, prepare a new scene, enter the stage armed with a new set of ontological insights—and fail again. As readers, we have no other narrative option but to join in this bumpy ride.
>
> —Judith Butler, *Subjects of Desire: Hegelian Reflections in Twentieth-Century France*

chapter 1

Judith Butler: Queer Feminism, Transgender, and the Transubstantiation of Sex

Transgender and the Queer Moment

> Queer is a continuing moment, movement, motive—recurrent, eddying, troublant. The word "queer" itself means across—it comes from the Indo-European root *twerkw*, which also yields the German *quer* (transverse), Latin *torquere* (to twist), English athwart.
>
> —Eve Kosofsky Sedgwick, *Tendencies*

In its earliest formulations, in what are now considered its foundational texts, queer studies can be seen to have been crucially dependent on the figure of transgender. As one of its most visible means of institutionalization, queer theory represented itself as traversing and mobilizing methodologies (feminism, poststructuralism) and identities (women, heterosexuals) already, at least by comparison, in institutionalized place. Seized on as a definitively queer force that "troubled" the identity categories of gender, sex, and sexuality—or rather revealed them to be always already fictional and precarious—the trope of crossing was most often impacted with if not explicitly illustrated by the transgendered subject's crossing their several boundaries at once: both the boundaries between gender, sex, and sexuality and the boundary that structures each as a binary category.

Even in Eve Kosofsky Sedgwick's work, which has argued most trenchantly for "a certain irreducibility" of sexuality to gender, and thus one might deduce would follow a certain irreducibility of *homo*sexuality to *trans*gender, homophobic constructions are understood to be produced by and productive of culturally normative gender identities and relations.[1] The implications of this include a thorough enmeshing of homosexual desire with transgender identification. In its claim that women in the nineteenth century served to mediate desire between men, Sedgwick's *Between Men: English Literature and Male Homosocial Desire* suggests that the production of normative heterosexuality depended on a degree of male identification—and yet importantly, the disavowal of this identification—with woman as the object of desire.[2] At the beginnings of queer therefore, in what is arguably lesbian and gay studies' first book, heterosexuality is shown to be constructed through the sublimation of a cross-gendered identification; for this reason, making visible this identification—transgendered movement—will become the key queer mechanism for deconstructing heterosexuality and writing out queer.

Sedgwick's next book foregrounds this methodological function of transgender explicitly. *Epistemology of the Closet* presents transgender as one good reason for the development of a theory of (homo)sexuality distinct from feminism. The critical visibility of transgender—"the reclamation and relegitimation of a courageous history of lesbian trans-gender role-playing and identification"—poses a challenge to lesbianism's incorporation within feminism: "The irrepressible, relatively class-nonspecific popular culture in which James Dean has been as numinous an icon for lesbians as Garbo or Dietrich has for gay men seems resistant to a purely feminist theorization. It is in these contexts that calls for a theorized axis of sexuality as distinct from gender have developed."[3] Exceeding feminism's purview of gender, transgender demands and contributes to the basis for a new queer theory; paradoxically, transgender demands a new theory of sexuality. It is transgender that makes possible the lesbian and gay overlap, the identification between gay men and lesbians, which forms the grounds for this new theory of homosexuality discrete from feminism. And it is surely this overlap or cross-gendered identification between gay men and lesbians—an identification made critically necessary by the AIDS crisis—that ushers in the queer moment.

Most recently in her autobiographical narratives and performance pieces, Sedgwick has revealed her personal transgendered investment lying at and as the great heart of her queer project. Her confession of her "identification? Dare I, after this half-decade, call it with all a fat *woman's* defiance, my identity?—as a gay man" "comes out" with the transgendered desire that has been present in her work all along.[4] Similarly in its readings, *Tendencies* derives its queer frisson openly and consistently from an identification across genders: a mobility "across gender lines, including the desires of men for women and of women for men," a transgendered traversal that in its queering (skewing and unraveling) of apparently normative heterosexuality is simultaneously a movement across sexualities.[5] To summon the queer moment, the book begins with a figure for transgender—gay men wearing DYKE T-shirts and lesbians wearing FAGGOT T-shirts.

But Sedgwick is just the tip of the iceberg. The transgendered presence lies just below the surface of most of lesbian and gay studies' foundational texts. Early work on the intersections of race, gender, and sexual identities theorized otherness as produced through a racist, homophobic, and sexist transgendering, and thus again transgendering became the means to challenging this othering. Kobena Mercer's work on the fetishizing/feminizing white gaze of Robert Mapplethorpe at the black male body; Cherríe Moraga's description of the hermaphroditic convergence of the chingón and the chingada; Gloria Anzaldúa's memory of the mita' y mita' figure in the sexual, gender, and geographic borderlands: these various cross-gendered figures emerged both as constructions and, in their articulation by these critics, deconstructions of cultural ideologies that insist on absolute difference in all identity.[6] Other early lesbian and gay studies work invested in the transgendered subject's "trans" a transgressive politics. For Teresa de Lauretis, Sue-Ellen Case, Jonathan Dollimore, and Marjorie Garber whether appearing in contemporary lesbian cinematic representations of butch/femme desire, in theatrical crossdressing in early modern England, or as popular cultural gender-blending icons, the transgendered subject made visible a queerness that, to paraphrase Garber, threatened a crisis in gender and sexual identity categories.[7] Crucial to the idealization of transgender as a queer transgressive force in this work is the consistent decoding of "trans" as incessant destabilizing movement between sexual and gender identities. In short, in retrospect, transgender *gender* appears as the most crucial sign of queer *sexuality's* aptly skewed point of entry into the academy.

Without doubt though, the single text that yoked transgender most fully to queer sexuality is Judith Butler's *Gender Trouble: Feminism and the Subversion of Identity*.[8] *Gender Trouble*'s impact was enormous: published in 1990, appearing with the decade, it transformed transgender into a queer icon, in the process becoming something of an icon of the new queer theory itself. Yet how this actually happened, how *Gender Trouble* imbricated queer with transgender, and how the book itself was imbricated with transgender forms something of an intriguing critical phenomenon. For the embodied subject of transgender barely occupies the text of *Gender Trouble*—a book very much, after all, about subjects' failure of embodiment. As Butler herself states in remarking her surprise at the tendency to read *Gender Trouble* as a book about transgendered subjects, "there were probably no more than five paragraphs in *Gender Trouble* devoted to drag [yet] readers have often cited the description of drag as if it were the 'example' which explains the meaning of [gender] performativity." From this later point, her 1993 essay "Critically Queer," Butler clearly challenges the equation of transgender and homosexuality, or to be precise, the construction of transgender as the only sign of a deconstructive homosexuality: "cross-gendered identification is not the exemplary paradigm for thinking about homosexuality, although it may be one."[9] Yet the effect of *Gender Trouble* was precisely to secure transgender as a touchstone of lesbian and gay theory. How did *Gender Trouble* canonize, and how was it canonized for, a theory of transgender performativity that was apparently not its substance?

In the first essay appearing in the first edition of the first academic journal devoted to lesbian and gay studies, *glq: A Journal of Lesbian and Gay Studies*, itself a canonical moment in queer studies, Sedgwick comments on *Gender Trouble*'s canonically queer status: "Anyone who was at the 1991 Rutgers conference on Gay and Lesbian Studies [another canonizing mechanism], and heard *Gender Trouble* appealed to in paper after paper, couldn't help being awed by the productive impact this dense and even imposing work has had on the recent development of queer theory and reading." Surmising that these invocations were not indicative of an uncomplicated loyalty to *Gender Trouble* however, Sedgwick goes on to suggest that "the citation, the *use* of Butler's formulations in the context of queer theory will prove to have been highly active and tendentious."[10] That *Gender Trouble* was subject to a set of reiterations and recitations proliferating meanings beyond the intention of the "original" might be considered especially fitting given its own attraction toward Foucauldian proliferation as the effective means for denaturalizing copies that pretend to originality. Its argument about recitation lent an amenability to its own recitation. There's something very campy, very definitively queer, about readings that refused to adhere to the letter of Butler's argument, that refused, to use its vernacular, to "repeat loyally." The original underwent a certain overreading, playful exaggeration, a mischievous adding of emphasis, yet nevertheless remained a discernible referent.

Camp may in fact be quite fundamental to our reading of *Gender Trouble* and our understanding of its transgender import. In his introduction to his anthology on camp (one of two anthologies on camp that appeared soon after *Gender Trouble*) David Bergman nominates Butler as "the person who has done the most to revise the academic standing of camp and to suggest its politically subversive potential."[11] Bergman stakes that her success in queer studies comes in part from bringing to camp a high theoretical tone—and, we might add, from bringing camp to high theory. Pushing further on the connections between camp, queer, and the argument of *Gender Trouble*, it might be said that Butler's centrality in queer theory is in part an effect of queer's recuperation of camp and queer's recuperation *through* camp. The late eighties/early nineties, simultaneous with the beginnings of queer theory, saw the cultural and political reappropriation of camp, and the history of the term "queer" is most symptomatic of this. From homophobic epithet designating and reinforcing the other's social abjection to self-declared maker of community pride, "queer" was reclaimed precisely according to the transformative mechanisms of camp in which what has been devalued in the original becomes overvalued in the repetition. In turn, in its queer reevaluation, camp has proven a key strategy for queer theory's own institutionalization, a means by which to piggyback into the academy on (appropriating and redefining) already established methodologies. *Between Men*, for instance, deployed a distinctive camp style in subjecting canonical nineteenth-century literature to deliberate yet wonderfully subtle overreadings that brought to the surface its sexual subtexts. In its academic manifestation, camp actually comes to appear a form of queer deconstruction, not simply inverting the opposition between the original and the copy, the referent and the repetition but creating, according to Scott Long, a third space, "a stance, detached, calm, and free, from which the opposition as a whole and its attendant terms can be perceived and judged."[12] This third space, this queer deconstruction, is surely queer theory.

It is certainly this camp inversion of the expected order of terms to elucidate the construction of the original that forms the very pith of *Gender Trouble*'s theory: the subject does not precede but is an effect of the law; heterosexuality does not precede but is an effect of the prohibition on homosexuality; sex does not precede but is an effect of the cultural construction of gender. Butler's argument consistently reverses the expected history between the two terms in each formulation to bring them into a third space where each opposition as a whole can be perceived and judged. The binaries of sexual difference that undergird what Butler terms "the metaphysics of sex" are fragmented and mobilized with a Derridean flourish into sexual *différance* (*GT* 16). The driving sensibility of *Gender Trouble*'s theory is in this respect an archetypically camp one. Although the embodied transgendered subject doesn't occupy *Gender Trouble* in any substantial way, it is this camp reversal of terms that conveys the sense that the transgendered subject of drag is always in the margins of the text, the implicit referent (ironically given Butler's use of camp/drag's function to displace the referent). For it as the *personification* of camp—the third/intermediate term that reveals the constructedness of the binary of sex, of gender, and of the sex/gender system—that queer studies has anointed the transgendered subject queer. "Critically Queer" 's reading of *Gender Trouble*'s reception is thus absolutely right. Transgendered subjects, butches and drag queens, did come to appear the empirical examples of gender performativity, their crossing illustrating both the inessentiality of sex and the nonoriginality of heterosexuality that was the book's thesis. And those five paragraphs or so where *Gender Trouble* does explicitly address the subject in drag certainly do nothing to contradict this conception of transgender as exemplarily camp/queer/performative: "*In imitating gender, drag implicitly reveals the imitative structure of gender itself—as well as its contingency*" (*GT* 137). In this sentence (particularly given that the italics appear in the original), transgender's function is unambivalently and emphatically that of the elucidating example of gender performativity.

This chapter charts the achievement of and challenges that association, transgender/camp/queer/performativity. That transgender can emerge as a "studies" in the late nineteen-nineties, that the figure at the center of many of transgender's projects is the "gender troubler," is largely due to Butler's canonization (both the canonization of Butler and her inadvertent canonization of transgender): *"s/he"*—the transgenderist, the third camp term whose crossing lays bare and disrupts the binaries that found identity—threads prominently through the self-declared first reader in the new field of transgender studies.[13] My concern is the implication of this harnessing of transgender as queer for transsexuality: what are the points at which the transsexual as transgendered subject is not queer? The splits and shifts between the deployment of transgender and that of transsexuality within Butler's work are revealing on this count. Whereas in *Gender Trouble* the transgendered subject is used to deliteralize the matter of sex, in Butler's later *Bodies That Matter: On the Discursive Limits of "Sex,"* the transsexual in particular symbolizes a carefully sustained ambivalence around sex.[14] That Butler chooses to elucidate the limits of the transgendered subject's deliteralization of sex through the figure of a transsexual is a powerful indicator of the conceptual splitting between transsexual and queer and, indeed, of queer theory's own incapacity to sustain the body as a literal category. In transsexuality sex *returns*, the queer repressed, to unsettle its theory of gender performativity. In making Butler the substance of my first chapter, I intend both to mark the absolutely generative force her work has had for this book and to suggest that the limitations over the figure of the transsexual and the literality of the sexed body in her work make necessary my readings of the transsexual body narratives that follow.

Queer Gender and Performativity

> To realize the difference of the sexes is to put an end to play
> —Jacques Lacan and Wladimir Granoff, "Fetishism: The Symbolic, the Imaginary, and the Real"

Even though it is articulated only in the last of four sections in the final chapter ("Bodily Inscriptions, Performative Subversions" [*GT* 128–141]), that is in less than one-twelfth of the book, it is the account of gender performativity that is most often remembered as the thrust of *Gender Trouble*. Sedgwick illustrates: "Probably the centerpiece of Butler's recent work has been a series of demonstrations that gender can best be discussed as a form of performativity." More intriguing than the disproportionate emphasis accorded the final section of *Gender Trouble* in general remembrance, however, is the way in which *gender* performativity has become so coextensive with *queer* performativity as to render them interchangeable. Sedgwick, again, exemplifies the way in which "gender" has slipped rapidly into "queer." "Queer Performativity" (the title of her essay on James) she writes, is "made necessary" by Butler's work in and since *Gender Trouble*; and in *Tendencies* Sedgwick assigns Butler "and her important book" (*Gender Trouble*) a representative function, "stand[ing] in for a lot of the rest of us" working on queer performativity.[15] How does this slippage from gender to queer in the discussion of performativity come about, and how does *Gender Trouble* come to "stand in for" it?

While it argues that *all* gender is performative—that "man" and woman" are not expressions of prior internal essences but constituted, to paraphrase Butler, through the repetition of culturally intelligible stylized acts—*Gender Trouble* presents the transgendered subject as the concrete example that "brings into relief" this performativity of gender (*GT* 31). In retrospect we can note that, in concretizing gender performativity with transgender, *Gender Trouble* inadvertently made possible two readings that Butler later returns to refute: first, that what was meant by gender performativity was gender theatricality; and second, that all transgender is queer is syllogistically subversive. The first assumption, that gender performativity means acting out one's gender as if gender were a theatrical role that could be chosen, led to the belief that Butler's theory of gender was both radically voluntarist and antimaterialist: that its argument was that gender, like a set of clothes in a drag act, could be donned and doffed at will, that gender *is* drag. In this reading *Gender Trouble* was both embraced and critiqued. (Even before *Gender Trouble*, however, Butler had carefully argued against any conceptualization of gender as something that could be chosen at will).[16] In fact, Butler's notion of performativity is derived not from a Goffman-esque understanding of identity as role but from Austinian speech-act theory, crucially informed by Derrida's deconstruction of speech-act theory. Not cited in *Gender Trouble* but implicit throughout in its insistence on the cruciality of repetition as destabilizing is Derrida's reading of J. L. Austin and John Searle.[17] *Bodies That Matter* wastes little time before citing Derrida's reading (introduction 13), and in order to clarify this speech-act sense of performativity, the new work emphasizes gender's citationality throughout. To some extent in *Bodies That Matter*, the later term, "citationality," comes to displace the former of *Gender Trouble*, "performativity." Like a law that requires citing to be effective, *Bodies That Matter* argues, sex comes into effect through our citing it, and, as with a law, through our compulsion to cite it. Butler's refiguring of sex as citational law in *Bodies That Matter* is designed to derail the understanding of gender as free theatricality that constituted the misreading of *Gender Trouble*, to clarify how gender is compelled through symbolic prohibitions. The shifts in terms in the books' titles, from "Gender Trouble" to the "Discursive Limits of 'Sex' " (both the shift from "gender" to " 'sex' " and from "trouble" to "discursive limits") run as parallel attempts to account for gender's materiality, its nonsuperficiality, and at the same time to foreground the "limits" of the "trouble" subjects can effect to its constitutive prohibitions. That "sex" appears typographically inserted in citation marks suggests sex precisely as a citation.

It is the second assumption drawn from *Gender Trouble*'s illustration of gender performativity with transgender that concerns me most: the assumption that transgender is queer is subversive. For it is this syllogism that enables Sedgwick to make that slide from gender performativity to queer performativity and that effectively encodes transgendered subjectivity as archetypically queer and subversive. It should be understood that, although it never makes such an argument, *Gender Trouble* does set up the conditions for this syllogism: transgender = gender performativity = queer = subversive. We can begin to illustrate the first part of this, the equation of transgender with gender performativity, by examining *Gender Trouble*'s reading of Beauvoir's "One is not born a woman, but rather becomes one." In Butler's reformulation of Beauvoir's famed epigram on the construction of gender nearly half a century later, it is through the suggestion of a possible transgendering that gender appears not simply constructed but radically contingent on the body. To cite Butler: "Beauvoir is clear that one 'becomes' a woman, but always under a cultural compulsion to become one. And clearly, the compulsion does not come from 'sex.' *There is nothing in her account that guarantees that the 'one' who becomes a woman is necessarily female*" (*GT* 8; my emphasis). And again: "Beauvoir's theory implied seemingly radical consequences, ones that she herself did not entertain. For instance, if sex and gender are radically distinct, then it does not follow that to be a given sex is to become a given gender; in other words, *'woman' need not be the cultural construction of the female body, and 'man' need not interpret male bodies*" (*GT* 112; my emphasis). In both citations, Butler's suggestion of a possible transgendered becoming (that men may not be males and women may not be females) not only opens up a conceptual space between gender and sex and leaves sex dispensable to the process of gendering; it also conveys that gender is not a teleological narrative of ontology at all, with the sexed body (female) as recognizable beginning and gender identity (woman) as clear-cut ending. In Butler's reading transgender demotes gender from narrative to performative. That is, gender appears not as the end of narrative becoming but as performative moments all along a process: repetitious, recursive, disordered, incessant, above all, unpredictable and necessarily incomplete. "It is, for [Butler's version of] Beauvoir, never possible finally to become a woman, as if there were a *telos* that governs the process of acculturation and construction. Gender is the repeated stylization of the body, a set of repeated acts within a highly rigid regulatory frame that congeal over time to produce the appearance of substance, of a natural sort of being" (*GT* 33).[18]

If transgender now equals gender performativity, how does this formulation come to acquire the additional equivalencies of queer and subversion? In "Critically Queer," in correcting the tendency to misread *Gender Trouble* as about transgender, Butler underscores that there is no essential identity between transgender and homosexuality: "not only are a vast number of drag performers straight, but it would be a mistake to think that homosexuality is best explained through the performativity that is drag."[19] That she must return to make this qualification, however, is again precisely because *Gender Trouble* has already produced an implicit equivalence between transgender and homosexuality, so that transgender appears as the sign of homosexuality, homosexuality's definitive *gender* style. In one claim key to this imbrication of transgender with homosexuality, "parodic and subversive convergences" are said to "*characterize* gay and lesbian cultures" (*GT* 66; my emphasis). This characterization encodes transgender as homosexual gender difference, a kind of archetypal queer gender.

Where "straight" gender occults its own performativity according to a metaphysics of substance, queer transgender reveals ("brings into relief") the performativity of all gender. Transgender "dramatizes" the process of signification by which all gendered embodiment "create[s] the effect of the natural" or real; drag's imitative workings parallel the imitative workings that structure straight genders, for all "gender is a kind of persistent impersonation that passes as the real" (*GT* x). The metaphysics of substance undergirds the naturalization of sex and of heterosexuality. What Butler terms the "heterosexual matrix," building in particular on Monique Wittig's analyses of the straight mind's naturalization of a dimorphic gender system, sustains heterosexuality as natural and naturalizes gender as sex.[20] The naturalizing mechanism works both ways, shoring up the apparent naturalness of both sex/gender and heterosexual desire. The claim to "be" a man or a woman is made possible by the binary and oppositional positioning of these terms within heterosexuality. Sex, gender, and desire are unified through the representation of heterosexuality as primary and foundational. Female, femininity, and woman appear as stable and conjoined terms through their opposition to male, masculinity, and man. Gender, in other words, appears as *identity*. What stabilizes the association and keeps the two sets discrete and antithetical is the apparent naturalness of heterosexual desire.

Queer transgender's function in *Gender Trouble* can be summarized as twofold: to parallel the process by which heterosexuality reproduces (and reproduces itself through) binarized gender identities; and at the same time to contrast with heterosexuality's naturalization of this process. For whereas the constructedness of straight gender is obscured by the veil of naturalization, queer transgender reveals, indeed, explicitly performs, its own constructedness. In other words, queer transgender serves as heterosexual gender's subversive foil. Thus in the scheme of *Gender Trouble*, heterosexual gender is assigned as ground, queer transgender as figure, dramatizing or metaphorizing the workings of heterosexuality's construction. Even in "Critically Queer," in the very same paragraph that apparently seeks to disentangle homosexuality and transgender, Butler writes that drag "exposes or *allegorizes*" the process by which heterosexualized genders form themselves.[21] Queer transgender is allegory to heterosexual gender's (specious, for it only veils its performativity) referentiality or literality.

Biddy Martin has described her anxiety in response to Butler's and Sedgwick's work over this tendency of "antifoundationalist celebrations of queerness" to represent queer sexualities as "figural, performative, playful, and fun." Martin's anxiety specifically concerns the way in which feminism, gender, and, by extension, the female body, are stabilized in this dynamic, projected by queerness as "fixity, constraint, or subjection . . . a fixed ground."[22] While agreeing that the category of woman is often subject to a degree of a priori stabilization in the very writings that call for its destabilization and proliferation, my concerns, for the following reasons, are particularly with the effective appropriation of transgender by queer. In the first instance, transgendered subjectivity is not inevitably queer. That is, by no means are all transgendered subjects homosexual. While "Critically Queer" itself points this out, *Gender Trouble's* queer transgender illustrates a certain collapsing of gender back into sexuality that, in the particular process of *Gender Trouble's* canonization, has become a tendency of queer studies: a tendency that is, as Martin suggests, the queering of gender through sexuality (and I would add of sexuality through gender). And, more crucially in regard to this first distinction, in the context of a discussion of how gender and sexual subjects have been taken up in theoretical paradigms, by no means are transgendered subjects necessarily queer even in the sense that queer has come to signify in queer studies. That is, although "queer" as a camp term has to some extent lost that referent "homosexual" and now signifies not as homosexual *stricto sensu* but as a figure for the performative—subversive signifier displacing referent—by no means are all transgendered subjects queer even in this figurative, nonreferential sense. Butler's reading of Venus Xtravaganza in *Bodies That Matter* will work as an attempt to demonstrate just this: the way in which not every gender-crossing is queerly subversive. Yet it should be pointed out again that the fact that she must later return to disentangle transgender, queer, and subversion in *Bodies That Matter* as she must in the essay "Critically Queer," is due precisely to their prior entanglement in *Gender Trouble*. (Although, given the importance within Butler's theory of the dynamic of citation, the extent to which her own writing is generated through such reiterative returns should be noted as richly appropriate.)

My second reason for concern with queer's arrogation of transgender is that it allocates to nontransgendered subjects (according to this binary schema, straight subjects), the ground that transgender would appear to *only* figure; this "ground" is the apparent naturalness of sex. For if transgender figures gender performativity, nontransgender or straight gender is assigned (to work within Butler's own framework of speech-act theory) the category of the constative. While within this framework, this allocation is a sign of the devaluation of straight gender, and conversely queer's alignment of itself with transgender gender performativity represents queer's sense of its own "higher purpose," in fact there are transgendered trajectories, in particular *transsexual* trajectories, that aspire to that which this scheme devalues. Namely there are transsexuals who seek very pointedly to be nonperformative, to be constative, quite simply, to *be*. What gets dropped from transgender in its queer deployment to signify subversive gender performativity is the value of the matter that often most concerns the transsexual: the *narrative* of becoming a biological man or a biological woman (as opposed to the performative of effecting one)—in brief and simple the materiality of the sexed body. In the context of the transsexual trajectory, in fact, Beauvoir's epigram can be read quite differently as describing not a generic notion of gender's radical performativity but the specific narrative of (in this case) the male-to-female transsexual's struggle toward sexed embodiment. One is not born a woman, but *nevertheless* may become one—given substantial medical intervention, personal tenacity, economic security, social support, and so on: becoming woman, in spite of not being born one, may be seen as a crucial goal. In its representation of sex as a figurative effect of straight gender's constative performance, *Gender Trouble* cannot account for a transsexual desire for sexed embodiment as *telos*. In this regard *Gender Trouble* serves to prompt readings of transsexual subjects whose bodily trajectories might exceed its framework of the theory of gender performativity.

If *Gender Trouble* enables the syllogism transgender = gender performativity = queer = subversive, it stabilizes this syllogism through suggesting as constant its antithesis: nontransgender = gender constativity = straight = naturalizing. The binary opposition between these syllogisms proliferates a number of mutually sustaining binary oppositions between *Gender Trouble*'s conceptual categories: queer versus straight; subversive versus naturalizing; performativity versus constativity; gender versus sex. The first term in each opposition is ascribed a degree of generativity that puts in question the primacy of the second. The value of this intervention lies in our recognition that it is the second term that is customarily awarded primacy and autonomy over the first. But the transsexual, as Butler later realizes in Venus Xtravaganza, ruptures these binaries and their alignment.

Because it constitutes the focal point of the transsexual trajectory (to *be* a woman) among these binaries, it is the matter of sex that is of interest to me next before Venus, not simply in its conceptually associative opposition to transgendered subjects in *Gender Trouble* but as a conceptual category in itself. Transgender certainly allows Butler to displace an expressivist model of gender where gender is the cultural expression or interpretation of sex (consolidated as bedrock) with a performative model where sex can "be shown to have been gender all along" (*GT* 8). But *Gender Trouble*'s most thorough accounting for sex as discursive effect appears in the discussion of melancholia in the second chapter, "Prohibition, Psychoanalysis, and the Production of the Heterosexual Matrix" (*GT* 35–78). Here, although the transgendered subject is not explicitly marshaled to exemplify the theory, the figure of transgender haunts the analyses, and the particular conceptualization of sex as "gender all along," as we shall see, certainly has significant implications for any theory of transsexual subjectivity.

Heterosexual Melancholia and the Encrypting of Sex

> To recast the referent as the signified... —Judith Butler, "Contingent Foundations"

Butler has suggested that it was the tendency to skip over this central chapter that led to the conventional (mis)reading of *Gender Trouble* as about drag and promoting a "free play" model of gender. On two occasions she has stated that this tendency is enabled by the book's structure, by too great a thematic break between the discussion of drag and the discussion of melancholia: "The problem is that I didn't bring forward the psychoanalytic material into the discussion of performativity well enough"; "[W]hat I failed to do is to refer the theatricality of drag back to the psychoanalytic discussions that preceded it, for psychoanalysis insists that the opacity of the unconscious sets limits to the exteriorization of the psyche."[23] Butler's later work has gone on to make these moves back and forth between drag and psychoanalysis, to work the connections between gender performativity and melancholia. Melancholia later becomes a way of delimiting the "play" of gender performativity (one section in "Critically Queer" is subtitled "Melancholia and the Limits of Performance"), a means for Butler to unstick the notion of performativity from the literal performance (external display) to which it had become fixed and resituate performativity within the interior workings of the psyche. If, as Butler later writes, the drag sections of *Gender Trouble* "did not address the question of how it is that certain forms of disavowal and repudiation come to organize the performance of gender," drag as it is reworked though melancholia becomes interesting not so much for what it reveals as for what it reveals as repudiated—or rather, to follow Butler's specific psychoanalytic distinction, foreclosed. For although drag is later said to expose or to allegorize heterosexuality, now elaborated as heterosexual melancholia, melancholia is itself constituted by the "unperformable," by what it reveals as that which cannot be revealed as such.[24]

Even without Butler's later underscoring its importance and her continued reworking of melancholia and gender performativity, however, it is difficult not to conclude that, in its thorough accounting for the construction of sex via a thorough accounting of the construction of heterosexuality, this second chapter represents the primary achievement of *Gender Trouble*. While the construction of gender and sexuality is often asserted in poststructuralist theory, this chapter details how the process of construction actually takes place through the categories of culture, the psyche, and body, setting up a complex and brilliant exchange between their domains and, by extension, structuralist and psychoanalytic theory. The analyses stem from these difficult questions: If sex is "gender all along," not a prior ontological substance that gender interprets but rather gender in masquerade, how is it that gender comes to pass so effectively as sex? How does sex appear as biological bedrock, and gender as its a posteriori cultural interpretation?

The deft interlocking of theoretical paradigms, namely, Lévi-Strauss, Lacan (and to a lesser extent, Joan Rivière), and Freud gives to Butler's answering of these questions a comprehensive and authoritative feel. Her beginning premise, undergirding the work of Lévi-Strauss, Lacan, and Freud—and of course Foucault—is the productivity of cultural prohibitions. However, where psychoanalysis and structuralism both posit incest as the prohibition that produces heterosexuality, Butler argues that the incest taboo is preceded by the taboo on homosexuality, for it is this that inaugurates the positive Oedipus complex, that is, the incestuous desires in the first place. The child's compliance with the taboo on homosexuality ensures that his/her object-cathexis is directed toward the opposite-sexed parent. In a move designed to refute the primacy of heterosexuality over homosexuality, Butler asks: What then is the productive effect on heterosexuality of the prohibition of homosexuality? What happens to the once-desired, now-outlawed homosexual love object? Where within the subject does this object-cathexis go?

Via Lacan, Butler asserts that the lost object is incorporated through a melancholic strategy of masquerade crucial to the production of sexual difference. In Lacan's "The Meaning of the Phallus," women appear to be the phallus through a masquerade effected by a melancholic incorporation. Incorporated are the "attributes of the object/Other that is lost," and significantly for Butler, Lacan exemplifies the lost object with a female homosexual cathexis (*GT* 48).[25] The lost object, in particular "the signification of the body in the mold of the Other who has been refused," is incorporated as a mask via "melancholic identification" (*GT* 50). Lacan's account enables Butler to locate "the process of gender incorporation within the wider orbit of melancholy" and to suggest that the unresolved homosexual cathexes outlawed by the taboo on homosexuality effect the production of heterosexually invested genders: symbolic sexual difference (*GT* 50). From Lacan, Rivière's famous refusal of the distinction between the masquerade of femininity and "genuine womanliness" (and Stephen Heath's elaboration of this assertion) allows

Butler to consider the mask not as concealing an interior authentic gender essence but rather as that which masquerades as this essence; the mask itself constitutes gender (*GT* 53).[26]

So far in Butler's chapter the argument has stayed within the bounds of the construction of *gender*. Butler now begins to account for the construction of *sex*, that is how sex is "gender all along." She does so by turning to Freud's writings on melancholia and incorporation ("Mourning and Melancholia" and *The Ego and the Id*, particularly its chapter, "The Ego and the Super-Ego [Ego Ideal]"), and by layering over these two other sets of psychoanalytic texts: Nicolas Abraham and Maria Torok's work on mourning, melancholia, and the processes of introjection and incorporation; and Roy Schafer's descriptions of psychic internalization and the psychoanalytic language of internalization.[27] My questions here—what happens to the matter of sex in *Gender Trouble* and what are its implications for the subject of transsexuality—can be addressed by our careful retracing and elaboration of Butler's steps through these texts.

Freud's 1917 "Mourning and Melancholia" distinguishes these two eponymous psychic states. He defines mourning as a normal finite reaction of grief, which has as its goal the resolution of the death of a loved object. Melancholia differs from mourning on all counts. First, the object is lost not necessarily through death but through, for instance, love. Second, the melancholic does not know for what he grieves: the loss remains opaque to consciousness. And thus third, in not knowing what he has lost, the melancholic *preserves* his object-loss by encrypting it and incorporating it as an identification. In this incorporation of the once-desired lost object as an identification, the melancholic regresses to an oral phase where object-cathexis and identification are confused. In 1923 in *The Ego and the Id*, Freud returns to this essay in order to normalize the workings of melancholia. He discards the opposition between mourning and melancholia and suggests that the processes distinct to melancholia should now be reconceived as part of the process of mourning. Depathologizing melancholia, he argues that its dynamic of substituting an object-cathexis for an identification is central to the formation of the ego. In fact, "it may be the sole condition under which the id can give up its objects." In particular, the dynamics of substitution and incorporation should be understood to produce normative—that is nonpathological—gendering; they function to resolve the object-cathexes of the Oedipus complex and to consolidate gender positioning. Surely significantly for Butler, although she doesn't cite this passage, Freud's example of how identification through incorporation functions to consolidate gender is one of a moment of transgendered identification: "Analysis very often shows that a little girl, after she has had to relinquish her father as a love-object, will bring her masculinity into prominence and identify herself with her father (that is, with the object which has been lost), instead of with the mother."[28]

Freud's generalization of the dynamics of melancholia, his understanding of their role in gendering (through transgendering), allows Butler to select melancholia as the response to the taboo on homosexuality in generating normative (that is heterosexual) gender positions. Heterosexuality is ensured by the cultural prohibition on homosexuality, but the once-loved homosexual object must nevertheless be processed. Because of the cultural prohibition on homosexuality, because of the cultural unnameability of homosexuality, the lost homosexual love-object (always already lost in the sense that it is forbidden) cannot be mourned—that is, articulated or named. The taboo on homosexuality effects a denial of its desired status; grief over the loss is instead turned back in on itself in an unarticulated and unconscious melancholia. At this point Butler enlists Abraham and Torok's description of mourning and melancholia as characterized by two antithetical dynamics of internalization; where mourning introjects the lost object, melancholia incorporates it. Introjection, Abraham and Torok argue, clearly developing Freud's 1917 understanding of mourning as a consciousness of loss, works on a recognition or consciousness of the absence of the object. The void left by the loss of the object is not so much "filled" by articulation of the loss—that is, language—as it makes possible language—that is, the expression of loss. The original loss (the loss of the breast) is resolved through the child's cry. The loss of the real object (originally the mother's body) is thus displaced into language or metaphorized; the mouth emptied of the breast makes possible the mouth filled with words. Melancholia, on the other hand, sets in motion a fantasy of incorporation. As a means of denying the loss, the subject imagines or fantasizes taking in the object. When the loss cannot be acknowledged and articulated via mourning, the subject imagines literally "swallowing" the object, a melancholic fantasy of literalization. As a refusal to displace loss into language, incorporation, Abraham and Torok argue, is fundamentally antimetaphoric. In this sense incorporation is a magical resolution of loss; the loss is actually not resolved at all, remaining unacknowledged and unspoken. As prohibited desire that thus cannot be mourned, Butler uses Abraham and Torok to suggest, the lost homosexual cathexis is incorporated (rather than introjected) as prohibited identification.

But if this identification is incorporated, where exactly is it incorporated? Butler asks: "If the identifications sustained through melancholy are 'incorporated,' then the question remains: Where is this incorporated space? If it is not literally within the body, perhaps it is *on* the body as its surface signification such that the body must itself be understood *as* an incorporated space" (*GT* 67). Having established that melancholia is one psychic effect of the prohibition on homosexuality in the production of heterosexual identity, this, then, is Butler's most engaging proposal. Melancholia for the lost homosexual love-object literalizes sex on the (heterosexual) body. Through Freud and Abraham and Torok, the incorporation that does the work of melancholia appears as an antimetaphorical activity "precisely because it maintains the loss as radically unnamable. In other words, incorporation is not only a failure to name or avow the loss, but erodes the conditions of metaphorical signification itself" (*GT* 68). Incorporation enacts a literalization of the loss. "As an antimetaphorical activity, incorporation *literalizes* the loss *on* or *in* the body and so appears as the facticity of the body, the means by which the body comes to bear 'sex' as its literal truth" (*GT* 68).

This interchangeability between "on" and "in" ("*on* or *in*"), this slippage between, in other words, the surface of the body and its interiority, is crucial. It sets up an equivalence between surface and interiority that is absolutely pivotal both to Butler's description of sexing as a fantasy of incorporation and to her figuring of the body *as* a psychically "incorporated space." In Abraham and Torok the literalizing dynamic of incorporation is crucially a *fantasy* of literalization. Nothing is ever literally taken in during this process of incorporation. Rather, as a means of denying its absence, the subject fantasizes "swallowing" its loss. Corporeal interiority, in this case the notion that the body has a sex, is thus indexical of the literalizing fantasy of heterosexual melancholia, its incorporative response to the prohibition of homosexuality. It is only via this fantasy of literalization that the body comes "to bear a sex" as literal truth, that gender gets inscribed on the body as sex and sex appears as the literal embodiment of gender:

> The conflation of desire with the real—that is, the belief that it is the parts of the body, the "literal" penis, the "literal" vagina, which cause pleasure and desire—is precisely the kind of literalizing fantasy characteristic of the syndrome of melancholic heterosexuality. The disavowed homosexuality at the base of melancholic heterosexuality reemerges as the self-evident anatomical facticity of sex, where "sex" designates the blurred unity of anatomy, "natural identity, "and "natural desire." The loss is denied and incorporated, and the genealogy of that transmutation fully forgotten and repressed. The sexed surface of the body thus emerges as the necessary sign of a natural(ized) identity and desire. The loss of homosexuality is refused and the love sustained or encrypted in the parts of the body itself, literalized in the ostensible anatomical facticity of sex. Here we see the general strategy of literalization as a form of forgetfulness, which, in the case of a literalized sexual anatomy, "forgets" the imaginary and, with it, an imaginable homosexuality. (*GT* 71)

The denied homosexual love is thus incorporated as the "surface" of the body that yet masquerades as interior literal sex. Heterosexuals who believe that their penises and vaginas are the "cause" of their pleasure or desire literalize them and "forget" an/other body: both the (once-loved) homosexual body, the body of the other, and their own imaginary or phantasmatic body (there is an implicit binding of the homosexual to the imaginary).

Because she grounds it on a misrecognition, a mistaking of the signifier of gender for the referent of sex, of the metaphorical for the literal, Butler's description of heterosexual sexing through melancholia inevitably raises mind-boggling questions about what (nonerroneous) recognition might entail. What imaginary body (parts or surfaces) does the heterosexual male who literalizes his penis forget? Is the forgotten imaginary necessarily other than what masquerades as the real? Does this body correspond to a gendered one? Are the imaginary and the phantasmatic already gendered? Later in *Gender Trouble*, in "The Body Politics of Julia Kristeva" (*GT* 79–93), Butler critiques Kristeva's premise of a pre-Symbolic body, one situated in the murky maternal space of the semiotic before the paternal law. Butler reverses Kristeva's temporality, positioning the semiotic or the imaginary as an effect of the Symbolic, the (zone of) prohibition again productive of (the zone of) the prediscursive Kristeva conceives as primary. As this section of the final chapter of *Gender Trouble* suggests that no imaginary body can signify outside of gender, it would follow that the imaginary body in the second chapter is already gendered. Indeed Butler asserts as much in the final pages of "Prohibition, Psychoanalysis, and the Production of the Heterosexual Matrix" when she figures the imaginary or fantasized body as "an altered bodily ego . . . within the gendered rules of the imaginary" (*GT* 71). In literalizing his penis, then, might the straight man be said to forget an imaginary or fantasized vagina? Does he also forget to literalize (invest sex in) body parts that he might be said to already "have" (more than he can be said to "have" a vagina)—feet for instance? And how are *these* parts gendered in the imaginary? What exactly *are* the "gendered rules" of the imaginary? The question of the precise relations between actual heterosexual subjects and the theory of heterosexual melancholia is prompted by, though not addressed in, *Gender Trouble*'s description.

For transsexual embodiment, Butler's harnessing psychoanalytic discussions of melancholia and incorporation to the processes of gendering has two interdependent significant effects: it refigures sex from material corporeality into phantasized surface; and through this it reinscribes the opposition between queer and heterosexual already at work in *Gender Trouble*, sustaining it by once again enlisting transgender as queer.

First, Butler's deliteralization of sex depends upon her conceiving the body as the psychic projection of a surface. This conceptualization derives from a rather eclectic reading of Freud's description of the bodily ego in *The Ego and the Id*. I cite the Freud passage in full:

> A person's own body, and above all its surface, is a place from which both external and internal perceptions may spring. It is *seen* like any other object, but to the *touch*, it yields two kinds of sensations, one of which may be equivalent to an internal perception. Psycho-physiology has fully discussed the manner in which a person's own body attains its special position among other objects in the world of perception. Pain, too, seems to play a part in the process, and the way in which we gain new knowledge of our organs during painful illnesses is perhaps a model of the way by which in general we arrive at the idea of our body.
>
> The ego is first and foremost a bodily ego; it is not merely a surface entity, but is itself the projection of a surface.[29]

In the apparent periphery of a footnote, *Gender Trouble* cites from the second paragraph of this passage Freud's assertion, "the ego is first and foremost a bodily ego" (*GT* 163, n. 43). But then, in a substitution crucially significant to her conceptualization of the body as the psychic projection of a surface, Butler replaces the referent "it" in the subsequent part of the cited sentence, *which in Freud clearly refers back to the ego as bodily ego* ("The ego is first and foremost a bodily ego; *it* . . .), with the word (square bracketed, demoted—in my citation of Butler's note—to parenthetical) "body." Butler's recitation of the passage reads: "Freud continues the above sentence: '(*the body*) is not merely a surface entity, but is itself the projection of a surface'" (*GT* 163 n. 43; my emphasis). Butler's reading of Freud's assertion thus figures the body as interchangeable with the ego. That is, the body appears not only as a surface entity but as itself *the psychic projection of a surface*. Yet that it is precisely Freud's concern at this point in his essay to articulate the bodily origins of the ego, the conception of the ego as product of the body not the body as product of the ego, is underscored by the explanatory footnote added by his editor James Strachey that appeared first in the 1927 English translation of this text immediately following the above passage—a note authorized by Freud. The note reads: "I.e. the ego is ultimately derived from bodily sensations, chiefly from those springing from the surface of the body. It may thus be regarded as a mental projection of the surface of the body."[30] Butler's reading therefore inverts the note's representation of the body as productive of the psyche ("the ego is derived from bodily sensations") and, through that square-bracketed substitution, conversely images the body as a psychic effect. The body itself becomes commensurable with the psychic projection of the body. Whereas Freud's original assertion maintains a distinction between the body's real surface and the body image as a mental projection of this surface (a distinction between corporeal referent and psychic signified), Butler's recitation collapses bodily surface into the psychic projection of the body, conflates corporeal materiality with imaginary projection. In so doing, it lets slip any notion of the body as a discernible referential category.

Her later use in *Bodies That Matter* of this same passage in *The Ego and the Id* repeats and indeed heightens this reading, even though she here (again in a footnote) addresses directly that 1927 footnote—and even though she here reads it directly as Freud's: "Although Freud is offering an account of the development of the ego, and claiming that the ego is derived from the projected surface of the body, he is inadvertently establishing the conditions for the articulation of the body as morphology" (*BTM* 258, n. 4). The modifying subordination in her syntax ("although") to which her summary of the manifest meaning of the note is confined makes clear that she recognizes that what she desires the note to articulate is not deliberate but "inadvertent." Yet in spite of this recognition, Butler continues to read against the manifest sense of the note—the description of the ego as derived from the body—in order to emphasize the antithesis: the body as morphology. This notion of body as morphology derives from a Lacanian conceptualization of the body as illusory psychic projection. Indeed, her citation of Freud appears here in her chapter on imaginary morphology, "The Lesbian Phallus and the Morphological Imaginary," where Freud's concept of the ego as a bodily ego is said to "prefigure" Lacan's mirror stage in which the body is an "idealization or 'fiction' " (*BTM* 73). But Freud's configuration of the relations between psyche and body is quite different from Lacan's. If in Lacan's mirror stage the body is the ego's misconception, in Freud's *The Ego and the Id* the body is the site of the ego's conception.[31]

Butler's inversion of Freud's formulation of the relations between psyche and body in *Gender Trouble* may also be influenced by Roy Schafer's reading of Freud's bodily ego to illustrate the illusory status of the distinctions the subject makes (and the language of psychoanalysis sustains) between what is interior and what is exterior to the body. Butler enlists Schafer's critique of internalization (in addition to Abraham and Torok's analyses) to argue that incorporation is a fantasy. Schafer proposes that, in its language of internalization, psychoanalysis literalizes the always-imaginary projections on the part of the subject between what is inside and outside. For Schafer Freud's description of the bodily ego exemplifies the original way in which the subject deludes itself into believing in the facticity of corporeal interiority. The bodily ego constitutes a perception or rather a construction of the body espoused (falsely) by the subject, not a product of the body at all but rather a misreading of it; for via the bodily ego the subject assumes wrongly that the self can be conceived as occupying a body, a materiality in space.[32] My contention is that it is precisely this point that the 1927 footnote approved by Freud seeks to emphasize. Freud's bodily ego is designed not to dematerialize the body into phantasmatic effect but to materialize the psyche, to argue its corporeal dependence.

In her critique of the queering of gender Martin has remarked on the tendency in queer studies for "surfaces [to] take priority over interiors and depths and even rule conventional approaches to them [i.e., interiors and depths] as inevitably disciplinary and constraining."[33] Butler's conceptualization of sex as a heterosexual melancholic fantasy of literalization, of sex as the phantasmatic encrypting of gender in the body, implicitly designates corporeal interiority as "disciplinary and constraining" and, conversely, privileges surface as that which breaks up interiority and reveals its status as fantasy. This prioritization of surface is emphatically occularcentric, as is *Gender Trouble*'s concomitant investment in the transgendered subject of the power to reveal sex as "gender all along" (i.e., interiority as incorporated fantasy). *Gender Trouble*'s theoretical economy of gender relies heavily on a notion of the body as that which can be seen, the body as visual surface. This is possibly most marked in its deployment of the transgendered subject to illustrate gender performativity: girls who *look like* boys and boys who *look like* girls. In this sense then, in its dependence on the visible, on body-as-surface, the theory of gender performativity does in fact work out of a definitively theatrical arena. Any claim to a sense of sexed interiority, any *feeling* of being sexed or gendered (whether "differently" or not), along with other ontological claims, is designated phantasmatic, symptomatic of heterosexual melancholia. Yet, to return to that passage in *The Ego and the Id*, Freud underlines that the bodily ego derives not so much from the perception of the body (an "external perception"), that is, from what can be seen, but from the *bodily sensations* that stem from its touching—touching here in both an active and passive sense—(an "internal perception"): "[A person's body] is *seen* like any other object, but to the *touch*, it yields two kinds of sensations, one of which may be equivalent to an internal perception."[34]

The transsexual doesn't necessarily *look* differently gendered but by definition *feels* differently gendered from her or his birth-assigned sex. In both its medical and its autobiographical versions, the transsexual narrative depends upon an initial crediting of this feeling as generative ground. It demands some recognition of the category of corporeal interiority (internal bodily sensations) and of its distinctiveness from that which can be seen (external surface): the difference between gender identity and sex that serves as the logic of transsexuality. This distinction is tactically, ingeniously, and rigorously refused by *Gender Trouble*; it is this refusal that allows for a refiguration of sex into gender. In its one mention of transsexuality *Gender Trouble* uses transsexuality to exemplify not the constitutive significance of somatic feeling but the reverse, the phantasmatic status of sex: the notion that pleasure exceeds material body parts.[35] The transsexual's often declared capacity to experience his or her body as differently sexed from its materiality certainly supports Freud's notion of a bodily ego. But, because the subject often speaks of the imaginary body as more real or more sensible, I argue that this phenomenon illustrates the materiality of the bodily ego rather than the phantasmatic status of the sexed body: the material reality of the imaginary and not, as Butler would have it, the imaginariness of material reality. That the transsexual's trajectory centers on reconfiguring the body reveals that it is the ability to feel the bodily ego in conjunction and conformity with the material body parts that matters in a transsexual context; and that sex is perceived as something that must be changed underlines its very un-phantasmatic status.

Butler's deliteralization of sex, her displacement of sex from material interiority into fantasized surface, is enabled by the production of a binary between queer and heterosexual. The second important ramification for a theory of transsexual embodiment following the refiguring of the body as visual surface, is the alignment once again of transgender with queer. Heterosexuality is engendered via the literalizing strategies of melancholia, strategies that queer through its transgendered performativity brings into relief. Heterosexuality operates by attempting to literalize sex *in* the body; queer transgender reveals this depth as surface. It is not that heterosexuality is natural and queer denaturalizing; rather, heterosexuality is naturali*zing*, concealing the masquerade of the natural that queer makes manifest. Even so, heterosexuality and queer are represented as, respectively, restrictive interiority and playful surface. If gay and lesbian cultures are said to be *characterized* by camp, parodic subversive—that is, transgendered—performances that deliteralize the apparently real of sex, heterosexuality is said to be *characterized* by a literalizing of the apparently real: "The conflation of desire with the real . . . is precisely the kind of literalizing fantasy characteristic of the syndrome of melancholic heterosexuality" (*GT* 71). This attribution of character effects a certain hypostatization of queer and heterosexual, simultaneously impacting queer more thoroughly with transgender. In effect Butler subjects heterosexuality to a certain degree of grounding in order to read queer *through* transgender as refiguring this ground. In operation is a generic antithesis, the queer performative coinciding with the comedic staging of the impossibility of identity, heterosexual literalization with the melancholic attempt to sustain it as absolute ground. As Butler herself implicitly acknowledges when she considers how transgendered subjects also reliteralize the gender norms in her essay on *Paris is Burning*, this pivotal antithesis of *Gender Trouble* is too neat.[36] If in *Gender Trouble* the transsexual is not distinguished from the queer transgendered subject, in *Bodies That Matter* the transsexual is specifically elected as the subject who most succinctly illustrates the limitations of the queerness of transgender. It is to this delimiting and the transsexual that I now turn.

Venus is Burning: The Transubstantiation of the Transsexual

> I don't feel that there's anything mannish about me except what I might have between me down there. I guess that's why I want my sex change, to make myself complete.
> —Venus Xtravaganza, *Paris is Burning*.

Because it was released in 1990, hot on the heels of the publication of *Gender Trouble*, Jennie Livingston's film *Paris is Burning* often got taken up in discussions of queer identities in conjunction with Butler's book, as if the subjects of the drag ball—again, the lure of the visual example in transgendered contexts—illustrated Butler's theory of gender performativity.[37] Both texts in their transgendered themes captured what seemed definitive of the queer moment. For this reason they were subject to a certain yoking together in feminist/queer studies—in our readings, course syllabi, conferences, and so on. Butler's chapter in *Bodies That Matter* on the ambivalent effects of transgender in *Paris is Burning*, "Gender is Burning: Questions of Appropriation and Subversion" (*BTM* 121–142), serves by association therefore as a return to the subject of transgender in *Gender Trouble* to mark out *its* ambivalent effects. In this sense "Gender is Burning" functions to complicate those binary syllogisms of *Gender Trouble*. The essay's thesis is that crossing identifications in the film both denaturalize and renaturalize identity norms: "*Paris is Burning* documents neither an efficacious insurrection nor a painful resubordination, but an unstable coexistence of both" (*BTM* 137).

While Butler uses *Paris is Burning* in general to document the ambivalent significance of performative crossings, she uses Venus Xtravaganza as the specific lever to articulate this ambivalence: "Venus, and *Paris is Burning* more generally, calls into question whether parodying the dominant norms is enough to displace them; indeed, whether the denaturalization of gender cannot be the very vehicle for a reconsolidation of hegemonic norms" (*BTM* 125). For Butler it is the particular configuration of Venus's body, gender presentation, desires, and fate that best exemplifies how transgressive crossings can simultaneously reinscribe symbolic norms. The film's representation of this Latina transsexual delimits the subversive possibilities of parodic repetitions. Yet although its argument about ambivalence pivots on the specific material ambivalence of the transsexual body, Butler's essay encodes transsexuality as metaphor in a way that sublimates into theoretical allegory the specific materiality of Venus's sex and of her death as a light-skinned Latina transsexual.

The revelation of Venus's murder in the second part of *Paris is Burning* (filmed in 1989, two years after the first encounter with Venus) is indisputably the moment that most cuts through any sense of the performativity, the fictionality of identities the film provides elsewhere, particularly in the ball scenes. That Venus is killed for her transsexuality, for inhabiting a body which, as that of a preoperative male-to-female transsexual, is not coherently female, is strongly supported by the film's narrative. Angie Xtravaganza, the mother of Venus's house, to whom the film turns to provide an account of the occurrence, firmly fixes Venus's death in the context of a transsexual narrative: "That's part of life. That's part of being a transsexual in New York City." The implication is that Venus is murdered in her hotel bedroom on being "read" by her client, killed for having a body in excess of the femaleness he imagined he was paying for; killed, then, as a transsexual. Butler isolates Venus's death as the most prominent instance in the film in which the symbolic precludes its resignification: "This is a killing that is performed by the symbolic that would eradicate those phenomena that require an opening up of the possibilities for the resignification of sex" (*BTM* 131). Yet while Butler's isolation of this moment and this citation suggest that what matters (to the client, to the film, and to Butler the critic) is Venus's transsexuality and the particular configuration of her sexed body as a male-to-female, Butler's reading of Venus's killing situates Venus's body along a binary of queer man/woman of color, in the split between which Venus's Latina, passing-as-white, transsexual body falls.

Butler attributes Venus's death first to "homophobic violence," staking that it is Venus's "failure to pass completely [that renders her] clearly vulnerable" to this violence (*BTM* 129–130). By "failure to pass completely," Butler clearly intends Venus's penis; yet the presence of the penis on Venus's body renders neither her a homosexual man (a literalization of gender surely symptomatic of the heterosexual melancholia *Gender Trouble* critiqued) nor her death an effect of homophobia. Venus presents herself unambivalently as a transsexual woman, not as a gay man or drag queen. Although the only "genetic girl" is behind the camera, it does not follow that all the bodies in *Paris is Burning* are male. Rather, the film presents a spectrum of bodies and desires, heterosexual and homosexual, in-drag, transsexual, and genetic male, with the subjects frequently articulating the distinctions between these categories in a careful self-positioning. Stating that there's nothing "mannish" about her except what she has "down there," Venus describes looking forward to sex reassignment surgery to make her "complete": in other words, a complete woman. Her identification not as a gay man or a drag queen but as an incomplete (preoperative transsexual) woman highlights the impossibility of dividing up all identities along the binary homosexual/heterosexual. If it applies to Venus at all, her desire—to be a complete woman for a man—is heterosexual, and it is more this desire in combination with her transsex that kills her: not as a homosexual man, then, but as a transsexual woman whose desire is heterosexual—or, as *the failure to be* (an ontological failure) a biological woman.

It is therefore equally inadequate to read Venus's death as equivalent to that of a woman of color, as Butler does in the second instance: "If Venus wants to become a woman, and cannot overcome being a Latina, then Venus is treated by the symbolic in precisely the ways in which women of color are treated" (*BTM* 131). Without disputing that women (of color or white) can be treated identically to Venus, and while underlining that it is crucial that Venus's passing be acknowledged as doubleleveled—a race and sex crossing—again, it is not for *being* a woman of color but for failing to be one that Venus is murdered; it is the crossing, the trans movement that provokes her erasure. Her death is indexical of an order that cannot contain crossings, a body in transition off the map of three binary axes—sex (male or female), sexuality (heterosexual or homosexual), and race (of color or white): a light-skinned Latina transsexual body under construction as heterosexual and female. At work in Venus's murder is not fear of the same or the other but fear of bodily crossing, of the movement in between sameness and difference: not homo- but transphobia, where "trans" here signifies the multileveled status of her crossing. This interstitial space is not foregrounded in Butler's reading of Venus's death.

If for Butler Venus's death represents the triumph of the symbolic, "Gender is Burning" discovers the symbolic asserting its norms through Venus even before this moment—in particular, in her expressed desires to become a "complete woman," to marry and attain financial security. The second two are of course crucially dependent on the first: a Latina transsexual's desires for sexed realness and domestic comfort. It is to set the realization of these desires in motion that Venus is turning tricks to earn enough for her lower surgery, sex work being a not uncommon, indeed often the only means by which poor/working-class male-to-females can afford to change sex. For Butler these desires reveal the extent to which Venus, even before her murder, is subject to "hegemonic constraint":

> Clearly, the denaturalization of sex, in its multiple senses, does not imply a liberation from hegemonic constraint: when Venus speaks of her desire to become a whole woman, to find a man and have a house in the suburbs with a washing machine, we may well question whether the denaturalization of gender and sexuality that she performs, and performs well, culminates in a reworking of the normative framework of heterosexuality. (*BTM* 133)

Venus's fantasy as a Latina transsexual of becoming "real" (both achieving coherent sexed embodiment and middle-class security) and her corporeal progress in realizing this fantasy mark her out from the drag ball performers who "do" realness and who "resist transsexuality" (*BTM* 136). Butler's presupposition is twofold here: first, that inherent to *doing* realness is an agency resistant to and transformative of hegemonic constraint that the desire to *be* real lacks; and following this, that the transsexual's crossing signifies a failure to be subversive and transgressive of hegemonic constraint where it *ought* to be. Hegemony constrains Venus through the "normative framework of heterosexuality." If resisting transsexuality produces a denaturalizing agency, it is because in Butler's scheme transsexuality is understood, by definition, to be constrained by heterosexuality. By extension, to fail to resist transsexuality fully (as Venus does in hoping for a sex change) is to reliteralize sex (to be rather than perform it) according to the workings of heterosexual melancholia. While Venus's murder symptomizes the triumph of the heterosexual matrix, in her desires Venus is duped by this same heterosexual ideology into believing that a vagina will make her a woman. The heterosexual matrix is therefore already asserting its hegemony in Venus's transsexuality even before her death.

From this scheme it might appear that the binary of heterosexual = literalizing/queer = performative is still in operation in *Bodies That Matter*, with transsexuality standing in for the first term. The transgendered subject, here exemplified in the transsexual, would accordingly appear simply to have been switched from one side of the binary to the other since *Gender Trouble*. Yet Butler's essay works not to reinforce but to demonstrate the ambivalence of this binary, to delimit (not negate) the queer performativity of transgender. It is the literal ambivalence of Venus's transsexual body that allows for this new theoretical ambivalence. Venus's death represents the triumph of hegemonic norms only as it simultaneously illustrates Venus denaturalizing these norms: it is a "killing performed by the symbolic that would eradicate those phenomena that require an opening up of the possibilities for the resignification of sex." Venus's body, with penis intact, is such a phenomenon that would resignify sex. Even in her death, because of her transsexual incoherence between penis and passing-as-a-woman, Venus holds out for Butler the promise of queer subversion, precisely as her transsexual trajectory is incomplete. In her desire to complete this trajectory (to acquire a vagina), however, Venus would cancel out this potential and succumb to the embrace of hegemonic naturalization. In other words, what awards Venus the status of potential resignifier of the symbolic in Butler's scheme is the fact that Venus doesn't get to complete her narrative trajectory and realize her desires, because she still has a penis at her death. What matters for Butler is the oscillation between the literality of Venus's body and the figurative marks of her gender. Conversely, Venus's desire to close down this tension (what I am calling her desire for sexed realness, for embodied sex) curtails her capacity to resignify the symbolic. That Butler figures Venus as subversive for the same reason that Butler claims she is killed, and considers indicative of hegemonic constraint the desires that, if realized might have kept Venus at least from this instance of violence, is not only strikingly ironic, it verges on critical perversity. Butler's essay locates transgressive value in that which makes the subject's real life most unsafe.

Butler's essay itself is structured on an ambivalence toward transsexuality in its relation to the literal, caught (twice over), both between reading transsexuality literally and metaphorically and between reading the transsexual as literalizing and deliteralizing. That Butler assigns Venus the function of ambivalence in her effect on the literal is encapsulated in the essay's reliance on the theme of transubstantiation, a term that is conjoined to transsexuality twice in the essay, that indeed stands in for transsexuality: first, in reference to Venus; and second, in reference to Jennie Livingston's camera. First, then, Butler writes that Venus's transsexual fantasy of realness is one of transubstantiation: "Now Venus, Venus Xtravaganza, she seeks a certain transubstantiation of gender in order to find an imaginary man who will designate a class and race privilege that promises a permanent shelter from racism, homophobia, and poverty" (*BTM* 130). Venus's desire is here said to represent a transubstantiation of gender in that her transsexuality is an attempt to depart from the literal materiality of her sexed and raced body (and as her class is intricated with these corporeal materialities, thus also a move away from her social materiality) precisely according to a strategy that reliteralizes sex: the acquisition of a vagina to make her a "complete woman." The term "transubstantiation" sustains exactly such antinomy: it conveys both literalization and deliteralization, is both performative and constative. In the Eucharistic sense of transubstantiation, that the bread and wine stand for Christ's body and blood is simultaneously a metaphorization of the materials and a literalization of the Godhead. The exchange of speech during the Eucharist between the priest ("The body of Christ") and the recipient ("Amen") contracts both into agreeing that the materials *are* literally this body. Thus, to make a connection to my discussion of melancholia and mourning, the Eucharistic transubstantiation functions as an incorporation of the lost object (Christ), which is *also* an introjection: the object is taken in and literalized, yet at the same time the articulation of its representation ("the body of Christ") ensures its resymbolization. If Venus's transsexuality "transubstantiates" in Butler's account, then, it is because transsexuality is perceived (ambivalently) as seeking out a heterosexual melancholic literalization of sex (the vagina) precisely through a queer resignification (the quest for the vagina is the penis's deliteralization). The antithesis structuring *Gender Trouble* is rendered ambivalent through transsexuality, specifically through the representation of transsexuality as transubstantiation.[38]

Butler's essay goes on to displace its discussion of transsexuality and transubstantiation from the literal transsexual body of Venus to the metaphorical body of Jennie Livingston. Butler takes up bell hooks's criticism that *Paris is Burning* is the product of a white gaze that yet occults the situatedness of this gaze, that the film is a white scripting of black bodies into a play(ground) of Otherness for white pleasure. For hooks Livingston's exclusion of her own white body from the cinematic frame misrepresents the fact that the film is a white perspective on blackness and is thereby symptomatic of the dominant cultural production of whiteness as disembodied:

> Jennie Livingston approaches her subject matter as an outsider looking in. Since her presence as white woman/lesbian filmmaker is "absent"

from *Paris is Burning* it is easy for viewers to imagine that they are watching an ethnographic film documenting the life of black gay "natives" and not recognize that they are watching a work shaped and formed by a perspective and standpoint specific to Livingston. By cinematically masking this reality (we hear her ask questions but never see her), Livingston does not oppose the way hegemonic whiteness "represents" blackness, but rather assumes an imperial overseeing position that is in no way progressive or counter-hegemonic.[39]

Seemingly driven by the wish to read the film as more ambivalent than hooks's reading allows (that is both reinscriptive and subversive), Butler seeks an exception to hooks's premise of the disembodiment of the white author. Butler suggests that Livingston's body—or at least its allegorical delegate—might be discovered in the scene in which the other transsexual protagonist, Octavia St. Laurent, poses for a swimsuit shoot: "The one instance where Livingston's body might be said to appear allegorically on camera is when Octavia St. Laurent is posing for the camera, as a moving model would for a photographer. We hear a voice tell her that she's terrific, and it is unclear whether it is a man shooting as a proxy for Livingston or Livingston herself" (*BTM* 134–135). My viewing of the film differs strongly from Butler's. In my experience of this scene, the body that's shooting (and the voice that's shown originating from it) is quite *clearly* that of a white male photographer, whose photographic camera appears in the cinematic frame while Livingston's cinematic camera and her directorial body continue to remain clearly outside the frame. Livingston remains omniscient and unsituated. For Butler, however, the photographer's camera metaphorically embodies Livingston's own desire through the feminization and eroticization of Octavia's transsexual body:

> What is suggested by this sudden intrusion of the camera into the film is something of the camera's desire, the desire that motivates the camera, in which a lesbian phallically organized by the use of the camera (elevated to the status of disembodied gaze, holding out the promise of erotic recognition) eroticizes a black male-to-female transsexual—presumably preoperative—who "works" perceptually as a woman. (*BTM* 135)

If the camera as subject of the gaze is the phallus, then not only is the photographic camera's appearance within the cinematic frame the allegorical instantiation of Livingston's body, in its eroticization of the male-to-female transsexual as model perfect, the photographic camera metaphorically phallicizes Livingston's body. For in representing the male-to-female transsexual as woman as object of desire, Livingston, Butler writes, "assumes the power of 'having the phallus.' " (*BTM* 135). The camera's feminization/eroticization of the male-to-female transsexual circulates the phallus from transsexual to lesbian, a circulation that amounts to a "transsexualization of lesbian desire": "What would it mean to say that Octavia is Jennie Livingston's kind of girl? Is the category or, indeed, 'the position' of white lesbian disrupted by such a claim? If this is the production of the black transsexual for the exoticizing white gaze, is it not also the transsexualization of lesbian desire?" (*BTM* 135). Livingston's desire for the transsexual is apparently also her identification with the transsexual; or rather the moment enacts an exchange of identities, with the "real girl" acquiring a phallus (becoming transsexualized) as she represents the transsexual as a "real girl." Extending her metaphorization of transsexuality, Butler designates the camera (photographic symbolizing cinematic) the tool of this (s)exchange, the "surgical instrument and operation through which the transubstantiation occurs" that produces Octavia as woman, which "transplants" the phallus from Octavia's body to Livingston's lesbian body.

Transsexuality and transubstantiation are thus brought together for a second time in Butler's essay, now in a metaphorical context. As in Butler's discussion of Venus's fantasy, transsexuality is again implicitly defined as, rendered equivalent to, transubstantiation. How is the double dynamic of literalization and deliteralization played out in this second moment of transsexualization as transubstantiation? I suggest that Butler's reading here again depends on the literal sexed ambivalence of the preoperative male-to-female transsexual body (the woman with a penis). Yet Butler's metaphor of transsexualization, its application to the lesbian body—and the refiguring of surgery into the camera's look—in effect displaces the materiality of transsexuality, and thus the materiality of sex, to the level of figurative. First, in figuring the phallus as circulated from Octavia to Livingston, the metaphor of transsexualization pivots on, and actually originates in, Octavia's penis. We know that Octavia, like Venus, is indeed preoperative for likewise in her narrative Octavia speaks of looking forward to the surgery that will make her a "complete" woman. However, as in its process of circulation in Butler's essay this penis becomes the phallus (Livingston's camera is said to accord her the phallus, not the penis), this penis is clearly subject in its translation to Lacanian sublimation itself. Butler's metaphor of transsexualization depends upon this crucial substitution of fleshly part with symbolic signifier, a confusion between phallus and penis that certainly does not take place in the film. For while Octavia (like Venus) may yet have a penis, in no way can she be said to "have the phallus": that is, in no way is she accorded or does she assume the position of delegate of the symbolic order. Conversely, while (presumably) Livingston has no penis, her capacity to represent Octavia, Venus, and the rest of the cinematic subjects as embodied others via her authority as disembodied overseer, as hooks's essay argues so convincingly, situates her precisely in this position of the symbolic's delegate—the one who appears to have the phallus. In the context of this film by a white lesbian about black and Latino/a gay men, drag queens, and transsexuals, the penis and phallus might be said to remain not only discrete but oppositional. Worlds apart from her subjects in her whiteness, her middle-classness, her educatedness, and her "real" femaleness, Livingston's position behind the camera is that of an authority with absolute powers of representation.[40]

Moreover, Livingston appears to wield this phallic power most heavily in her representation of the transsexuals, Octavia and Venus, in particular in her representation of their fantasies. The section in the film in which Octavia and Venus are cataloguing their desiderata stands as the most explicitly edited and authored moments in the film. Their sentences, most of which begin "I want," are rapidly intercut with each other's and their visual images likewise interwoven. The technique suggests an identity of their fantasies—not only that there is a generic transsexual fantasy but that the transsexual might be conceived according to what she *lacks*; "I want" reveals all that the subject lacks. At the same time, in its location of these scenes, the cinematic apparatus occults its own framing/authoring function. Both Octavia and Venus are filmed reclining on beds in bedrooms (the viewer is led to believe the subjects' own); Octavia is even dressed for bed. The setting allows the audience to assume an intimacy with the subjects, to forget the extent to which these moments are mediated through Livingston's white female gaze—exactly the dynamic of occultation that provides fodder for hooks's critique. Elsewhere in the film it becomes evident how Livingston's camera mediates what of their lives the subjects reveal. Before her death, for instance, Venus informs Livingston that she no longer works the streets, a claim that her death, of course, proves drastically untrue. (The question of whether Venus would have continued to work the streets to save for her surgery, *of whether Venus would have been killed, had Livingston contracted her* along with the film's subjects as actors is ultimately unanswerable, though the fatal ending of Venus's narrative demands its asking.) To summarize, then: in having the power to represent the other and conceal this power, Livingston not only "has the phallus," this having enables her to represent the transsexual other—Octavia and Venus—as crucially lacking: not so much in spite of, as because of their penises. Along with race and class, the crucial structuring difference between Livingston on the one hand and Venus and Octavia on the other is sexed coherence or biological realness: the difference between the nontransgendered and the embodied transgendered subject.

If phallus and penis are antithetical in *Paris is Burning*, Livingston's "phallicization" in no way reveals her embodiment—even allegorically—as Butler claims. The difference between reality and the allegorical, between the fleshy intractability of the penis and the transcendence of the phallus could not be more marked. As her position behind it renders her unrepresented, only a disembodied voice popping questions, the camera is precisely Livingston's means to disembodiment not to her embodiment. Thus hooks's critique of the filmmaker's bodily erasure still holds. Indeed, Butler's allegorization of Livingston's body in the very vehicle for her disembodiment only places further out of reach the filmmaker's literal corporeality, the notion that Livingston has a "body that matters." And although rendering the camera a lesbian phallus might well disrupt Livingston's identity as a lesbian, it does nothing to disrupt its transcendent whiteness: the reason why hooks has problems with its overseeing position in the first place. Indeed, Butler's wish to curtail hooks's critique of Livingston's disembodiment seems queerly motivated (in both senses)—that is, until she reveals an identification with Livingston: both "white Jewish lesbian[s] from Yale" (*BTM* 133). This moment—exceptionally autobiographical for Butler—suggests that perhaps something quite personal is at stake in Butler's discovering an exception to the disembodied gaze of the auteur representing transgendered subjects. For Butler as much as for Livingston the personal investment in this representation of transgendered subjects may well be there; but the point is that in neither is it ever shown and in both this elision of whatever autobiographical stakes there are exacts the cost of objectification and derealization on the represented subjects.

Most significantly, the essay's metaphorical shifting of transsexuality from Venus's body to Livingston's camera displaces transsexuality to a realm that has nothing to do with the materiality of the body. In the context of a discussion of a film during the making of which one of the protagonists is killed for her transsexuality, for the literal configuration of her sexed body, this sublimation of transsexuality appears more prominent and, in my experience anyway, proves the most disturbing moment in Butler's oeuvre. The critic's metaphorization of the transsexual body transcends the literality of transsexuality in precisely a way in which Venus cannot—Venus who is killed for her literal embodiment of sexual difference. Even in the film we might notice that the literality of Venus's transsexual body and the facticity of her death are already subject to a glossing over. As hooks points out, the film glides over the reality of Venus's death, the moment is rapidly overridden by the spectacle of the ball, and, now that she can no longer function in the service of this spectacle, Venus is abandoned. Indeed, it might be said that not only does the filmic narrative fail to mourn Venus, it markedly includes no scenes of others' bereavement over Venus. We simply have Angie Xtravaganza's terse account of what happened to Venus overlaying footage of Venus filmed on the Christopher Street piers while she was still alive, this montage itself threatening to deny the reality, the finality of Venus's death. In metaphorizing transsexuality, Butler inadvertently repeats something of this deliteralization of the subject, her body, and her death. The substance of the transsexual body is sublimated in the move from the literal to the figurative. In the critical failure to "mourn" her death, Venus's body (surely the lost object of *Paris is Burning*), the most prominent representation we have in this film of the pain and anguish of embodying the experience of being differently sexed, is encrypted in Livingston's camera. And what is not kept in view in the film or the theory on it is the intractable materiality of that body in its present state and its peculiar sex.[41]

Queer Feminism and Critical Impropriety: Transgender as Transitional Object?

> The institution of the "proper object" takes place, as usual, through a mundane sort of violence.
> —Judith Butler, "Against Proper Objects"

In her work since *Bodies that Matter* Butler demonstrates how the founding of lesbian and gay studies as a methodology distinct from feminism has involved a privileging of subjects and categories to the exclusion of others. Her essay in the "More Gender Trouble" issue of *differences* edited by her in 1994, "Against Proper Objects," critiques the way in which lesbian and gay studies has arrogated sexuality as its "proper object" of study, defining itself through and against feminism by assigning gender as feminism's object of study. What comes to appear quite critically improper in Butler's essay is this very investment in theoretical property: both the assurance with which that attribution of the object to the other is made (in effect a restriction of the other to the object) and the claims staked in the name of this attribution and restriction—namely, lesbian and gay studies' claims to "include and supersede" feminism.[42]

Butler's essay implies that it might never be possible to claim methodological distinctness without bringing into play a degree of aggression, that every theory that grounds itself by allocating "proper objects" will be prone to this kind of critical impropriety. Undoubtedly, my attempts to wrest the transsexual from the queer inscription of transgender—and here, my criticisms of Butler's writing on Venus—are not free of aggression. From the point of view of this project, what subtends the difference in such readings is quite primal (theoretical, political, and admittedly personal): concerns about territory, belonging, creating homes; indeed, the extent to which identity is formed through our investment in external "objects"—a fundamental tenet of psychoanalysis, that definition depends on defining and "owning" objects. The question is perhaps quite simple: Where (best) does the transsexual belong? In seeking to carve out a space for transgender/transsexual studies distinct from queer studies, inevitably terrain must be mapped out and borders drawn up (a fact that doesn't render them uncrossable). Representations, subjects, and bodies (such as Venus) serve as the all-important flags that mark the territory claimed. It is additionally inevitable that the establishment of methodological grounds involves the attempt early on to circumscribe neighboring methodologies and approaches, the emphasizing of what *they* do *not* as opposed to what *we do*.

Significantly, "Against Proper Objects" conjures transsexuality in order to complicate articulations of methodological difference (although Butler's language of "domestication" suggests not my frontier-scale struggles but tiffs in the kitchen). Butler presents transsexuality as a category that, because of its "important dissonance" with homosexuality (tantalizingly, but importantly for my readings which follow, she doesn't say what this is), falls outside the domain of lesbian and gay studies ("APO" 11). Insofar as lesbian and gay studies delimits its proper object to sexuality and "refuses the domain of gender, it disqualifies itself from the analysis of transgendered sexuality altogether" ("APO" 11). Transsexuality and transgender are invoked as illustrations of the exclusions that lesbian and gay studies has performed in fixing its proper object as sexuality. Transsexuality and transgender number among the categories of "sexual minorities" Butler rightly understands Gayle Rubin insisting in 1984 made necessary a "radical theory of the politics of sexuality."[43] These categories, Butler believes, get sidelined, ironically in lesbian and gay studies' appropriation of Rubin's essay as a foundational text. As I outlined at the beginning of this chapter, my sense of the role of transgender in lesbian and gay studies is quite different: that is, the figure of transgender has, rather, proven crucial to the installation of lesbian and gay studies—its installation *as* queer. Even work purporting to focus exclusively on sexuality and not gender—I suggested Sedgwick's in particular—implicitly engages this transgendered figure and, correlatively, the axis of gender. (In her other mention of transgender and transsexuality Butler writes of Sedgwick's antihomophobic critique that "[b]y separating the notion of gender from sexuality, [it] narrows the notion of sexual minorities offered by Rubin, distancing queer studies from the consideration of transgendered persons, transgendered sexualities, transvestism, cross-dressing, and cross-gendered definition" ["APO" 24, n. 8]). Although it strongly suggests that "an analysis of sexual relations apart from an analysis of gender relations is [not] possible," Butler's essay does not address how lesbian and gay studies might *already* be engaged in gender analyses, if largely unconsciously ("APO" 9). Indeed, toward the end of Butler's interview of Gayle Rubin in the same "More Gender Trouble" issue of *differences*, Rubin provocatively hints that Butler's critique of lesbian and gay studies' exclusion of gender might amount to a tilting at windmills:

> As for this great methodological divide you are talking about, between feminism and gay/lesbian studies, I do not think I would accept that distribution of interests, activities, objects and methods. . . . I cannot imagine a gay and lesbian studies that is not interested in gender as well as sexuality. . . . I am not persuaded that there is widespread acceptance of this division of intellectual labor between feminism, on the one hand, and gay and lesbian studies on the other.[44]

That s/he has received considerably less critical attention than the cross-dresser or drag artist(e), that s/he has not been subject to the same deliberate and concentrated queer recuperation, and indeed, as is demonstrated in Butler's own work on Venus, that s/he is more likely to be deployed to signal the *unqueer* possibilities of cross-gender identifications, suggests that, above all transgendered subjects, the transsexual is more of the limit case for queer studies: the object that exceeds its purview. Yet my sense is that the reasons for transsexuality's exceeding queer lie not so much in queer's refusal of the category of gender (and thus transgender), as Butler argues, as in queer's poststructuralist problems with literality and referentiality that the category of transsexuality makes manifest—particular in relation to the sexed body. Butler's metaphorical displacement of the literality of Venus's sex can serve to exemplify just this.

Indeed, according to Butler, it must remain "an open question whether 'queer' can achieve these same goals of inclusiveness" imagined by Rubin's radical theory of sexual politics, whether queer studies can incorporate all of the "sexual minorities" among which transgender and transsexuality might be categorized ("APO" 11). For Butler the concern is queer's *capacity* to include, a question about queer's elasticity, about how far the term "queer" will stretch. What is not a concern is whether queer *should* even attempt to expand; expansion, inclusion, incorporation are automatically invested with value. One wonders to what extent this queer inclusiveness of transgender and transsexuality is an inclusiveness *for* queer rather than for the trans subject: the mechanism by which queer can sustain its very queerness—prolong the queerness of the moment—by periodically adding subjects who appear ever queerer precisely by virtue of their marginality in relation to queer. For does not this strategy of inclusiveness ensure the conferral on queer of the very open-endedness, the mobility, and—in the language of "Against Proper Objects"—the very means by which to "rift" methodological "grounds" that queer has come to symbolize? If, as Butler writes, "normalizing the queer would be, after all, its sad finish," the project of expansion enables queer to resist this normalization (what Butler fears will be "the institutional domestication of queer thinking") that would herald its end ("APO" 21). Yet if we conceive of "finish" and "end" here not as a limitation in time but a limitation in institutional space, this limited reach is inevitable and arguably necessary for the beginnings of other methodologies, for reading other narratives from other perspectives.

What Butler does not consider is to what extent—and on what occasions—transgendered and transsexual subjects and methodologies might not wish for inclusion under the queer banner. "Against Proper Objects" assesses inclusion and the resistance to inclusion solely from the perspective of queer; it does not imagine possible resistance stemming from the putatively excluded "sexual minorities." Our discussions should address not only—or perhaps not primarily—queer's elasticity but also what is gained and lost for nonlesbian and gay subjects and methodologies in joining the queer corporation. In the case of transsexuality there are substantive features that its trajectory often seeks out that queer has made its purpose to renounce: that is, not only reconciliation between sexed materiality and gendered identification but also assimilation, belonging in the body and in the world—precisely the kinds of "home" that Butler's essay holds at bay in its critical troping of "domestication." There is much about transsexuality that must remain irreconcilable to queer: the specificity of transsexual experience; the importance of the flesh to self; the difference between sex and gender identity; the desire to pass as "real-ly-gendered" in the world without trouble; perhaps above all, as I explore in my next chapter, a particular experience of the body that can't simply transcend (or transubstantiate) the literal.

Since *Gender Trouble*, "domestication" has figured as something of a specter in Butler's work. Domestication appears to represent the assigning of subjects and methodologies to specific categorical homes, the notion that there is an institutional place to which they belong. For the Butler of 1990 what was at stake was the domestication of gender, and concomitantly the domestication of feminism through gender's domestication beyond sexuality. *Gender Trouble* sought "to facilitate a political convergence of feminism, gay and lesbian perspectives on gender, and poststructuralist theory" to produce a "complexity of gender[,] . . . an interdisciplinary and postdisciplinary set of discourses in order to resist the *domestication* of gender studies or women['s] studies within the academy and to radicalize the notion of feminist critique" (*GT* xiii; my emphasis). As a means of resisting gender/women's studies' domestication, *Gender Trouble* marshaled lesbian and gay sexuality and, as I have suggested, lesbian and gay genders, in effect troubling or queering gender. In analyzing the way in which the sex/gender system is constructed through the naturalization of heterosexuality and vice versa, *Gender Trouble* performed its work in an interstitial space between feminism and lesbian and gay studies, producing a new methodological genre—hence my term for this: queer feminism. In this sense *Gender Trouble* constituted an attempt to queer feminism. Yet although Butler's work might be said to have always conceived of domestication—what we might term object-constancy to push further on the psychoanalytic metaphor—as restrictive, it is interesting to note that in 1994 it is no longer *feminist* but *queer* studies that she perceives to be under threat of domestication: the shift indexes the change in values of the currencies of these methodologies, the ways in which queer and gender studies have "circumscribed" feminism. In "Against Proper Objects" it is (trans)gender that returns as the supplement to trouble the domestication of (homo)sexuality, gender that "troubles" queer. This shift in Butler's theoretical "object-cathexis" is a sure a sign of queer's institutionalization (Oedipalization? with feminism as [M]Other?) if ever there was one.

To resist queer's incorporation of trans identities and trans studies is not to refuse the value of institutional alliances and coalitions (in the form of shared conferences, journals, courses, and so on). But an alliance, unlike a corporation, suggests a provisional or strategic union between parties whose different interests ought not to be—indeed, cannot totally be—merged, sublimated for cohering—or queering—the whole. In closing, it needs emphasizing that it is precisely queer's investment in the figure of transgender in its own institutionalization—and above all the methodological and categorical crossings of Butler's queer feminism—that have made it possible to begin articulating the transsexual as a theoretical subject. It can be said that, in its very origins and its early attempts at self-definition, transgender studies is allied with queer.

> To be oneself is first of all to have a skin of one's own and, secondly, to use it as a space in which one can experience sensations.   —Didier Anzieu, *The Skin Ego*

> The layer which I really needed to take off was what can only be described as a second skin. But no matter how hot or how cold or how uncomfortable it makes you feel, you cannot get it off. I yearned for the pure relief you get from ripping off some really uncomfortable piece of clothing, except, I couldn't because that last layer was me.   —Raymond Thompson, *What Took You So Long?*

> Why should the area of the skin, which guarantees a human being's existence in space, be most despised and left to the tender mercies of the senses?   —Yukio Mishima, *Sun and Steel*

chapter 2

A Skin of One's Own: Toward a Theory of Transsexual Embodiment

Surface Material

In December 1993 "Orlan: Omnipresence" brought to the Sandra Gering Gallery in New York the latest work of the French surgical performance artist, Orlan. This consisted in the surgical reconstruction of her face to resemble a computer composite of five canonical representations of beautiful women (the Mona Lisa and Botticelli's Venus among them). At the exhibition a video of the operation, originally relayed live to multiple international art galleries, showed a surgical team fitted out in black robes and conical hats performing on Orlan's laid-out body. The video of the surgery and its live broadcast, as Julia Epstein observes, "literaliz[ed] the term 'operating theater.' "[1] Underlining this theatricality, a surgeon's bloody robe stretched and pinned to the wall at Gering's bore the legend, "The body is but a costume." To be sure, by her own account, Orlan seems to divest herself of her lineaments with an ease in keeping with this figure: "Skin is a mask of strangeness, and by refiguring my face, I feel I'm actually taking off a mask."[2] Yet like the robe's disavowal of the body's materiality, Orlan's image for the superficiality of her face only raises anxious questions about the meaning of bodily matter for identity. If skin is a mask, where is the self in relation to the body's surface? Deeper than the skin (underneath the mask)? Or not "in" the flesh at all? In her surgical performance of the body (this was I think her sixth set of procedures), in her literalization of the body as a costume, Orlan appeared to provide an insane personification of the poststructuralist insistence on the absolute constructedness of the body.

Contrary to the robe's and Orlan's assertions, the body's materiality (its fleshiness, its nonplasticity, and its nonperformativity) was anyway much in evidence elsewhere in the gallery: in the gruesome video itself; in the photographs of Orlan's face, much swollen, bruised, and misshapen, which served as a daily record of her very gradual postsurgical recovery; and (evidently a recovery not yet completed) in Orlan herself, (omni)present at the gallery the day I went, her face mostly hidden behind dramatic big dark glasses, what wasn't, still puffy and luminous, oddly large. In the question and answer session following the artist's talk, after mentioning the work I was then beginning on transsexuality, I asked Orlan about the relation of body and identity in her work. Did she feel any sense of identity transformation, of an internal shifting, as her face underwent its successive alterations? Was the transformation really only skin deep? (I wondered what it was like to wake up to a different face each morning; I wondered how she sustained her self in the face—literally—of such change). Skimming over the substance of my question (there were problems in translation) but picking up my reference to transsexuality, Orlan replied simply that she felt like "une transsexuelle femme-à-femme." It was a striking reformulation. But what was the import of transsexuality here? On the one hand, eliding the element of sex change but nonetheless suggesting a total identity (ex)change (she changed from one woman to another), her identification with a substantial transsexual transition implied that something of her self was indeed invested in the surgery, that the transformations were not simply skin deep. On the other hand, the readiness of her embrace of transsexuality and the ease with which transsexuality translated into a context that made of surgery a spectacle brought to the surface a commonplace assumption about transsexuality: that is, that transsexuality is precisely a phenomenon of the body's surface. In the cultural imagination that figure of the body as costume is surely welded most firmly to the transsexual. The transsexual changes sexed parts like a set of clothes, treats the body as tractable, provisional, immaterial: "For transsexuals a book may be read by its cover, and the bodily frame is thought of as another article of clothing, to be retouched at will."[3] If the Orlan/transsexual analogy could have worked either way—to substantiate Orlan's transformation or to unsubstantiate (transubstantiate?) the transsexual's—what is the status of the body for transsexuals? Does sex reassignment suggest the body as a surface in which the self is substantially invested or conversely the body's substance as superficial to the self? What does transsexuality, the fact that subjects do seek radically to change their sex, convey about sex, identity, and the flesh?

Upon sex reassignment surgery, upon assumptions concerning its mechanics and effects, pivot popular attitudes to transsexuality. More than the potentially dramatic somatic effects of the long-term hormone therapy that necessarily precedes it, sex reassignment surgery is considered the hinge upon which the transsexual's "transsex" turns: the magical moment of "sex change." At the same time contemporary conceptualizations of sex make it difficult to believe that surgery, through the simple excision and restructuring of body parts, can miraculously and wholly alchemize one sex into "the other." Sex is currently ascribed a complex of meanings that push the category beyond the surface of the body. For a start, in science sex is no longer located monolithically in the genitals but disseminated through the inscrutable parts of the body: the gonads, the chromosomes, even the brain—parts of the body that cannot be exchanged in sex reassignment. On the basis of this multiplication and encrypting of sex, the transsexual can alter sex only partially and superficially, only in the limited sense of hormonal and genital sex. Second, our belief in the importance of the cultural and psychic in identity formation has left us wary of reducing sex to the body *tout court*. "Gender" has made it routine to ask how much of sex is socialization, cultural construction, and personal history. How can surgical intervention into biological material alter the accretion of this sociocultural matter, the experiences that make up our lives as men and women? Third, since feminism has complicated the status of difference in sexual difference (antithesis or likeness? difference from or difference within?), isn't the naturalization of sexual difference into a binary twoness anyway a cultural construct? Ann Fausto-Sterling argues that even medical narratives of sex reveal the dimorphic sex model as arbitrary.[4] The transsexual would seem to assume a binary difference that doesn't even exist in biology: how, then, can s/he cross a space that is not clearly there? Finally—and most important since this constitutes the theoretical zeitgeist—if sex as much as gender is performative, an effect of our doing not a fact of our being ("gender all along"), how can we conceive of the transsexual as intervening in sex at all?[5] If there is no sex left over, no immanent sexed part to the self that is not already gender, what substance is there for the transsexual to change?

Because sex has become irreducible not only to the sex organs accessible to surgical remolding but to the body itself, the transsexual's attempted sex reassignment may serve to illustrate the very failure of sexual difference. Elizabeth Grosz deploys the transsexual to this effect. Conceiving of sexual difference as "a problematic . . . entail[ing] a certain failure of knowledge to bridge the gap, the interval, between the sexes," she claims: "At best the transsexual can live out his fantasy of femininity—a fantasy that in itself is usually disappointed with the rather crude transformations effected by surgical and chemical interventions. The transsexual may look like a woman but can never feel like or be a woman."[6] Looking like a woman but not really one, yet, after the "crude transformations" have "disappointed" his "fantasy" of gender, hardly looking like a man, the transsexual as transmogrified, hermaphroditic prodigy falls into that very space/time ("gap," "interval") of sexual difference. This "gap" is not only between man and woman but between signifier and referent: it is in this Lacanian sense (the fact that the signifiers of man and woman can never fully or fixedly inscribe themselves on referential bodies) that sexual difference is said to fail. In her Lacanian reading of transsexuality, Catherine Millot argues that the transsexual's quest for sex reassignment is a psychotic refusal to recognize the law of the symbolic that makes us subjects—that is, that the referent *is* symbolic, that sexual difference is a matter of signification only.[7] Following Millot therefore, Parveen Adams reads Orlan's reformulation of transsexuality (the exhibition I attended was televised) to suggest Orlan as the better transsexual. Where the transsexual, in attempting to move substantively from one sex to the other, would seek to render literal a difference that is representational, Orlan's performative female-to-female transition "transform[s] the confident existence of one sex . . . towards the gap in representation which signifies sexual difference." *She* keeps open the gap, or rather reveals that the referent *only* figures: "[A]n image trapped in the body of a woman," Orlan demonstrates that "there is nothing beneath the mask."[8] Ironically, this poststructuralist deliteralization of sex (its detachment from referentiality) can often seem like a further mystification of sex. Irreducible to the body, by definition indefinable, sex has become in excess, that which we cannot "know" about gender; as Grosz illustrates, "There remains something ungraspable, something outside, unpredictable, and uncontainable about the other sex for each sex."[9]

Yet what is the status of the body's surface that the transsexual in changing sex reconfigures? Is our corporeal outside simply a "mask," so detachable from, so insubstantial for the self? Writing against the grain of most poststructuralist theories of the body informed by psychoanalysis, Didier Anzieu suggests the body's surface as that which matters most about the self.[10] His concept of the "skin ego" takes the body's physical skin as the primary organ underlying the formation of the ego, its handling, its touching, its holding—our experience of its feel—individualizing our psychic functioning, quite crucially making us who we are. Bordering inside and outside the body, the point of separation and contact between you and me, skin is the key interface between self and other, between the biological, the psychic, and the social. It holds each of us together, quite literally contains us, protects us, keeps us discrete, and yet is our first mode of communication with each other and the world. A Freudian psychoanalyst, Anzieu derives his skin ego from Freud's description of the ego in *The Ego and the Id* as "not merely a surface entity, but . . . the projection of a surface" and from Strachey's explanatory note later attached: "I.e. the ego is ultimately derived from bodily sensations, chiefly from those springing from the surface of the body. It may thus be regarded as a mental projection of the surface of the body, besides, as we have seen above, representing the superfices of the mental apparatus."[11] If in her reading of this passage, Judith Butler connects the notions of "surface" and "mental projection" to transform the body into a projected image, Anzieu provides a quite different, non-Lacanian trajectory to Freud; Anzieu emphasizes "the projection of a surface" as "*derived from* bodily sensations" to represent the image of the body as derived from the feeling of the body. With a wonderfully uncomplicated literalism Anzieu renders Freud's "surface" as the skin. The body's physical surface or encasing provides the anaclitic support for the psychic apparatus: the ego, the sense of self, derives from the experience of the material skin. The body is not only not commensurable with its "mental" projection but responsible for producing this projection. The body is crucially and materially formative of the self. Anzieu's means of demonstrating that all psychic structures stem from the body, the skin ego returns the ego to its bodily origins in Freud.

According to Anzieu the central tenet of Freudian psychoanalysis, that "[e]very psychical activity is anaclitically dependent upon a biological function," has been forgotten in psychoanalysis's structuralist assumption: the body has become "the great missing, unrecognized, unacknowledged element in education, everyday life, the rise of structuralism" (*SE* 40, 21). Anzieu underwent the trainee-analyst analysis with Lacan, but it was precisely this experience that prompted Anzieu to develop a critique of Lacan's work, particularly of Lacan's centralization of language. Reversing Lacan's substitution of language for body as psychoanalysis's key material, Anzieu positions his work in direct antithesis: "I myself would oppose the formula: 'the unconscious is structured like a language' with a formulation that is implicit in Freud: 'the unconscious is the body.' The unconscious seems to me to be structured like the body."[12] If in poststructuralism (Anzieu seems to date desomatization from the "rise of structuralism") and in particular in psychoanalysis in the wake of Lacan, we have recast the body's referentiality as psychic and cultural signified, Anzieu works to reconstitute and sustain the material body as discrete, generative, or productive referent.[13]

In her bodily ego footnote in *Gender Trouble* Butler cites Anzieu's *The Skin Ego* as "a provocative account ... which, unfortunately, does not consider the implications of its account for the sexed body."[14] Along with Grosz's reading of Anzieu (in its inversion of "the primacy of a psychical inferiority by demonstrating its necessary dependence on a corporeal exteriority," Grosz's "corporeal feminism" is a model for me here in spite of its brief deployment of transsexuality),[15] Butler's note prompts my attempt to read Anzieu to provide such an account. Stories of sex change, transsexual narratives provide the perfect matter for this task. "Sex change" entails a transformation of the body's surface. Hormone therapy begins this process, dramatically contravening the functioning of the gonads, refiguring the body's contours, altering tissue structure (muscle, fat, breast, genital), redistributing hair, changing skin texture in body and face. Surgery continues and radicalizes the transformation: removing sex organs (genital and secondary, internal and external), reshaping the remains and/or relocating other bodily tissues—nerves, skin, flesh—to form others. The making of these new transsexual parts (vaginoplasty, phalloplasty, mastectomy) consists in the surgical manipulation of the body's surface: the grafting, stretching, inverting, splitting, tucking, suturing of the tissues. How does sex reassignment surgery as a manipulation of the body's surface change the transsexual's sex? Of what does this "moment" of sex change consist? In its turn Anzieu's skin ego allows us to consider the significance of sexed embodiment in transsexual accounts: to explore the feeling and experience of being transsexed.

From the prevalent perspective in gender theory the transsexual's story of becoming sexed can only appear naively overdetermined. Butler asserts that if "there is no body prior to its marking [,] . . . we can never tell the story of how it is a body comes to be marked by the category of sex."[16] Relating first how the body comes to be marked by sex wrongly, then how it comes to be marked correctly, transsexual narratives take up poststructuralism's untellable story. What makes it possible for a female-to-male transsexual to name the somatic material (skin, tissue, and nerves) transplanted from his forearm or his abdomen to his groin "my penis," or for a male-to-female transsexual to name the inverted remains of her penis "my vagina" is a refiguring of the sexed body that takes place along corporeal, psychic, and symbolic axes. Gendered becoming, becoming a man or a woman, occurs for the transsexual at these points of intersection, complex crossings for sure but the investment of sex in the flesh is undeniable. Narratives that immerse us (subject and reader alike) in the bodily matter of sexual difference, transsexual autobiographies challenge theory's cynicism over identity's embodiment. In that s/he seeks to align sex with gender identification; in that the somatic progression toward these goals of sexed embodiment constitutes the transsexual narrative, the transsexual does not approach the body as an immaterial provisional surround but, on the contrary, as the very "seat" of the self. For if the body were but a costume, consider: why the life quest to alter its contours?

Second Skins: Transsexual Body Image

In what is surely one of the most disturbing recent representations of the transsexual, the psychopathic figure at the center of Jonathan Demme's 1990 film, *The Silence of the Lambs*, a former psychiatric patient refused sex reassignment surgery kills fat girls, skins them, and is shown loonily sewing their skins together to form a costume of womanness to clothe his own body.[17] Jame Gumb's activity reifies what has become the formula for transsexual ontology: the subject trapped in—and trying to escape— the wrong (sexed) body. A topos of transsexual autobiographies, the wrong-body formula is used by transsexuals themselves to express the sensory experience of transsexuality. The transphobic stereotype in *The Silence of the Lambs* is particularly noxious because it arrogates and psychopathologizes figures immanently significant to transsexual accounts, inscribing the somatic trouble of the transsexual into the transsexual as trouble for the social corpus.

The detail of this Hollywood corruption—its particular focus on the skin as crucial surface for the fantasy of sex change—further replicates details from transsexual accounts. Gumb is refused the medical technology to enable him to throw off his own skin (to escape his "wrong body"). His recourse is to fabricate (to make up and produce as a fabric) a layer of female skin to cover his male skin.[18] Transsexual subjects frequently articulate their bodily alienation as a discomfort with their skin or bodily encasing: being trapped in the wrong body is figured as being in the wrong, or an extra, or a second skin, and transsexuality is expressed as the desire to shed or to step out of this skin. Fantasies of excoriation punctuate transsexual autobiographies. Pretransition, Jan Morris writes that she "began to dream of ways in which I might throw off the hide of my body and reveal myself pristine within—forever emancipated into that state of simplicity."[19] Leslie Feinberg writes of a desire for disembodiment in terms of shedding the body like a skin: "I think how nice it would be to unzip my body from forehead to navel and go on vacation. But there is no escaping it, I'd have to pack myself along."[20] Shifting from the body as a single piece of clothing to the body as a suitcase full of clothing with the "self" packed inside, Feinberg's imagery suggests the true self as en-cased in a restrictive or burdensome outer layer. And in one oral transsexual account an anonymous male-to-female expresses her alienation from her male body in terms of being encased, surrounded by a false skin: "I used to look at my body and think it was a bit like a diver's suit, it didn't feel like me inside."[21] The image of the body as diver's suit suggests that the subject's authentic self might be revealed if only the outer layer of the visible body could be peeled off, like a diver's suit. Yet the speaker goes on to interpret her own simile startlingly: "it didn't feel like me inside." The "me" is not inside, either; indeed, the "real me" seems to have disappeared from the picture altogether—so fundamental is the bodily alienation, I would suggest. One is left with the disturbing image of the body as a false outer casing with nothing inside: a hollow shell or empty skin. What is disturbing is the extent to which identity has truly vacated its "case" (the body).

What is the currency of this genre of body image in transsexual narratives? Why does it recur and what relation of self to body does it posit? Certainly an inquiry into the value of the wrong body formula should acknowledge at the outset its status as powerful medicodiscursive sign. Transsexuality entered the cultural lexicon first as a form of extreme (body) transvestism, with the body's skin as the "clothing" that the subject needed changing. Christine Jorgensen, the subject with whom transsexuality became popularized in the early 1950s, was diagnosed and changed sex as a "genuine transvestite" before being reclassified as transsexual.[22] And as a formula that continues to trope transsexuality in its medical narrative version, being trapped in the wrong body has become the crux of an authenticating transsexual "rhetoric": language, narratives, and figures that the subject deploys to obtain access to hormones and surgery. Yet in the history of the subject even with the category of transsexual in place, and in the individual subject's history even once the transsexual has achieved sex reassignment, the figure of being trapped in a wrong body, of being wrongly encased, continues to be evoked in transsexual accounts. A transsexual leitmotif appearing across transsexual narratives, the proliferation of the wrong-body figure is not solely attributable to its discursive power.

My contention is that transsexuals continue to deploy the image of wrong embodiment because being trapped in the wrong body is simply what transsexuality feels like. If the goal of transsexual transition is to align the feeling of gendered embodiment with material body, body image—which we might be tempted to align with the imaginary—clearly already has a material force for transsexuals. The image of being trapped in the wrong body conveys this force. It suggests how body image is radically split off from the material body in the first place, how body image can feel sufficiently substantial as to persuade the transsexual to alter his or her body to conform to it. The image of wrong embodiment describes most effectively the experience of pretransition (dis)embodiment: the feeling of a sexed body dysphoria profoundly and subjectively experienced.

More dramatically than any other, female-to-male Raymond Thompson's transsexual autobiography substantiates this constative dimension of the image of entrapment in the wrong body. Thompson's narrative presents him as embodying the image, feeling it; he suffers claustrophobia in his body precisely as a false outer skin or enclosure locking inside an authentic "inner body":

> I needed to be out of my body, to be free. It felt as if my "inner body" was forcing itself to the ends of my limbs. It was growing ever larger inside

of me, making me feel I was bursting at the seams and wanting out . . . out . . . *out*!

Because this was impossible, this process would abruptly reverse and I would start to shrink inside myself. My whole inner body shrank until I became very small inside. It was as if I became so small I had to find some safe place to hide inside myself. My tiny inner body was in unfamiliar surroundings, in a place it didn't belong and I felt utterly unsafe. I became like a little shadow inside my physical body, a shadow running around everywhere trying to find somewhere inside.[23]

This image of an internal body attempting to force its way out of the referential flesh and then of its recoiling is Thompson's attempt to convey what is obviously an intensely sensory, visceral experience. As Thompson's own descriptive term for these sensations underlines—"body feelings," a term that comes startlingly close to Freud's "bodily sensations"— the transsexual trope of the subject trapped within the wrong body is materialized as somatic feeling (253). *What Took You So Long?* fleshes out transsexuality into a psychophysiological condition, one that alters the body's physicality as much as a sickness. Pretransition, Thompson is struck by moments of semiparalysis in which he is unable to move or feel his body. Attributed to his transsexuality, these moments stem from the conflict between the true body within and the false body without, between sentient body image and insentient visible body. As though more real and substantial, body image appears to bear the agony and material body is correlatively dematerialized. Note that the autobiographical "I" in the above passage (as in the entire narrative) is located in the internal body image not in the alien outer body.

The conflict between inner and outer body is incarnated and the figure of authentic body seeking to break out of its outer body prison dramatically enacted. In an incident lasting several days Thompson takes to his bed, refuses food and drink, as though body image is driven to deny body-prison its necessary material fortifications, as if death is its only means of release from improper embodiment. Only the intervention of his family prevents this precipitation into suicide, by which time Thompson's inner body, in an assertion of its authenticity and dominance over visible body, has succeeded in metamorphosing the latter into a flimsy, barely containing shell: his body is now "positively emaciated" (202). Unable to break out of its "prison of flesh and bones" (165), body image punitively reconstitutes material body into flesh and bones.

When body image transforms fleshly matter and inscribes its struggle on the material body, it exteriorizes what is conceived as internal. In a remarkable instance of quasihysterical symptomization, Thompson's narrative literalizes this psychic/corporeal inside-out-ness. Rising from his bed, seeing his reflection in the mirror, Thompson finds his face covered with weeping blisters. As the narrative provides no somatic reason for their presence, and as Thompson himself presents them as signs of the externalization of his internal state ("my internal stress [was showing] on the outside" [202]), the reader is asked to accept these physical marks as evidence of his "inside" on his "outside," the trace of body image acting on material body: symptoms of bodily representation wounding or punishing the literal body that pitifully fails to embody it. Not simply marking the dissociation between physical body and body image, the blisters reproduce in their very microstructure that dynamic of an inner body pushing up against, trying to escape from the material outer body: vesicles filled with bodily fluids bursting up and out from their internal course through to the body's surface, overflowing their assigned passage. It is as if the figure of the inner body striving to break out of its container has erupted on the surface of its container, broken out literally in blisters on the skin. "Because my body was becoming more and more alien to me as I developed, there was an urge to rip off my own skin, for lack of a better description. The frustration and anxiety were tearing me to bits" (54). In fact, as the blisters literally tear him to bits, producing the splitting or bursting of the skin as a kind of unconscious material effect of this "urge," Thompson's description of this psychic/somatic agon couldn't be better.

But if the trope of being trapped in the wrong body can be materialized, what are the mechanics of this catachresis—of this figure that is at the same time a physical experience? The pivotal connective term is "surface"; and as Thompson's dermatological condition suggests, the pivotal connective surface is the skin. In medicine the skin, the material surface of the body, is a psychic/somatic interface. Psychodermatology and much dermatology assumes a relation between dermatological disorders and psychic upheaval. Many skin conditions are accepted among medical workers as psychosomatic: not "made up" but somatized, the body's manifestation of, its bringing to the material surface deep psychic disturbance. Even skin conditions with certain organic causes are thought to be exacerbated by psychic stress. In turn skin conditions bring with them their own psychic distress. Psychotherapy is thus very often indicated as a treatment to alleviate if not the skin disorders themselves, at least their psychological costs. On all levels the psyche is firmly correlated to the skin.[24]

Sited on the borders between psyche and body, skin appears as an organ enabling and illustrating the psychic/corporeal interchange of subjectivity. Formulated first during his training as a psychologist on a hospital dermatological unit, Anzieu's skin ego is based upon the conception of skin as such an interface. Apprehending the figure of the wrong body as part of a transsexual unconscious according to Anzieu's concept of the skin ego emphasizes not the imaginariness of the figure (rhetorical image) but its sensibility (embodied image); for in Anzieu's topography of the subject the unconscious is isomorphic to ("structured like") and materially supported by the body through the psychosomatic surface of the skin. If the urge to break out of one's skin or bodily encasing is not simply a metaphor, the skin—as the surface mediating "inside" and "outside" the body—presents itself as the point of contact between material body and body image, between visible and felt matter. Anzieu's skin ego provides an explanation, one that schematically melds the organic with the psychic, for the purchase of images of wrong embodiment in transsexual accounts. That is, the skin is the locale for the physical experience of body image and the surface upon which is projected the psychic representation of the body. As the skin represents this nexus, it makes sense that such psychic discomfort as feeling trapped in the wrong body, first, can be physically felt, and second, may be transcribed unconsciously and apparently miraculously onto the literal skin as is the case with the blisters that appear on Thompson's face.

Skin is a sense organ, our most vital, not only generative of touch but our largest and most multifunctioning: "one can live without sight, hearing, taste or smell, but it is impossible to survive if the greater part of one's skin is not intact." (*SE* 14). Because skin is a psychic/somatic interface, not being able to live without one's skin is not just a physical but a psychic state. If psychic damage can inscribe itself on the skin, conversely and unsurprisingly, damage to the material skin (such as burning, scarring—and we might add, psoriasis, eczema, and acne) is likely to damage the subject's body image, to alter his or her bodily sense and presentation. From the mutuality of this exchange Anzieu hypothesizes a precise correspondence between material body surface and body image: "the seriousness of damage to the skin . . . is in direct relation to the extent, both quantitative and qualitative, of the flaws in the Skin Ego"

(*SE* 35). According to this proportioning, psychic/corporeal harmony can be rendered as the feeling of being at home in one's skin: "To be oneself is first of all to have a skin of one's own and, secondly, to use it as a space in which one can experience sensations" (*SE* 51). Subjectivity is not just about having a physical skin; it's about feeling one owns it: it's a matter of psychic investment of self in skin.

If I feel confined in the wrong body on a fundamental level, it must be said that I fail to own my skin, to accept it as my own. Thompson captures this sense of having no skin, of being skinless, lacking a proper (that is not only "right" but "owned") bodily surround or container: "it felt as if I came into this world with no physical form to protect me. I was not a solid, tangible human being, like everyone else seemed to be. I felt vulnerable and alone" (26). He feels this unprotected, uncontained body image somatically. His "body feelings" are characterized by coldness and immobility, a semiparalysis. He is unable to get his limbs to function normally, as though his bodily alienation consisted of the physical failure to "know" his body as his own: "Since my body is not my own I cannot feel the warmth of it, so I am cold, very cold on the inside. . . . I could simply never be comfortable and warm in my own skin. . . . There is a sense of disconnectedness and unreality, of being left out in the cold. Most of the time I couldn't get my body to move from my chair, whilst panic was raging inside me" (249). The figure of somatic non-ownership is emphatically not a metaphor in Thompson's narrative, but constitutes his pretransition bodily experience. The skin ego marks the point at which self-image meets the grounds of the body.

How does one function without feeling surrounded by a proper body? How does the subject survive without a skin of his or her own? Anzieu outlines how the subject with a damaged or flawed body image, the subject who imagines him or herself skinless or with a broken skin, develops defenses—psychic but sometimes enacted—against this state: means of producing an imaginary skin for rekindling bodily belonging. Surely the most traumatic of these compensatory measures consists in producing "[m]utilations of the skin—sometimes real, but more often imaginary—[which] are dramatic attempts to maintain the boundaries of the body and the Ego and to re-establish a sense of being intact and self-cohesive" (*SE* 20). As a transsexual who fails to feel ownership of his skin, Thompson performs repeated acts of real self-directed violence, turning against his pretransition body precisely as if it were not his own, hitting his head against a wall, punching himself in the face, throwing himself down ravines, coating his body with mud. His skin serves as locus for this self-reflexive aggression. He inscribes his skin with tattoos (in his words they are "self-inflicted"), covering the entire area on the backs of his hands, his thumbs, his knuckles: "This was done by first writing or drawing the tattoo on the skin with a pen. Then I punctured my skin along the lines with a needle so that it would draw blood. These hundreds of pin pricks were then stained with paint or indian ink" (52). Following these on his hands, he acquires chest and neck tattoos.

The ability to give oneself pain, to harm one's own body, surely depends upon a great degree of bodily alienation; yet the tattoos, like the self-directed pain more generally, function as part of Thompson's attempt to feel his body as his own—quite simply, to feel it. In the absence of feeling his body surrounded and supported, feeling its limits and attachment to self (or rather in the feeling of the absence of this feeling), this self-directed inscriptive violence uses pain to establish bodily boundaries for the self. Thompson tattoos his skin as if he would have his body bear/bare the true self hidden within: his authentic signature. Such acts of marking the body's surface in an effort to feel belonging in it prefigure the surgical inscriptions of sex reassignment: on a larger and of course medically officiated scale, the transsexual's way of (re)making the body/skin in order to feel at home in it. When Thompson decides to have the tattoos from his neck and hands removed, this surgery does not erase but exacerbates the skin damage; the skin is slit and stitched to leave painful and prominent scarring. One scar on his right hand splits open and becomes infected, leaving "a large oozing hole in my hand" (83). During later phalloplasty procedures, when the suture on the underside of Thompson's penis comes loose and the skin splits, Thompson dreams that the skin on his hand along the scar of the tattoo removal has reopened, this time revealing a horrifying ball of fat beneath the skin. Displacing the split surface from penis to hand, the dream constructs as symbolic parallels the subject's own interventions on his body's surface and his substantial transsexual surgery: both appear as inscriptive attempts at bodily ownership and belonging, both take place via the psychically rich material skin. Skin surfaces, Anzieu suggests, are the fabric of many dreams. Such dreams of splitting and graftable skin here describe a specifically transsexual desire to get out of the wrong body and into a new one: a desire to trade skins.

Surely not incidentally, Thompson's attempts to inscribe his own skin occur before he has begun hormone treatment and testosterone has androgenized (coarsened, hardened, thickened) his skin. Once Thompson no longer bears a visibly female skin, this sense of skinlessness recedes and the direct physical self-abuse, as if correlated to the gendered appearance of the body, ceases. It is startling to grasp the extent to which the skin's appearance determines gendered reading, to which skin is a gendered text. Even so, posthormones and presurgery constitute a weird transitional zone for the transsexual body, a time and place in between sexual difference in which its naked sex can be perceived as neither/nor or both. Passing during this period entails covering or concealing this nakedness so that the body might be accepted as uniformly gendered. In Thompson's case passing as a man presurgery is achieved not only through testosterone therapy but through disguising what is still a female morphology. The daily layerings of binder, several T-shirts, and thick work shirt, the reshaping his body that still has a female chest into male contours form a kind of provisional, transitional male skin or surround, protective (it hides the hated body and prevents his discovery) and at the same time restrictive, stifling (he can't move without it, it's a skin-tight second skin). The significance of this second skin is thus (aptly) twofold. As it allows for passing, it also entraps and prevents *being*.

Simultaneous with Thompson's successful passing in the narrative, the images of damaged or disintegrating surfaces and containers are refracted away from his body and projected onto inanimate objects. Thompson achieves most of his transition exceptionally early, beginning hormone therapy at sixteen and undergoing a double mastectomy at twenty-one. But as a penis is essential to his body image (from late childhood, he packs the front of his trousers, filling in for what he feels should be already there), more than half of the autobiography concerns itself with his long, distressing wait for this surgery. When his prospects for phalloplasty appear most tenuous, Thompson directs his urge to rip and tear up his skin onto his home, smashing furniture, windows, and crockery, his narrative itself recognizing the displacement of destructiveness from self-protection to concrete protection: "The walls of protection that I had carefully built about myself, I was now breaking down" (248). In spite of his building skills he lives for some years without adequate material walls of protection, in the midst of broken windows, collapsed ceilings (through which fall rain and snow), piles of dirt and rubble: in other words within a damaged, fragmented, and inadequate container. Yet once the course of phalloplasty surgeries gets underway, Thompson sets to reconstructing the house, confirming that its physical condition is inextricably tied up with his own, as if this "envelope" of home can be reintegrated only alongside the envelope of body image.

Selfhood, according to Anzieu, is fundamentally entangled with images of integrity, of bodily wholeness. Conversely, states of depersonalization, of not feeling real, are enmeshed with images of inadequate containers on which boundaries are blurred, surfaces flawed, envelopes perforated. "A reality of the order of phantasy" (a psychic projection of the body derived from the body), the skin ego as the unconscious "figures in phantasies, dreams, everyday speech, posture, disturbances of thought" (*SE* 4). In *What Took You So Long?* the images of damaged, broken surfaces before Thompson's phalloplasty proliferate. Some, like the progressive dilapidation of Thompson's house, his grandfather's heavily scarred and curled-in hand, and his father's loss of his fingers in the steel-work machinery, make sense as significant events in the subject's life-plot. Others—eggs with ruined "crinkled skin" that Thompson remembers from a TV program ("I am the crinkled egg that nobody wants . . . but I am as good on the inside as all the other eggs" [254]), a toad with no legs he finds in the road as a child and carries with him everywhere—appear more phantasmagorically, free-floating oneirically in the narrative, their significance intimately bound up with Thompson's psychic reality. Onto the surfaces of such "others," Thompson projects "this ugly, fragmented body of mine" (191), a body glaringly incomplete when overlaid with the integrity of his male body image, a body in bits and pieces that only phalloplasty, as Thompson writes after this procedure, makes "whole" (309). Pausing over incidents of amputation in others' bodily forms— the legless toad, the father's fingerless hand—the narrative implicitly refigures Thompson's own female contours as a transsexual man into a case of amputation, as though his material body has "lost" what his male body image rightfully possess, namely, a penis: a loss that surgery will then be represented as restoring.

If the skin is the organ enabling the sense of touch, how does one touch, how is one touched, in a skin not one's own? Legendarily, the genital parts of the presurgical body remain for transsexuals untouchable; genital eroticism, writes Anzieu, is possible only for those who feel a basic level of security and comfort in their own skins. Male-to-females

Caroline Cossey and Renée Richards both describe their acute discomfort at having their penises touched pre-surgery. "I found that part of my body so repulsive that [my lover's] desire for me began to sicken and repel me"; "I discouraged any fondling of my penis. . . . I felt similarly about oral sex. Here again, my objections probably boiled down to the fact that this action represents such an intense focus on my penis."[25] The significance of sex on the pretransition body is then complex for it is both too real and yet not real enough. On the one hand the delimiting of touchable areas refuses to sex these areas with feeling: the genitals remain unsexed, both nonerogenous and not included in the imaginary "true sex" morphology. On the other hand this nonerogenization implicitly acknowledges those genital parts as already materially sexed (that is male or female); it is the substantiality of bodily sex that renders them untouchable. Regarding this split, we might say that it is what is *not* "gender all along" about the body's sex (the fact that that material sex is not commensurable with gender identity) that drives the transsexual trajectory. For Thompson, his female parts are not simply untouchable, they are inconceivable, blank spaces in body image:

> While my body was the way it was, there was no way that anyone would be allowed to see or touch the parts of it that didn't belong to me. I had rejected them myself so long ago, and had learned to close off from my mind the fact that they were there. I never looked at the parts of my body which were wrong—it was hard enough to wash them. . . . My body didn't exist in the way it was born; for me it only existed in my inner identity as a male. Having a woman touch me sexually would not only have seemed perverse to me, but also it would have broken my detachment.
>
> (75).

This dis-ownership of sex, the untouchability of the body, maintains the integrity of the alternatively gendered imaginary. As the contours of body image are outlined as fundamentally noncoincident with material body, it is this sense of im-proper-ness—the conceptualization of the sexed morphology as not the property of the subject's body image—that is captured so succinctly in the wrong-body formula. It becomes a description simply of the refusal of body ego to own referential body: I do not recognize as proper, as my property, this material surround; therefore I must be trapped in the wrong body. Since inappropriateness is located in the material body, the entire configuration explains why the subject seeks surgical intervention to alter the flesh rather than psychological intervention to transform body image. If the body is not owned, it is in this experience of body—not *my* body—that surgery intervenes.

"What is more important for us, at an elemental level, than the control, the owning and operation, of our own physical selves?" asks neurologist Oliver Sacks.[26] Feeling one's body as one's own, Sacks's work on severe body image disturbances demonstrates, is a core component of subjectivity, perhaps its very basis. Conversely, the sentient feeling of disembodiment, what Sacks terms "bodily agnosia" (*a-gnos*: the unknown; here, the body as unknown, that which in our everyday life we take for granted as the base for perception and knowledge) interferes with basic bodily functioning. In Sacks's case histories somatic unknowing entails not only the loss of limbs in the subjects' bodily representation—or on one occasion, the totality of the body image—but also the loss of control and feeling in body parts.[27] The effect of this erasure in bodily representation is, above all, profoundly, bizarrely, and sometimes comically (in a blackly humorous way) material, as in the case of "The Man who Fell out of Bed." Having "lost" his leg in his body image, the patient finds what he takes to be a foreign leg in his bed: his own. Deciding it to be a severed limb planted by medical students as a practical joke, he throws it out of the bed, only to find himself, much to his bewilderment, on the floor. Such instances of the failure of body image to know the limits of the physical body graphically reveal not only the material force of body image in the subject's imaginary but the neurophysiological base of body image. More than an imaginary construction, more than psychic excess, the feeling of knowing one's body as one's own, Sacks's neurology emphasizes, is essential to the body's successful sensorimotor functioning. It constitutes the "vital 'sixth sense' by which the body knows itself." For this substantial bodily feeling Sacks uses C. S. Sherrington's "proprioception"—a term that retains the notion of ownership (*proprio*), of the body as the subject's property.[28] While, like Anzieu, Sacks never writes of sexual anatomy, the transsexual might be grasped via his terms as a subject who has "lost" sex proprioception: s/he can't feel her or his sex; it's the felt/unfelt "blind spot."

Yet proprioception is body image residing in the sentient rather than the visual. Sacks states that the feeling of owning one's body is more foundational than visual body image to our body's operation: visual body image is "normally rather feeble (it is of course absent in the blind), and normally subsidiary to the proprioceptive body-model."[29] This sense of the body thus concerns less body *image*—the visual, the phenomenological—than the feeling of the body: the postural schema. Anzieu likewise insists on the supremacy of touch over sight in the development of body image: "Skin is the touchstone (literally) to which the various sensory data are referred back ... the skin possesses a structural primacy over all the other senses"; and it is touch that engenders the skin ego, beginning at birth ("an all-over body massage"), even perhaps in the final stages in utero.[30] In thinking body image, we seem to have emphasized "image" at the expense of body, rendering the body equivalent to that which can be seen (the body in the eye of the other) and omitting to account for the subjective experience of the body, the body as it is (or is not) felt. It is surely Lacan's work that lies behind this privileging of sight; he has already been much criticized for his occularcentric account of the origins of the subject, most substantially by Luce Irigaray.[31] In their inversion of the conventional privileging of sight over touch, Sacks and Anzieu recover the bodily "sensations" that form Freud's bodily ego, which, following Lacan, have been overlooked (even in Sacks's neurological model, Freud's psychoanalytic ego is given a foundational place: proprioception is said to be equivalent to Freud's "body-ego").[32] The passage from *The Ego and the Id*, in which Freud suggests a nonidentity between seen and felt body and sustains the importance of feeling, needs to be understood, therefore, as seminal. Like Anzieu's and Sacks's prioritization of touch over sight, Freud's distinction between what can be seen of the body and what it can feel, and his alignment of the sensory with internal perception, explicates the strange materiality of transsexual wrong embodiment. Together they suggest why the transsexual's gender identity, originally invisible but deeply felt, can wield such a material force: why "feeling like" in the face of such opposition from the visible body can be experienced as a core self.

Not only do they allow the substantiation of the figure of the wrong body into a transsexual ontology in which body image, while still a psychic projection, is nevertheless deeply felt, Anzieu and Sacks elucidate the cruciality of the feeling of bodily integrity to successful and happy functioning in general. In their work splitting and fragmentation in the body ego (the difference between "perceptions" of the body) are unlivable states. Sacks underlines that proprioception is "the fundamental organic mooring of identity—at least of ... corporeal identity";[33] Anzieu likewise underscores the essentiality of feeling identity as one's own. In a passage that challenges the contemporary theoretical skepticism toward the grounded, integral subject, Anzieu distinguishes carefully between the productive theoretical project of interrogating the subject and the devastating loss of belief in one's self: "Belief is a vital human need.... One is not a person if one does not believe in the identity and continuity of the self.... The human being who holds these beliefs has certainly to question them. But the person who does not have them has to acquire them before he can experience his own being and his own well-being" (*SE* 131). Appropriating the Moebius-strip configuration from Lacan's representation of the normative structure of the ego, the torsion and unborderedness (it has no inside nor outside) of which has meant its promotion to an archetypal symbol of the poststructuralist disbelief in the integrity and continuity of the subject, Anzieu uses this configuration specifically to denote the ego in impaired, self-destructive psychic states. His case histories illustrate that the subject's inability to distinguish "inside" from "outside" is most often responsible in "borderline" conditions for acute psychic suffering: a suffering that Anzieu's psychoanalytic practice understands as its task to lessen, to smooth out this torsion and reestablish the boundaries of self and body. The lability and confusion in the post-Lacanian subject are in Anzieu profoundly negative disturbances. Operative in Sacks's and Anzieu's practice as clinicians is that same narrative drive held as most precious in transsexual autobiography: from fragmentation to integration; from alienation to reconciliation; from loss to restoration. Both neurologist and psychoanalyst perceive their patients' discomfort or suffering to be intimately bound up with some form of corporeally effective loss; recovery consists in an equipollent corporeal reappropriation. It is this notion of corporeal reappropriation that inhabits the logic of sex reassignment surgery: attaining that feeling of a coherent and integral body of one's own.

From Mutilation to Integration: The Poetics of Sex Reassignment Surgery

Sharon Olds's poem, "Outside the Operating Room of the Sex-Change Doctor," begins with envisioning a tray of severed penises, the imagined remnants from a series of sex reassignment surgeries. Although manifestly rejecting the scene's comparability to those of historical locations world-renowned for their systematization of torture ("This is not Vietnam, Chile, Buchenwald"), in the very invocation of these sites of horrific mutilations, the poem conjures up grand-scale barbarism and (in spite of the refutation of similarity) blurs "sex-change" surgery into their backdrop.[34] The poem's pivotal image of the severed penises, which misrepresents the mechanics of male-to-female sex reassignment surgery (for the last thirty years these have included orchidectomy—castration—but not penectomy—full surgical removal of the penis; rather, the penis is hollowed out, its skin surround preserved attached, and inverted to form the vaginal lining), portrays sex reassignment surgery not as the refashioning of bodily sex but as its literal removal, as if the surgery were a matter of desexing rather than resexing the body. In keeping with this position the poem's interest is not with the transsexual bodies recovering from the surgery but with their severed sex. The body of the poem (so to speak) goes on to bring to life the seven severed penises, animating them with their transsexual subjects' thoughts as if these severed parts could speak *for* their former "owners"; as if the truth of the subject lay not with her postreassignment body but with the severed sex; as if the penis were the "seat" of her true sex and subjectivity. In this way the poem picks up on and plays to the cultural stigmatization of transsexuality and the misconceptions that underpin this: that transsexuality consists in the brutal mutilation of healthy bodies, that sex reassignment surgery does not so much effect sex change as it transmogrifies "normal" men and women into unsexed or hermaphroditic monstrous others simply through the excision of their "natural" functioning sex.

Without doubt what renders transsexuality most unnatural in the cultural imagination is sex reassignment surgery. The logic of its conception as mutilation is that if the bodies operated on are not already wounded or deformed, then the surgery itself must wound or deform. Sex reassignment surgery is differentiated from curative reconstructive surgery on the basis that it is not seen to resolve any physical defect. Like other forms of perceived "nonfunctional" surgery, but because it meddles with the intricate, intimate, and rarefied domain of sex to a much greater degree, sex reassignment surgery on the healthy body can only disfigure. This association of sex reassignment surgery with the cosmetic enables many health insurance companies to classify it as such in an attempt to evade funding responsibilities for transsexual clients—and this in spite of the fact that transsexuality continues to be classified according to a disease model by the American Psychiatric Association: an illness requiring a medical remedy.[35] Ironically, the notions of sex reassignment as "superficial" and "mutilating" shore each other up in this catetory of the cosmetic. As Kathy Davis's work on women and cosmetic surgery reveals, the category of cosmetic surgery in general is shot through with deeply moralizing judgments about the perceived inessentiality of its intervention. Whereas plastic surgery, which emerged as a specialty from mass warfare at the beginning of this century, is accepted as necessary for correcting malfunctioning or disfigured bodies, its offshoot, cosmetic surgery, is devalued as an elective procedure for "the aesthetic improvement of otherwise healthy bodies."[36] This devaluation is suggested in the very term "cosmetic," so named in order to keep it distinct from the substantive form, "plastic." Even though the procedures for plastic and cosmetic surgery may be identical, "cosmetic" implies a greater superficiality, as if cosmetic surgery intervened in an even more "surface" surface of the self. Hence to elect for cosmetic surgery is perceived as being superficial.

Precisely as it intervenes in the body's surface tissues (a locale that Anzieu's skin ego shows has a profound importance for sense of self), the plastic aspect of sex reassignment surgery—the restructuring of breasts/chest and genitals, the manipulation of surface tissues—is transformative. Even in cases of the "cosmetic" surgery described by Davis's research, the reasons for and effects of reconstructive surgery may run psychically deep. The realization of identity hoped for and/or brought about as a result of the manipulation of the material surface of the body can be substantial; skin is anything but skin deep. For transsexuals surgery is a fantasy of restoring the body to the self enacted on the surface of the body. If the dominant body image pretransition is that of being trapped within an extraneous "other" skin, sex reassignment surgery is figured as bringing release from this skin. Of his sense of his body after mastectomy, Thompson writes: "It was like shedding an annoying and uncomfortable garment and being back in my own self" (177). Likewise, female-to-male Martino metaphorizes his "not-me" breasts as clothing extraneous to bodily self that the surgery removes: drowsily coming to after his mastectomy, he wonders whether the surgery has indeed taken place, "[O]r was I still *wearing* those unsightly breasts?"[37] Figuratively releasing the female-to-male from this restrictive second skin, mastectomy also literally gives him freer movement of body. Both Martino and Thompson indicate that much of their postsurgical relief resides in being able to leave aside the layers of binding and clothes required to compress and conceal their breasts. The physical experience of being able to wear fewer layers, in addition to and as the beneficial effect of the surgical removal of the breasts, contributes to the shaping of the postmastectomy body image as disburdened. Body image is a product of and produces physical experience.

Surgery strips the body bare to what it should have been. Transsexual autobiographies inscribe the event(s) of surgery as a return: a coming home to the self through body. Given the transsexual's failure to own material body, surgery appears as an attempt quite specifically to reestablish the "not-me" body as me; as a restoration of the "proper" body after the configuration of transsexual wrong embodiment, somatic transition makes narrative sense. Inverting common perception, transsexual accounts write against assumptions of mutilation with a poetics of reassignment. Images of wholeness and bodily integration pervade descriptions of sex reassignment surgery and after: "Elated, completed at last"; "I was all of a piece"; "[A] new life in the body of a complete man."[38] Filling in the gaps, removing the excess, sex reassignment surgery fleshes out in the visual the transsexual's already felt body image. Male-to-female Kim Harlow reveals how surgery directly concretizes and completes her body-picture of herself as a woman. Before sex reassignment surgery her dreams cut short her body above the waist. Close to surgery she begins to dream of the operation itself, but still without realizing her female sex: "each time the operation was interrupted, leaving me sexless." After the surgery, while still wrapped in bandages and without even having seen her female genitals, Harlow dreams for the first time of herself "naked and whole, with my women's sex." Surgery directly intervenes in body image, immediately integrating its "lost" parts.[39]

What makes the transsexual able and willing to submit to the knife—the splitting, cutting, removal, and reshaping of organs, tissues, and skin that another might conceive as mutilation—is the drive to get the body back to what should have been. What makes possible the psychic translation of the surgical incursions into the body into a poetics of healing is a kind of transsexual somatic memory. Surgery is made sense of as a literal and figurative re-membering, a restorative drive that is indeed common to accounts of reconstructive surgeries among nontranssexual subjects and perhaps inherent in the very notion of *reconstructive* surgery. From rhinoplasty to postmastectomy breast reconstruction, the subject seeks out through surgery an idealized body/face from the past. Lucy Grealy, for instance, describes the process of some thirty reconstructive surgeries on her cancer-disfigured face as a "journey back to my face," a progression toward a face that never grew because as a child most of her jaw was surgically removed.[40] An autobiography concerning psychical recovery from a disfigured body image (or more precisely facial image) more than a narrative about surgical recovery from actual facial disfigurement (for the surgeries fail in succession), *Autobiography of a Face* has much in common with transsexual autobiographies: Grealy begins trapped in her body, feeling intense somatic shame and alienation from her reflected image. Her struggle is also toward integrity. What the transsexual wants in remembering an originally felt body image may therefore be quite unexceptional.

Memory is crucial to how we experience our bodies. In his work on phantom limbs Sacks has pointed to the key role of somatic memory in structuring body image. The phantom limb (like transsexuality, also a phenomenon in which body image is incongruous with its corporeal referent) may be understood as a sensory memory of the lost body part, a feeling of presence that remains in its very absence. Cases of phantomization reveal the body (the experience is that of an unconscious involuntary sensation) engaged in the struggle not to forget its original body image. Phantomization may be grasped as the mirror image inversion of agnosia. Whereas agnosia represents the forgetting in the body image of somatically attached, functioning parts, leaving the subject a kind of " 'internal' amputee" (for s/he "loses" limbs from her or his inner or representational body), the phenomenon of the phantom limb represents the remembering in the body image of parts actually lost from the material body.[41] In the case of the transsexual the body constructed through sex reassignment surgery is not one that actually existed in the past, one that is literally re-membered, but one that should have existed; sex reassignment surgery is a recovery of what was not. The body of transsexual becoming is born out of a yearning for a perfect past—that is, not memory but nostalgia: the desire for the purified version of what was, not for the return to home per se (*nostos*) but to the romanticized ideal of home. Memory annealed in imagination, nostalgia re-collects the fragments of the past and welds them into an imaginary whole. Grosz also suggests that the phantom limb phenomenon represents a psychic nostalgia for somatic wholeness: "The phantom is an expression of nostalgia for the unity and wholeness of the body, its completion. It is a memorial to the missing limb, a psychical delegate that stands in its place."[42]

Based on a double conceptualization—of sex reassignment surgery as a nostalgic return to the sexed contours that should have been; and of phantomization as an expression of nostalgia for the idealized somatotype in its physical absence—might the transsexual's postreassignment body be reconceived as already phantomized prereassignment? Although phantom limbs are generally conceived as debilitating in that the feeling "in" the severed body part's spatial absence remains—often painfully, uselessly, distressingly after its physical loss—Sacks focuses on the enabling aspects of phantoms for amputees: positive phantoms. In order to use a replacement artificial limb, the amputee needs to appropriate the prosthesis as his or her own, to incorporate it into his or her body image. To do so, s/he needs to experience a phantom presence in the physical absence of the somatic limb. As one of Sacks's patients with a leg amputation explains, it is his positive phantom leg that "animates the prosthesis, and allows me to walk."[43] To use the prosthetic leg, the subject must "re-member" what it was like to use that leg. Does this not suggest the means by which the transsexual is able to incorporate the newly shaped parts into his or her body image, to claim the rearranged material as "my penis" or "my vagina"? How would s/he be able to feel postsurgical constructions as these parts, unless these parts were already phantomized? There must already be in a felt imaginary, for the transsexual to appropriate the rearranged somatic material as his or her new sex, a prior phantomization of sex, which is not to undermine but to underline the felt presence of transsex precisely in the very space of its physical absence. For if the natal sex represents an agnosic or alien part for the transsexual (the wrong body), leading him or her to experience the material body in bits and pieces as s/he dis-(re)members his or her sexed parts, the transsexual's "true" sex, the body trapped within, realized in theory by sex reassignment, might be understood to complement this agnosia as his or her phantom sex: the parts felt as more real, the parts that "complete" the transsexual body image. The phantomization of sex would appear as the concomitant of the not-knowing (the agnosia) of the real. Both conditions produce a body image radically noncoincident with the material body, a body image that pushes past the limits of material contours—and pushes the transsexual past these limits. Both conditions combine to produce a body image experienced as real enough to cause the transsexual to seek the reshaping of his/her material body. Sex reassignment surgery may then be grasped as healing and changing the transsexual subject in that it serves as the antidote to both of these body image distortions, simultaneously effecting the ablation of the disowned organs ("removing everything that didn't belong" [Thompson 161]) and the realization of the already phantomized sexed parts. Surgery deploys the skin and tissues to materialize the transsexual body image with fleshly prostheses in the shape of the sentient ghost-body. The surgical grafting of materials endows the transsexual with the corporeal referents for these imaginary or phantomized signifieds, restoring their substance. These parts become nameable for the transsexual only when realized by surgery. For the surgery-opting transsexual, however potent, the phantomized sex is insufficient in and of itself to transform the meaning of bodily matter. "If I could have lived in my own inner reality I might have survived without surgery," Thompson explains (178). But he cannot. Not residing wholly in the imaginary, sex must be felt in the body, must find its externalization, its substantiation, in material flesh. Sex reassignment surgery by definition recognizes the material body as a substantive and de facto sexually significant, although tractable and reconstructible, domain.

This cooperation between surgery as material intervention and body image as the phantomization of sex is responsible for enabling the transsexual to feel transsexed. "How new and wonderful it seemed," Katherine Cummings recalls of her feelings after her vaginoplasty, "to be thinking of 'my vagina'!"[44] "My vagina" becomes thinkable and nameable in response to the surgical construction as the transplanted, restructured tissue is recognized both as self ("my") and sexed ("vagina"). That Cummings, like other male-to-females can think "vagina" of what is in fact the inverted skin of her penis reveals how crucial is the dynamic of mutual enablement between the material and the psychic in the constitution of transsex. The surgical procedure for vaginoplasty, by retaining the erogenous skin of the penis as the vaginal lining and transplanting the penile glans into position as clitoris, encourages the subject's psychic investment in the material as erogenous parts. Mimesis is important as regards not only the appearance of transsexual genitals but their sexual function; the surgery is designed as much as possible to imitate vaginal and clitoral orgasm. Yet the restructured penile tissues can be said to become a vagina/clitoris for the transsexual only inasmuch as she already imagines and feels these parts as her own. Likewise, contemporary phalloplasty techniques for female-to-males encourage erotogenicity psychically and materially: the clitoris is typically relocated onto the surface of the penis or left intact underneath the penis and connected to nerves transported from the donor site—forearm, thigh, or abdomen—that form the phalloplasty. Insofar as body image takes as its psychic/corporeal interface the surface of the body—the skin and surface tissues of the body—surgery addresses body image precisely through the manipulation of these tissues; the transsexual's sex is changed as the subject feels this surface to be significantly altered.

So potent is the psyche/bodily surface correspondence effected by the sex reassignment surgery that the investment of body image in transsexed parts can begin even while these parts are still under construction—that is, before the part even looks like a vagina or a penis. During one of the final stages of his phalloplasty Thompson is told he could lose the penis surgery has so far produced for him. Created from tissues harvested from his thigh in the form of a pedicle tube flap, the "penis" is attached at one end to his groin and at the other to his hip, while the central section, the prospective penile body, is lifted free on its underside from the abdominal skin. At this stage, it looks like a suitcase handle (as it is often described in medical literature): a tube joined at either end to the body. The next stage involves cutting the penis loose from its transitional root at Thompson's hip and allowing it to hang free from his groin. The risk to the penis is necrosis (tissue death and tissue loss), which may result when it loses its blood supply from the hip end. As the surgeon explains this, Thompson—not surprisingly, having battled through three previous operations over some eighteen months—panics. For a moment he considers halting his quest for a penis then and there and living with the pedicle tube flap attached to his hip and groin, the "penis" a piece of flesh slung sideways across the right side of his mid-body, immobile, indeployable, and of course looking nothing like a penis. "Even though it had felt somewhat unnatural to have my penis attached to my leg, I had grown accustomed to it, and I felt I didn't want to lose even that. Even in its abnormal position I was more 'me' than I would have been without it" (300). Even at this stage of the procedure, when the pedicle tube flap resembles and functions as a pedicle tube flap—a tissue transplant in transitional attachment on the body on its way to becoming something else—the surgery has already enabled Thompson to invest in this thigh material as his penis: as with Cummings's vagina, both his ("more 'me' ") and as a penis. In the circular fashion of transsexual becoming the suitcase handle has already filled the place of the phantom penis in the body image, replacing the "packing" with real flesh: "I already saw my penis [the flap] as an entity with a life of its own, like a little human being. It was as if I had to breathe life into this part of my body, which should always have been there, should have been mine from birth. This was meant to be, I was a man" (300). Not only is the pedicle tube flap immediately psychically incorporated into his body image as a penis, it *personifies* (almost a being apart) his transsexed self, comes to stand for his authentically gendered subjectivity. This claiming and naming of the penis is in stark contrast to the unnamability and inconceivability of his female genital parts and functions: Thompson's autobiography unfailingly euphemizes vagina, menstruation, and breasts. If agnosia renders unnameable what is, phantomization renders nameable what is not—or at least not yet.

In postsurgical scenes the transsexual virtually installs his or her transsexed subjectivity in the new tender parts, precisely as if s/he becomes these parts (in the same sense that Grealy writes that her succession of facial surgeries leads her to "become" her face). Immediately postreassignment, the transsexual trajectory itself appears to be at stake in these organs. The subject's intense focus on them is to be expected, considering the fact that these organs are most often hard-gained and that these areas have been subject to such intense surgical attention. However, the concentration of subjectivity in transsex is also a response to a dramatically altered physical body that is at this point that which is blatantly most precious about the self. Reassignment is a restoration of body; nevertheless on a mechanical level the new longed-for organs present themselves as unfamiliar zones, and the transsexual must undergo—proprioceptively, gingerly—some adjustment to the remolded contours of this new bodily geography. Cummings's problems with vaginal dilation following surgery (required to keep the vagina from closing in on itself) stem from her unfamiliarity with her new genitals. Frankly, she's at a loss as to what her vagina feels or looks like. Having no bodily sense of the depth of her vagina, she's not sure when the dilator is inside; the limits of this new invaluable flesh are as yet strange. In a comparable moment, once his penis has been detached successfully from its vascular roots on his thigh, Thompson finds he must rethink the most automatic of movements such as getting out of the bath. How is he supposed to "handle" this new fleshy addition? Should he let the penis fall naturally, or should he support it as he stands up? Such postreassignment episodes, common in the autobiographies, both comic and frightening, mark the surgical body off as unfamiliar in a way that echoes its prereassignment unfamiliarity. But whereas the prereassignment body's unfamiliarity is alien (the foreign, to be abjected), the postreassignment body is the not yet known that is yet already most precious about the self.

And thus if gender reassignment is transsexuals' "rite of incorporation," as Ann Bolin suggests in her anthropological study of male-to-females ("Surgery . . . is their access to normalcy. They can finally be treated as if they had always been women. The value of the rite . . . lies in the 'incorporation it permits' "), it is so in a layered sense.[45] Surgery is a rite of social incorporation; it promises the ultimate passing—a passing in the flesh, one that allows the discarding of external passing devices involving concealing, strapping, wrapping, and padding the body—sex reassignment enables assimilation into the world of gendered realness. The skin itself becomes the article of gendered passing as gender shifts from doing to being, from performance to the flesh. Touching her genitals after her vaginoplasty, it is this skin-deep passing that Dawn Langley Simmons celebrates as the achievement of her surgery: "Nobody would be able to tell the difference.... I knew I was like all other women ... Not a blemish, not a scar; the vaginal lips perfection."[46] And in this bodily trajectory one cannot get deeper than the skin. Not being able to tell the difference on the surface bestows the security of a profound identity sameness; the fantasy of sex reassignment surgery is that it erases the difference of transsexuality, covers its traces with a seamlessly sexed body. Constructed in the medical narrative as the apogee of transsexuality, sex reassignment surgery in theory allows the transsexual to pass as nontranssexual, to appear as a "real" man or a "real" woman. One might be said to become most fully a transsexual through this rite when one is able to leave that identity, that body, most completely behind.

Yet sex reassignment surgery is a rite of incorporation for the transsexual in another sense, in the immediate sense of embodiment, incorporation: a rite of bodily appropriation, a grappling with the materiality of the body itself. Harrowing scenes of near-death experiences (Richards's tracheal shave, Martino's mastectomy), of botch-job medical interventions (Julia Grant's vaginal probe,[47] Martino's first phalloplasty), or simply of some of the routine but nonetheless terrifying problems entailed in any major surgery (malfunctioning catheters in Cossey and Thompson); descriptions of the pain, the shock, the discomfort to the body; the cycle of suffering and recovery, of the wounded body healing: in repetition these features give to sex reassignment surgery a certain ritualized structure, so that it does take on the form of *the* definitive transsexual experience, a transsexual rite of passage, as if it were the surgery that makes the subject most fully a transsexual. Before he can receive authorization from his psychiatrist for his phalloplasty, Thompson is required to state his willingness to tolerate the physical pain and distress that accompanies the surgery. It is as though the experience of such surgery and the compulsion to undergo it were the symbolic vehicle for transsexual transformation—the identifying marker of transsexuality—as much as its mechanics; for this corporeal distress is surely nothing next to that of the prereassignment body.

Body Politics and Personal Prosthetics

Previous theoretical descriptions of sex reassignment surgery overwhelmingly conceive of the transsexual as fragmenting the sexed body. Arguing that "transsexualism is fetishization par excellence," Janice Raymond claims that in their focus on genital parts transsexuals approach the body in bits and pieces.[48] Marjorie Garber similarly concludes that transsexuals, both male-to-female and female-to-male, overestimate the penis: " 'The absolute insignia of maleness' [the penis] *is* for them the index of male identity."[49] Although from lesbian feminism to queer theory, 1979 to 1989, the charge against transsexuals has shifted from fetishism to essentialism (now the problem lies not in transsexuals' fragmenting the body per se but in their metonymizing the fragment—mis-taking the sexed parts for the gendered whole), the assumption is still that sex reassignment surgery produces the body as an aggregate of exchangeable and overvalued parts. Most recently, in the more eccentric regions of postmodern theory, the transsexual has been celebrated precisely for cutting up the sexed body into detachable and artificial parts. Figuring the transsexual as a kind of cyberhacker, his/her manufactured sex wrecking what's real, what's natural about the body, Arthur and Marilouise Kroker read the transsexual's technosurgery as the ultimate deconstruction of the sexed body. The Krokers suggest transsexuality as "transgenic gender," that is "a virus free gender," the virus nothing less than the material body itself, living flesh. Recombinant sex taking place without the body is the "only good sex today": "Sex without origin, localizing gender, or referential signifier." Through the transsexual's "morphing" as they understand sex reassignment, the Krokers glimpse a "new sexual horizon, post-male, post-female," and crucially post-human(ist), the dawning of a new virtual age of which the transsexual will be hero.[50] If the reconstructions of reassignment surgery secure the transsexual in Raymond's lesbian feminist paradigm as patriarchal stooge and in Garber's queer theory as conventionalist, in the Krokers's postmodern vision of bodiless, originless subjectivity, surgery elevates the transsexual to postmodern outlaw. Now the material flesh—frighteningly, considering the current climate in which AIDS has made sexed body parts in and of themselves to be feared as infected/infectious—has become the marker of retrogressive identities; the discourse of transgenics (which in its quest for purer species ends up resembling that of nineteenth-century *eu*genics) is deployed against the biological body that has become but an impurity to be transcended.

For the process of changing sex to be like morphing, for it to be as systematized, clean, insouciant, and unbloody as the transformation of data on a computer screen, is surely—at least at one point or another—every transsexual's dream. "If I could just snap my fingers . . ."; "If there was a closet where we could go in one thing and come out another"; "Beam me up, Scottie": fantasies of immaculate transformation, of immediate materialization, and of perfect sex change are commonly voiced and exchanged, with self-deprecating humor although perhaps never without yearning. As medicine fast forwards into the future, the new biotechnological sciences can surely only facilitate sex change, making it more successful—that is, more convincing and more comprehensive. Even now, as a transsexual who religiously keeps tabs on medical research, I myself look to the new art of tissue engineering to revolutionize sex reassignment procedures. A masterful interdisciplinary alliance of chemical engineering, cell biology, genetics, and surgery, tissue engineering takes human cells from the body, treats them with tissue-inducing biochemicals to manufacture living organs and surfaces that are missing or damaged apart from the body on "scaffolds" (plastic structures of body parts), and transplants the organs back into the body. Because they share the subject's DNA structure, when reattached, these artificially manufactured parts immediately adapt to their environment and grow in proportion to the body. The first organ to have been successfully manufactured thus is skin (there is an entire industry in artificial bodily surfaces), but work is already underway on more complex organs: the liver, the pancreas, and most famously, an ear for a boy born without one—an experiment responsible for the recent surreal pictures on British television screens of a laboratory mouse scurrying back and forth with a human ear the size of its own body transplanted onto its back.[51] It is not difficult to imagine that sex organs would be included in this manufacture of body parts, if not first for transsexuals then for burn or accident victims who suffer from lost or damaged genitals, eventually becoming part of transsexual procedures as with plastic surgery in a trickle-down fashion.

More than any contemporary medical practice, tissue engineering fragments the integrity of the body into a collection of disconnected and detachable parts. It is a near literalization of what Rosi Braidotti has conjured with her inversion of Deleuze and Guattari's "bodies without organs" as "organs without bodies": a nightmarish vision of the biosciences' production of an ever more dismembered, fragmented body. Yet as its goal is bodily integrity, its purpose to restore the body to an original unity, tissue engineering would promise to fulfill the very task that Braidotti urges contemporary thought to address in the face of such technological fetishism: "the urgency to reformulate the unity of the human being."[52] Rendering obsolete the free-flaps and skin grafts that are the mainstay of current reconstructive surgery, tissue engineering will erase most effectively the differences of those bodies upon which surgical work is performed, enabling all bodies to pass as integral and original: whole. Behind this most cutting-edge technology is the quite nostalgic aim of restoring lost, absent, or malfunctioning material flesh, the integrity of the human being.

For the time being, however, changing sex remains very much a bodily affair: from the patient's perspective, a material intervention into living flesh that in the process reveals sex as quite real, quite embodied, and sometimes (especially in the case of female-to-male phalloplasty procedures as Thompson's account suggests) quite resistant to being changed. The recurrent problem with theoretical visions of sex reassignment surgery is their blithe elision of this perspective and of the experience of sex reassignment. Raymond, Garber, and the Krokers all argue the implications of sex reassignment surgery for a generic human body from a nonmedicalized subject position: none consider the body's surface experientially. Their vision of surgery as fragmenting the body is therefore not surprising; for from the point of view of the other watching the surgical procedure, the body laid out on the operating table is always going to appear as an integrity and surgery as an incursion into this integrity: holes made in a whole, rather than (as it is portrayed in transsexual autobiography) the transformation of an unlivable shattered body into a livable whole. And surely what has facilitated the elision of the experience of embodiment (of how bodies actually feel) in contemporary theories of transsexual and other bodies is such a splitting between our experience of our bodies and our theory, a failure to relate our bodily surfaces to our conceptual surfaces. Adrienne Rich's urging that we turn from an abstracted theory of the body to a situated, personal account of our own bodies might still prove useful in moving theory away from the generalized notion of "bodyhood" that characterizes bodily discourses to attend to subjective bodily experience: "Perhaps we need a moratorium on saying 'the body.' For it's also possible to abstract 'the' body. When I write 'the body,' I see nothing in particular. To write 'my body' plunges me into lived experience, particularity: I see scars, disfigurements, discolorations, damages, losses, as well as what pleases me.... To say 'the body' lifts me away from what has given me a primary perspective."[53]

To close by moving more fully into a "primary perspective" on the body through the autobiographical (and to stay with the lesbian feminist thread: a nostalgic gesture for this transsexual theoretical trajectory perhaps), I want to suggest Audre Lorde's *The Cancer Journals* as a complex conjoining of these surfaces: a cultural statement on a particular form of embodiment drawn from an autobiographical meditation on personal bodily experience.[54] *The Cancer Journals* is Lorde's attempt to come to terms with mastectomy for a cancer that was to kill her twelve years after its publication. As a surgery memoir, an "autopathographical" narrative like Grealy's *Autobiography of a Face*, it also has in common with transsexual accounts the experience of emotional and psychic pain around a body noncoincident with body image—"Any amputation is a physical and psychic reality that must be integrated into a new sense of self" (16)—although Lorde's somatic journey is the reverse; surgery deals the blow of psychic and bodily loss. *The Cancer Journals* seeks to translate this personal loss into a lesbian feminist politics of the body, a politics summed up in Lorde's clear-cut opposition: "power vs. prosthesis" (55). Lorde opposes postmastectomy prosthetics for women, whether reconstructive surgery or cloth padding, on the grounds that they perpetuate the cultural fetishization of the female body (again, a reduction of the whole to the part), woman = breast, and discomfit women from working through their changed bodies and the psychic and cultural meaning of the change. Symptomatic of the sexist "patterns and networks ... for women after breast surgery that encourage us to deny the realities of our bodies" (41), "[t]he emphasis upon wearing a prosthesis is a way of avoiding having women come to terms with their own pain and loss, and thereby their own strength" (49). Arguing that the "socially sanctioned prosthesis is merely another way of keeping women with breast cancer silent and separate from each other" (16), *The Cancer Journals* urges the monobreasted or unbreasted woman to come out of the prosthetic closet and allow herself to be read as not less a woman but rather as one with a particular history of breast cancer. Only through this act of coming out can there be a politically mobilized postmastectomy women's community.

If for the transsexual the surgical prosthesis is a marker of bodily nostalgia, a memory of the somatotype that should have been that allows for assimilation, Lorde suggests that for postmastectomy women this prosthetic nostalgia is a systematically validated, even socially enforced mechanism for disavowing women's bodily experience of cancer. Nevertheless, she does allow that the desire for prosthesis to recreate what was may be quite viscerally felt in postoperative women, including herself: after a mastectomy, "there is a feeling of wanting to go back, of not wanting to persevere through this experience to whatever enlightenment might be at the core of it" (55). Indeed, while *The Cancer Journals* as political treatise argues that the bodily nostalgia enacted and secured by prosthesis serves to veil the postmastectomy woman's difference, Lorde's personal account of her experience candidly reveals her struggle to accept this very difference: not only the cancer and the early death it forebodes but more finely the psychic effects of the loss of her breast, the impact of changed body on body image. The loss of a breast is tightly intricated with Lorde's identity. Notched into the grain of her critique of the cultural representation of women's bodies as symmetrically breasted is the notion that the breast as part of *her* body is absolutely caught up with her self as a woman, feminist, African-American, lesbian, mother, writer. How to sustain the continuity of that identity—"a woman, a black lesbian feminist mother lover poet" (25)—when all its axes, all meeting at womanness in Lorde's experience of them as she writes about the mastectomy, transect the breasts? At points Lorde's body image appears to hold the breast as most cherished. She wraps the lost breast in the maternal: "The pain of separating from my breast was at least as sharp as the pain as separating from my mother" (25–26). The surgery performs a terrible second birth, cutting the body off from a productive, protective life-source. In the place of the mother the breast is symbolically entangled in women's relations with each other; Lorde worries about how the mastectomy will alter her relations with other women. How will the lesbian other feel about (and feel) her monobreasted body? How will she herself feel (emotionally and physically) loving a woman with her one breast? Although she later claims in *The Cancer Journals* that, "[a] lifetime of loving women had taught me that when women love each other, physical change does not alter that love" (56), a few days after her mastectomy she is less sure:

> I was thinking, "What is it like to be making love to a woman and have only one breast brushing against her?"
> I thought, "How will we fit so perfectly together ever again?"
> I thought, "I wonder if our love-making had anything to do with it?"
> I thought, "What will it be like making love to me? Will she still find my body delicious?"
> And for the first time deeply and fleetingly a groundswell of sadness rolled up over me that filled my mouth and eyes almost to frowning. My right breast represented such an area of feeling and pleasure for me, how could I never bear to feel that again? (43)

Yet while this loss of the breast is deeply felt in the absence of the actual body part, the feeling of the breast's presence proves irrecoverable. Lorde avows that she could never invest sensory feeling in a supplementary noncorporeal part: "not even the most skillful prosthesis in the world could undo that reality, or feel the way my breast had felt" (44). What lies behind her antiprosthetic politics is thus absolutely caught up in the contours of her personal body image: in what she can and cannot feel a part of her body (one can imagine, for instance, the male-to-female transsexual easily investing in a prosthetic breast). Indeed, perhaps it is because she is unable to phantomize the prosthesis that body image must be brought into line with the reshaped material body: "either I would love my body one-breasted now, or remain forever alien to myself" (44). Certainly Lorde's political resistance to wearing a breast prosthesis cannot be "cut off" from her initial, visceral psychic refusal (or failure) to incorporate into body image the cloth prosthesis immediately on offer—a pink lambswool puff. Most striking is the suggestion that Lorde's non-investment in this material padding is as inseparable from a racial body image as it is from a gendered one. The prosthesis, in all its pinkness, is immediately unassimilable with her body's surface, with her skin color as a black woman. Trying the pink puff on before the mirror, Lorde perceives it as all the more "not-me" because "it was the wrong color, and looked grotesquely pale through the cloth of my bra" (44). And indeed, as the scene urges us to consider, why should a racial body image not be as sentient as that of sex? Particularly if skin is as invested with psychic and social meaning as Anzieu suggests, there is no reason to suppose why the flesh should not be subject to the same kinds of racial investments as sexed ones.[55]

At what point do our body images underlie our theories of the body? At what point do our experiences of our bodies resist or fragment our theoretical generalizations, reveal them as displacements of experience, and demand from them new formulations? Even Lorde does not consider that from breast cancer could develop a politics other than feminist, that by no means can it be certain that all women will experience their breast cancer as women. Eve Kosofsky Sedgwick has written her story of breast cancer to affirm her queer identification with *gay men*, to conduit this bodily experience into her queer politics. Hearing the way in which breast cancer is appropriated by certain women and AIDS repudiated ("our" disease and "theirs"), Sedgwick reaches out through this masculine identification and the "loss" that disease brings to embrace, via transgender, that queer, repudiated, excised part: "as though AIDS were *not* a disease of women or lesbians! . . . I feel I must refuse to identify [as a woman] on this ground." A low erotogenicity in the breast zone; an open desire for and identification with gay men; a nonreproductive feminine identity, Sedgwick's investment in her breasts is clearly not strong to begin with and thus her body image thoroughly underlies this identification. Her breasts are, she writes, "relatively peripheral to the complex places where gender and sexuality really happen."[56] While we should not stop thinking the body as a culturally and politically significant text, we need to write out such points at which our theories back onto our personal investments. Not simply costumes for our experience of our bodies, our theoretical conceptions of the body are foundationally formed by and reformative of them. To talk of the strange and unpredictable contours of body image, and to reinsert into theory the experience of embodiment, we might begin our work through such autobiographical narratives.

part two **narratives**

> Narcissus, contemplating his face in the fountain's depth, is so fascinated with the apparition that he would die bending toward himself.... The author of an autobiography masters this anxiety by submitting to it; beyond all images, he follows unceasingly the call of his own being.
> —Georges Gusdorf, "Conditions and Limits of Autobiography"

> The most sexual act I did at these times was to regard myself in the mirror. I would stare, longingly I suppose, into the face of the little girl opposite me. Somehow, in the mirror my femininity was more real. Like Narcissus I was fascinated by that unattainable image, and like him I pined.
> —Renée Richards, *Second Serve: The Renée Richards Story*

> Like Narcissus, I had fallen in love with the image in the mirror, which showed me that all the dreams of my life could be realised for a few moments now and then. —Katherine Cummings, *Katherine's Diary*

chapter 3

Mirror Images: Transsexuality and Autobiography

Transsexual Mirror Stages

In her autobiography, *Conundrum: An Extraordinary Narrative of Transsexualism*, Jan Morris restages her final act before her sex reassignment surgery. Ensconced in Dr. Burou's famous clinic in Casablanca, anaesthetized, and with pubes freshly shaven, Morris rises from her bed and makes her woozy way to the mirror: "[I] went to say good-bye to myself in the mirror. We would never meet again, and I wanted to give that other self a long last look in the eye, and a wink for luck.[1] She, this self that writes, is to emerge "alive, well, and sex-changed in Casablanca in a new body" (141), the old one, not so much that of a man as of a "hybrid or chimera" (141), to be discarded like a snake's skin on Burou's operating table. Morris's mirror scene is memorable for graphically figuring the specific split of the transsexual subject and prefiguring the passage—or to use the appropriate term, the transition—that heals this split. The moment is Morris through the looking glass: Morris passes into surgery one self, an androgyne (a chimera, half male, half female [109])—s/he—

and out a new self, an integral subject (normal, clean [141])—she. But if Morris's mirror scene is the transitional point in her transsexual trajectory, it is also crucially the transitional point in her autobiographical narrative. For from this point on in the narrative, the "me" written about (James Morris) and the "I" that writes (Jan Morris)—so far separated by sex—are fused into a singly sexed autobiographical subject, an integral "I." In joining the split gendered subject, autobiography transmits—in narrative—the integrating trajectory of transsexuality.

While Morris's is doubtless the most legendary,[2] mirror scenes punctuate transsexual autobiographies with remarkable consistency. Almost to the degree of the expected surgery scenes, mirror scenes, we might say, constitute a convention of transsexual autobiography. They recur across the texts in strikingly similar fashion. A trope of transsexual representation, the split of the mirror captures the definitive splitting of the transsexual subject, freezes it, frames it schematically in narrative. The difference between gender and sex is conveyed in the difference between body image (projected self) and the image of the body (reflected self). For the transsexual the mirror initially reflects not-me: it distorts who I know myself to be. "My life was a series of distorted mirrors," female-to-male Mario Martino metaphorizes his life before transition: "I saw myself in their crazy reflections as false to the image I had of myself. *I was a boy!* I felt like one, I dressed like one, I fought like one."[3] The mirror misrepresents who I know myself *really* to be: at an angle to Lacan's mirror phase, the look in the mirror enables in the transsexual only disidentification, not a jubilant integration of body but an anguishing shattering of the felt already formed imaginary body—that sensory body of the body "image."[4] Yielding this recognition that I am not my body, the mirror sets in motion the transsexual plot: it is once it is shattered in its visual reflection, once the material body is seen not to be the felt body that the material body can be approached in bits and pieces—an assembly of parts to be amputated and relocated surgically in order that subject may be corporeally integrated.

But mirror scenes in transsexual autobiographies do not merely initiate the plot of transsexuality. Highly staged and self-conscious affairs, as Morris's self-staging indicates, mirror scenes also draw attention to the narrative form for this plot, to the surrounding autobiography and its import for transsexuality. Looking into the mirror is of course a figure for the autobiographical act: autobiography is ostensibly anyway the literary act of self-reflection, the textual product of the "I" reflecting on itself. In transsexual autobiography the trajectories of transsexuality and autobiography are entwined in complex ways, narrative and bodily form conducting each other. To begin with, the narrative transitions of autobiography allow the somatic transitions of transsexuality in an immediate and material sense. The autobiographical act for the transsexual begins even before the published autobiography—namely, in the clinician's office where, in order to be diagnosed as transsexual, s/he must recount a transsexual autobiography. The story of a strong, early, and persistent transgendered identification is required by the clinical authorities, the psychiatrists, psychologists, and psychotherapists who traditionally function as the gatekeepers to the means of transsexual "conversion." Whether s/he publishes an autobiography or not, then, every transsexual, as a transsexual, is originally an autobiographer. Narrative is also a kind of second skin: the story the transsexual must weave around the body in order that this body may be "read."

Consequently, the published transsexual autobiographies that *we* read are always the transsexual autobiography a second time around. Herein lies another redoubling, with the written autobiography mirroring, reproducing, that first oral autobiographical scene. In its published retelling (after the diagnosis, as a repetition, and in writing) the transsexual *bios*, not surprisingly, typically appears as itself a highly formalized narrative. Reproduced in autobiography, transsexuality emerges as an archetypal story structured around shared tropes and fulfilling a particular narrative organization of consecutive stages: suffering and confusion; the epiphany of self-discovery; corporeal and social transformation/conversion; and finally the arrival "home"—the reassignment. In their formality, in their function as figures of self-reflection, mirror scenes serve to elucidate this formalization of transsexuality as a plot. Nancy Hunt's *Mirror Image: The Odyssey of a Male-to-Female Transsexual* frames the transsexual trajectory in autobiography precisely as a progression though a series of mirror stages. Each scene schematically marks a successive moment in the author's becoming woman. From her failure to identify as a man; to her crossdressing as a woman; to her decision to transition and become a woman: the significant turning points in Hunt's transsexual transition are symbolized in highly stylized fashion with mirror scenes. Gradually but inexorably and formulaically, transition is shown to undistort the reflected self and bring into gender alignment (gendered identity) body and body image. The trajectory (transsexual and autobiographical) of *Mirror Image* thus appropriately reaches closure with a weightily signifying mirror scene: the representation of Hunt's attainment of full identification with her specular image, a figure (admittedly schmaltzy) of the transsexual "finding herself"—"I now see in that reflection a mirror image of the person that I have always been, no longer distorted by the flickering heat of society or the crazy lens of masculinity. For better or for worse, at least I am me, a woman."[5]

In their forms gender and genre mirror each other. The effect of the autobiographical act on the subject parallels that of looking into the mirror on the transsexual. Autobiography, like the transsexual's first look in the mirror, breaks apart the subject into the self reflected upon and the self that reflects; autobiography, like transsexuality, instantiates (or reveals) a difference in the subject. In transsexual autobiography the split between the "I" of the *bios* and the "I" of the *graph*, the past self written and the present self writing, is heightened by the story of sex change. Autobiography brings into relief the split of the transsexual life; transsexual history brings into gendered relief the difference present in all autobiography between the subject of the enunciation and the subject enunciating. I was a woman, I write as a man. How to join this split? How to create a coherent subject? Precisely through narrative. Over the course of the recounting, the narrative continuity, the trajectory of autobiography (tracing the story of a single self), promises, like the transsexual transition itself, to rejoin this split into a single, connected "life."

As they mark the successive stages of transition, some mirror scenes illustrate and indeed participate in this cohering narrative movement between past and present selves, the "I" of the *bios* and the "I" of the *graph*. As the young girl, Marie, Martino places an enema nozzle over his (her) clitoris to improvise a penis on his (her) naked body before the mirror. This act prefigures in the imaginary his acquisition of a fleshly penis recounted in the penultimate chapter ("Phalloplasty" [252–263]) in the real of the plot. The childhood mirror scene functions simultaneously as autobiographical and as transsexual prolepsis, foretelling and naturalizing this plot of sex change, suggesting that, in the imaginary (the mirror) the penis has been there all along. The scene coheres this young girl with the male subject writing. Similarly, in Renée Richards's *Second Serve: The Renée Richards Story*, a scene of crossdressing before a hotel mirror in which the young jock, Dick Raskind, transforms himself into the elegant Renée with a slow and painful set of rituals (tying the penis back tightly between the legs to get a smooth reflection) at once looks forward to the equally gradual and painful transformation of the subject through transsexual transition and looks back to an already feminized self. When Richards's autobiographical narrative, following the identity shifts of the transsexual story and analogously to the mirror in this scene, begins "to reflect the face of a different character"—that of a woman not a man, that of Renée not of Dick—the act of self-reflection in writing produces the narrative transitions that smooth this sex transition.[6] The retrospective structure of autobiography, in other words—this look back at the self—like the redressing act of crossdressing, allows the transsexual to appear to have been there all along.

Drawing formally now on a list of some fifty autobiographies published between 1954 and 1996—a wonderfully engaging, extraordinary body of work (I'm not uninvolved: reading autobiography is always a pointed engagement of the self, and these texts on several levels constitute *my* mirror scene)—this chapter examines the intricate fretwork of transsexuality as subjectivity and autobiography as narrative form. My concern here is the production of transsexuality both in and through autobiographical narrative. What are the implications of autobiography's indispensability to transsexual subjectivity? Why do (so many) transsexuals write autobiographies? What is the relation of the second published autobiography to the first oral autobiography in the clinician's office? What engenders, what elicits, this textual return? And what are the dynamics of reading in each autobiographical situation—how do we read transsexual autobiography and how does this differ (or not) from the clinician's initial reading of the transsexual? If transsexuality is symptomized in narrative, how do we/they decide who—what sex(es)—is the subject of this story? Man, and/or woman, and/or transsexual? In sum, what kind of autobiographical narrative is the transsexual? The conventions of transsexuality are thoroughly entangled with those of autobiography, this body thoroughly enabled by narrative. Like two mirrors autobiography and transsexuality are themselves caught up in an interreflective dynamic, resembling, reassembling, and articulating each other.

Autobiography as Symptom: Telling Stories

We must begin our reading of autobiography where the transsexual begins its telling: in the clinician's office. There's an important conjunction of body and narrative here, a strikingly direct way in which narrative does the body's work. Although transsexuality concerns the deliberate transformation of the material body more than any other category catalogued by the American Psychiatric Association's *Diagnostic and Statistical Manual of Mental Disorders* (DSM), transsexuality does not symptomize itself in the subject's body, at least not visibly or reliably so. The diagnosis required for this transformation must instead derive from the patient's narrative: narrativization as a transsexual necessarily precedes one's diagnosis as a transsexual; autobiography is transsexuality's proffered symptom. If autobiography is transsexuality's proffered symptom, the process of diagnosing the subject should be understood above all as narratological. The primary diagnostic criteria for "Gender Identity Disorder" in *DSM-IV* under which transsexuality is now subsumed, "strong and persistent cross-gender identification" and "persistent discomfort with . . . sex or sense of inappropriateness in the gender role of that sex," must be substantiated through the subject's life history.[7] Boys playing with Barbie, wrapping their heads in cloths to simulate long hair, and hiding their penises between their legs; girls asking to be called boys' names, refusing to urinate sitting down, wanting to be Batman or Superman, and asserting that they will grow up to become men: such episodes find their place under the "Diagnostic Features" of Gender Identity Disorder as turns in transsexuality's classic plot. Gender dysphoria (acute gender discomfort) constitutes the medical narrative's overriding theme, and assertions of being "trapped in the wrong body," as we have seen, its most famous rhetorical trope. The story the transsexual tells the clinician must mirror or echo the diagnosis, its details matching or varying those of this master narrative. Clinicians (the first of transsexual autobiography's critics and setting a precedent in the exactingness of their approach) listen as narratologists for the recognizable transsexual plot, tropes, or themes, matching the subject's narrative against the narratemes of this archetypal story of transsexuality.

Given this original and thorough investment of transsexual subjectivity in narrative, for the cultural critic to fail to trace the specific importance of autobiography in the clinician's office is to miss the narrative kernel of transsexual subjectivity and the fraught struggle around plot that comes with being diagnosed. In her chapter describing the emergence of transsexual subjectivity, Bernice L. Hausman elides the function of autobiographical narrative to suggest instead that the transsexual emerges through demand—a demand for sex change in response to the existence of the diagnosis and the technology of sex change: "the demand for sex change is an enunciation that designates a desired action *and* identifies the speaker as the appropriate subject of that action . . .

[T]he demand for sex change was instantiated as the primary symptom (and sign) of the transsexual."[8] For Hausman the transsexual's claim to transsexual subjectivity is performative. The demand is that which, in a circular fashion, constitutes the subject as transsexual in the eyes of the clinician. As Hausman also reads demand via its Lacanian conception, however, the transsexual's demand for sex change paradoxically undermines this subjectivity (in Lacan demand displaces need and opens up the subject's desire; it is that about the subject which *by nature* cannot be met): "In the demand for sex change, the transsexual stakes a claim . . . that determines, indeed founds, subjectivity as the 'other sex.' . . . The demand itself, however, inaugurates in the subject a desire that cannot be met through the specific surgeries and endocrinological interventions that serve to relocate him or her in the opposite sex category" (136–137). In Hausman's description one becomes transsexual because one says one is; and yet the purpose of saying one is transsexual—to realize sex change—would appear to be unrealizable. The paradox assumes (and reproduces) a fundamental incompatibility between the transsexual's claims to gender identity made through language and the transsexual's need for technology to secure this gender as sex in the body.

My coinage "body narrative"—not an oxymoron but a deliberate conjunction—is intended to reflect, in contrast to Hausman, the ways in which body and narrative work together in the production of transsexual subjectivity. The narrative of a transsexual identification does not contradict but, rather, enables the realization of a sex-changed body. Narrative needs to be distinguished from Hausman's conception of demand on three counts. First, unlike demand, narrative is not coextensive with performativity. Narrative is diachronic, not instantaneous but an organized recounting of episodes of time over time. Second, narrative does not connote the "lack" of demand but is, rather, bound up with realization; in the development of its plot, in the progression of its episodes, narrative crucially seeks its own *telos*. Finally, more overtly than demand, narrative suggests an interlocution between author and reader, a dialogics of interpretation. The meaning of narrative is arrived at in a textual exchange. My description of how transsexuals become transsexuals may be formulated around these three properties of narrative: the transsexual must work to author a history of transgendered identification in order to receive a reading from the clinician directed toward the realization of transsexual subjectivity. Psychologist Ira Pauly's comments on the necessity of retaining the diagnostic criteria of transsexuality in DSM-IV certainly suggest a dynamic more in keeping with this narratological description than the simple, instantaneous act of demanding: "[t]he real issue [of the diagnosis] here is whether the gender dysphoric individual gives a clear-cut history of 'persistent discomfort and sense of inappropriateness [of his/her] assigned sex.' "[9] Demand omits both the recounting of a personal history of "persistent" identification and the interconstitutive although thoroughly contestatory relations between author and reader that characterize the transsexual diagnosis.

Indeed, the clinical literature shows that even before "transsexualism" first appeared in *DSM-III*, in 1980, demanding hormones and surgery could in fact obstruct treatment; for such demand attempts to bypass the narrative pas de deux between clinician and patient.[10] The first "standard" in the "Standards of Care," drafted in 1979 and still the authoritative guide alongside *DSM* for clinicians working with transsexuals, states categorically that "Hormonal and/or surgical sex reassignment on demand (i.e., justified simply because the patient has requested such procedures) is contraindicated": that is, demand works in itself as an indication *against* treatment. Even though, in presenting as transsexual, subjects originally self-author their transsexuality, to access hormones and surgery transsexuals must receive the clinician's all-important reading—must be authorized as authors. As the standard goes on, hormones and surgery may be administered only after the clinician's "careful evaluation of the patient's reasons for requesting such services"—evaluation here consisting of a thorough critical reading and interpretation of the transsexual's narrativization of his or her past life, of its assessment as transsexual plot.[11]

The entry of the diagnosis "transsexualism" into *DSM*-III in 1980 represents the medical formalization of transsexuality into such a plot. Boys playing with Barbie and girls wanting to be Batman: the description turns precisely on narrative episodes. This formalization of transsexuality has a double-edged significance. On the one hand the diagnosis critically recognizes sex change as a need—and not desire. (In declassifying homosexuality from *DSM-III* at exactly the moment transsexuality gained clinical classification, the medical establishment might be said to have remarked the difference between homosexuality as desire and transsexuality as dis-ease in need of treatment.) As it recognizes the patient's narrative as articulating need, the classification of Gender Identity Disorder (GID) is unique. Unlike treatment for other "disorders" (anorexia or schizophrenia for instance), the treatment proposed for the most serious manifestation of GID (transsexualism) doesn't try to cure us of the "disorder"; rather, it concurs with our own narrative, propelling us into it as a way of resolving it. As a consequence the diagnostic situation creates a narrative setting in which, not insignificantly, the intelligible transsexual life story is always already understood, not bizarre and foreign but familiar, anticipated, and—quite crucially—named. It gives us a place to tell and begin to realize our story.

I specify "intelligible," however, because on the other hand the standardization also renders some stories unintelligible, delimiting transsexual subjectivity, censoring the number of possible legitimate transsexual tales. As Sandy Stone remarks of this restriction, with *DSM*, "[e]mergent polyvocalities of lived experience, never represented in the discourse but present at least in potential, disappear."[12] When the subject's story diverges substantially from the clinical genre, when its details don't fit the specified requisites of what constitutes a transsexual story, its teller has traditionally had a hard time becoming (being a transitioning) transsexual. The diagnosis acts as a narrative filter, enabling some transsexuals to live out their story and thwarting others. In short, if the dependence of the diagnosis on autobiography suggests that one cannot be a transsexual outside the operations of narrative, transsexuality's entry into *DSM* hones this stipulation to a very set narrative.

The hub of the narrative exchange entailed in diagnosing transsexuality is formed by the intake interview. Published autobiographies highlight the delimiting and enabling effects of the narratological nature of this encounter between clinician and transsexual: sometimes at the same time as in Richards's *Second Serve*. In diagnosing Richards, Harry Benjamin is shown to be more than familiar with a transsexual narrative:

> As [Benjamin] listened to me reviewing my history, he tilted his head first one way and then another, sometimes nodding agreeably. Occasionally, when I would grope for words, he would supply them so casually that I didn't notice at first. Then I began to realize that the old man really did understand, so much so that he could probably have told the story without my help. The childish exploits, the futile years of psychotherapy, the driving compulsion, the skulking around—all these constituted a familiar refrain that accompanied his daily work. He listened intelligently, and he understood almost as well as I did. I began to gain respect for this little man. (164–165)

Benjamin relieves Richards, in both senses, of the need to detail her autobiography, anticipating themes and turns of plot, providing appropriate phraseology. As its original authority, the so-called "father" of transsexuality who had by then published the first book-length study of transsexuality, *The Transsexual Phenomenon*, he can indeed "tell the story" without her help.[13] At this point Richards portrays Benjamin's intimate knowledge as reassuring, a sign of his understanding—and crucially his authorization does allow her to begin transition. Yet when this same authority is later wielded to write Richards out of a transsexual narrative, it becomes apparent that Benjamin's filling in for Richards in the intake interview is also in effect a form of silencing her. Benjamin decides that, as a prominent professional (and with her unambivalently heterosexual past), Richards's story does not in fact fit Benjamin's preconceptions of the "true" transsexual plot. Forcing Richards to discontinue hormones and refusing to authorize her surgery, Benjamin interrupts the progress of her transition—in his capacity as primary author curtailing, at least temporarily, the specific plot she would live out.

The clinician's reading thus officially confers and by the same token may defer transsexual subjectivity. In this context, in which text stands in for body, everything is at stake in the production and reception of narrative in the clinician's office. A "misreading" can wreak irreparable psychological and emotional damage, can even (if a desperate subject is impeded in transition) indirectly kill or maim. As the past's recounting is compelled by the knowledge that the future of one's sex is to be determined by what one has to say for oneself, there has probably never been so much at stake in oral autobiography. Moreover, although this is never acknowledged in clinical texts, the diagnosis of "true" or "primary" or "core" transsexualism is surely derived not merely from a certain plot codifiable as transsexual but from an account that renders up this plot clearly and coherently—in other words, from narrative form: a strong, persuasive avowal of transsexuality, carefully supported by appropriate episodes presented in an orderly manner, sufficiently but not overwhelmingly detailed. In effect, to be transsexual, the subject must be a skilled narrator of his or her own life. Tell the story persuasively, and you're likely to get your hormones and surgery; falter, repeat, disorder, omit, digress, and you've pretty much had it, however "authentic" a transsexual you are. Erica Rutherford's account of her interview with the clinician in her *Nine Lives: The Autobiography of Erica Rutherford* suggests precisely the formal difficulties of rendering one's history in that oral encounter, as Pauly makes that all-important specification in his comments on the diagnostic criteria, "clear-cut":

> [The doctor] leaned back. "Tell me your story," he said.
> My mind spun. "My story." That would take all day. I was nearly fifty. What could he mean, "my story?" How could I condense it? I rambled on in a confused way, as best I could, while the doctor made notes and sometimes asked me to repeat something. I jumped from year to year and decade to decade, talking sometimes about my childhood and sometimes about my recent feelings. I was overwhelmed by the years of misery and the hours and hours of psychiatric sessions.[14]

But it is not merely the vicissitudes of memory, the recursive, associative structure of oral narrative, and the stakes of reception that make telling transsexual autobiography a fraught task. For some perhaps the most difficult aspect of the autobiographical requirement is simply speaking that which may constitute what is most unspeakable about the self. In his published autobiography Raymond Thompson returns to the clinical scene of this oral autobiography and underlines precisely these ways in which, as a compelled representation of the unrepresentable, it poses a disturbing dilemma. For Thompson transsexuality—even acknowledging as a female-to-male who never lives in the world as a woman that he ever *was* female—is too painful for words: "I didn't have the capacity, or the desire to talk about myself or specifically about my condition. I never described myself or my condition in any way and I could only express myself in monosyllables, never saying a word over and above what was necessary to anyone." Yet he must tell his story in order to get help: "Soon however, I was going to have to talk about myself and my condition, in order to ask for the help that I needed. . . . in order to get help, I had to speak." How to re-member the body one would forget—indeed, the agnosic body one is not?[15]

The recognition of what is at stake in self-articulation does not (unsurprisingly) loosen Thompson's tongue. Faced with the psychiatrist's request, Thompson remains unable to speak his birth name, choking on its feminine sound, his body (once again) punning on that which cannot be spoken. Fascinatingly, however, in this case it is Thompson's very delimiting of this name as unspeakable, his faltering, that catches the clinician's attention and begins the latter's authorization of Thompson's transsexuality:

> [The psychiatrist] was looking at his notes a lot while he was talking to me, but his interest picked up when I was unable to say the name given to me at birth. He had asked me matter-of-factly what the name was, and no matter how I tried to press it out of my lips, I just choked on it. I simply couldn't say it. I was struggling because there seemed to be a reason why I should say it. I finally agreed to write it down. He looked at the piece of paper for a minute and took in the name which I so detested, then looked at me and said, "You could have fooled me." I breathed a sigh of relief. Hearing him say that seemed a definite act of recognition.[16]

The clinician's interest is caught by Thompson's ellipses (presumably he looks up from his notes at this point); he begins to *read* transsexuality specifically only when Thompson cannot speak: the unspeakability of the female name symptomizes the unthinkability of the female identity of the subject before him. In his "act of recognition" ("You could have fooled me")—a repudiation along with Thompson of any trace of femaleness—the clinician signals his initial clinical approval of Thompson's "true" transsexuality. Notably, while Thompson eventually writes his female name in the clinician's office, his published autobiography, *What Took You So Long?*, leaves this name glaringly unwritten throughout; Raymond is always "Ray," is never given a female name and rarely a female pronoun. What is too painful for the spoken word before the clinician remains too painful for the written word in his book. In reproducing this aporia of what cannot be spoken in writing, Thompson's autobiography transparently elucidates—precisely through reenacting it—how traumatic may be that first scene of compelled narrativization of the transsexual past.

For the clinician the dependence of the diagnosis on narrative raises concerns above all of the autobiography's authenticity. How to be sure of the true sex of the transsexual body? How to know (*gnosis*) distinctively or apart (*dia*) transsexual identity? The diagnosis is premised on the belief that autobiography can and should function mimetically—narrative mirror to transsexual nature. While clinicians evidently fear the deliberate artifice of the transsexual narrator (author as fraudster), they yet appear to remain quite ignorant of the ways in which the autobiography is fundamentally constructed as narrative: a telling, a representation, the life thoroughly contingent on the form. Professional writings frequently contain strategies about how to detect the inauthentic transsexual via the inauthentic account, how to get the "true story."

Psychoanalyst and psychotherapist Leslie Lothstein suggests corroborating the patient's account with biographies produced by significant others; in one of his cases the subject's story comes to him via an unsympathetic brother's letter.[17] As may be imagined, however, because such others can have deeply vested interests in the presenting subject not realizing his or her transsexuality, this stipulation can lead to an even more vexed situation in which competing narratives tell blatantly different stories about the same subject, in which narrative appears even more opaque and the *bios* less retrievable. (Biography is of course no more authentic, no more the "life itself" than autobiography.) Along similar lines psychiatrist and specialized researcher of transsexual accounts Bryan Tully encourages the professional to use "authenticity checks" to weed out the "deliberate and skillful deception [that transsexuals may deploy] to achieve hormones and surgery"; to institute a system of cross-checking between different autobiographical versions. Truth will out in narrative repetition: "It is very difficult to sustain complex cover stories over a long time in the face of extended cross-examination. As police and espionage interrogators know full well, some 'leakage' of what is being covered up is almost impossible to prevent." [18]

Tully's policing model of reading transsexual autobiography, with the clinician as interrogator/detective, brings to the fore not only the clinician's fears of fraudulence in transsexual narrative but the peculiar unspoken violence these fears may structure into the diagnostics of reading. The patient's position is to confess, the professional's—half-priest holding the key to the patient's salvation, half detective decoding this clinical narrative—to listen, to take note—and precisely to police the subject's access to technology. Clinician as policeman is a shocking equation when we remember this is supposed to be a healthcarer/patient relation. If we follow through with the analogy, the transsexual occupies the place of criminal, is assumed to be a "suspect" text. Indeed, Lothstein's account considers transsexuality a cover for a profound psychopathology that can only be resolved psychotherapeutically, with talk and not transition; Tully's study of transsexual accounts also concludes questioning the necessity of transition. Psychologists Leah Cahan Schaefer and Connie Christine Wheeler have astutely observed that it is in part this tendency among some clinicians to approach the transsexual as a suspect text—a lack of understanding from the medical establishment of the difficulty in rendering transsexuality as story—that may provoke transsexuals to "falsify" histories in the first place.[19] Certainly, for any subject who experiences transition as essential, the importance of obtaining the right reading is inestimable. Yet this suspicion toward the transsexual narrator has a wider resonance outside the clinical situation. As we will see throughout the second part of this book (beginning with Hausman), that suspicion is the way to approach the transsexual text is repeatedly taken for granted, in the history of transsexual subjects and in contemporary readings of transsexual narratives, by cultural critics as much as clinicians. It is as if that redoubling of sex and gender, or perhaps the reliance of body on narrative, makes the transsexual an intrinsically unreliable text in the eyes of the reading other. If the transsexual narrative as much as the body is a second skin, the encounter with that very twofoldness seems to slide swiftly into assumptions of the transsexual's duplicity. As we move from narrative in the clinical situation to narrative in the published autobiographies, one published transsexual autobiography will serve to dramatize and elucidate the effect of this hermeneutics of suspicion on transsexual subjectivity.

Published during the 1970s at a juncture when in various disciplines (anthropology, sociology, and most pertinently in this context, psychiatry) the personal narrative began to be credited as a viable and authentic source of insider knowledge on institutions, Robert Bogdan's edition of Jane Fry's transsexual autobiography, *Being Different: The Autobiography of Jane Fry*, is transsexual autobiography repackaged as sociological document.[20] Sociologist Bogdan edits from interviews and follows transsexual Fry's narrative with a discussion of the clinicians' medical reports on her case. From this textual layering we read both the transsexual autobiography and the clinical reading of this autobiography; or, rather, the clinicians' refusal to read Fry's autobiography. For the professional notes compete with the autobiographical narrative; the doctors diagnose not transsexuality but psychosis, finding in Fry a subject in whom gender identity disorder is not what it seems but symptomatic, a signifier for something else (the performative demand in excess of the referential need again). Whereas for the subject feeling like a woman is concordant with a transsexual self—as Bogdan points out, Fry's narrative reveals that "Jane accepts her gender feelings 'for what they are,' that is, she takes them for granted"—for the clinicians Fry's gender feelings function as " 'immature verbalizations,' [symptoms of] a 'character disorder,' 'castration anxiety,' a 'psychotic profile,' and part of a 'repertoire' " (215). While they accept that Fry believes herself to be a woman, they themselves do not believe this, their disbelief radically throwing the truth of her belief into question. Unsatisfied with the literalism of Fry's transsexual autobiography, the clinicians seek out another interpretation, effectively rewriting her narrative: if in Fry's account her father does not figure significantly, in the clinical reports this very absence becomes key, a possible etiological cause for her psychic disturbance.

Not surprisingly, Fry's autobiography shows that her very life has, in a circular fashion, constituted an interpretative battle to shape her history to achieve the right reading and change her sex. The cause of her particular transsexual struggle rests with her shortcomings as autobiographer. Almost exceptionally among transsexual autobiographers, Fry is a blatantly poor narrator of her life: even if one allows for its status as transcription from oral recounting, her narrative is disorganized, repetitive, and defensive—in my experience, the hardest transsexual autobiography to read. Even the section of Fry's writing that Bogdan does include in the book proves equally hard to read. It is this narrative difficulty—or narrative deficiency—I suggest, that is at the root of the clinicians' delay in diagnosing her transsexuality (Fry does eventually obtain the diagnosis and subsequently hormone treatment from one sympathetic doctor; does his brief "case history" supply her with the narrative frame she needed? [130]). Bogdan, however, uses the juxtaposition of transsexual autobiography and clinical text to underscore the stakes of reading transsexual narratives carefully. Since through reading his transcribed interviews with Fry we have "spent more time with her and [have] more first-hand information about her than all the professionals whose comments have been presented here, we are in a position to look at them more skeptically and to give the patient's perspective more credence" (216–217). In effect, we are asked to perform the reading the clinicians didn't and restore meaning to her narrative (to read her as transsexual); at the same time we are asked to subject the readings of her to our skeptical reading, to read "the politics of diagnosis" (220). The hermeneutics of suspicion are reversed and reflected back on the clinicians themselves.

That narrative is the linchpin of the transsexual diagnosis has one unforeseen side effect. If the published transsexual autobiographies are typically so crafted and engaging it is surely because of the narrative rigors of this diagnostic situation: because *to be* transsexual, transsexuals must be arch storytellers—or if they are not, must learn to become passable ones. But, given that transsexual subjectivity originates in this compelled narrative situation in all its fraughtness, why would transsexuals make a voluntary return to narrative in writing their autobiographies? What is the function of the published return?

Transsexual Conformity: The Published Return

As expected, narrative has an even more textured presence when the transsexual writes the life story. Nevertheless, in Hausman's chapter on published transsexual autobiographies that follows her chapter on the transsexual's demand for subjectivity, the genre of this form of transsexual representation still remains transparent; it is as if (following the clinician) one could evaluate transsexuality even in transsexual autobiography without considering the import of the particular narrative frame. According to Hausman the autobiographies constitute transsexuals' attempts to naturalize their gender, to "cover over" their technological production with claims to always already really be the "other" sex (173). (Hausman rightly points out these claims to already really be a man or a woman are often inscribed in the narratives as a form of psychic or embodied intersexuality.) Her purpose in reading the autobiographies is to reveal and critique this cover-up. She suggests that the autobiographies' naturalization of gender effectively undermines the conception of transsexuality in two parallel ways. First, in the claims they make to already really be the other sex within the autobiographies—that is to *really* be a man or woman—transsexuals contradict their own (prior) demands for sex change. Second, such claims result in a tension between transsexual autobiographies and the professional representation of transsexuality. For if the clinical text lays out transsexuality as a narrative of sex change and defines transsexuals as subjects whose gender identity as different makes necessary this intervention into their sex, transsexual autobiographers' insistence on always already really being the other sex subverts this description and unsettles the very etiology of transsexuality: "transsexuals compromise the official understanding of 'gender' as divorced from biological sex by their insistent reiteration of the idea that physiological intersexuality is the cause of their cross-sex identification" (141). For Hausman the autobiographies are above all conformist texts: transsexual autobiographies are of a "closed nature" (147), "monolithic narratives" (156), texts in which "gendered meanings are unilinear and very clear" (158). Indeed, she considers the primary rhetorical function of transsexual autobiographies to get readers to conform *their* lives to the author's: "The purpose of the narratives is to force the reader to comply with the author's experience, to begin to interpret his or her own life along the same trajectory"—a purpose against which Hausman admits she finds "resistance" "exhausting" (156).

The troubling ramification of Hausman's reading is its conclusion that transsexual self-representation works to subvert not only the narrative of sex change offered by the clinician, not only the consistence and coherence of transsexual accounts but the very feasibility of transsexuality. Transsexual identity again appears untenable, founded and immediately unfounded on a contradiction; transsexual autobiography, like the demand in the clinician's office, a self-deconstructing, self-undermining opposition. However, in her very attentiveness to the contradictions within transsexual autobiographies and between transsexual autobiographies and the clinical narrative, in her very sense of the texts' "closed nature" and conformism, Hausman misses the crucial points about the conformism and contradictions of transsexual autobiographies. First, transsexual autobiographies conform as narratives to a generic form; they conform above all as autobiography. Second, the genre of autobiography operates precisely on a set of reconcilable and constitutive oppositions. These oppositions provide the larger framework within which Hausman's temporal "problematic" (always already and transformation) not only makes sense but is requisite. Third, the autobiographies' conformism to the oppositions within the genre of autobiography in turn plays an indispensable role in actuating transsexual transition. The autobiographies do not undermine but permit the realization of transsexual subjectivity. And finally, the autobiographies show the transsexual and medical narrative in collaboration: a relationship again complicated, but ultimately consolidated, by autobiographical conventions. In short, critical questions arise from the dependence of transsexuality on autobiographical narrative in the clinical situation that Hausman does not address: How do the particular conventions of autobiography underwrite the representation of transsexuality in the published autobiographies? What is at stake in transsexuals continuing to conform their lives specifically to this genre? It is not simply in the clinician's office but in the very conception of transsexual subjectivity that autobiography subtends (supports and makes possible) transsexuality.

Before critiquing transsexual autobiographies for conforming to a specific gendered plot, for writing narratives in which gendered meanings are "unilinear," we need to grasp the ways in which the genre of autobiography *is* conformist and unilinear. In that its work is to organize the life into a narrative form, autobiography is fundamentally conformist. "The original sin of autobiography," writes critic Georges Gusdorf in his classic description of autobiography's conventions, "is first one of logical coherence and rationalization."[21] Autobiography's primary purpose is to correspond life to textual form, to order the disorder of life's events into narrative episodes. In autobiography the desultoriness of experience acquires chronology, succession, progression—even causation; existence, an author. In other words writing endows the life with a formal structure that life does not indeed have. Published transsexual autobiography is no exception to this rule of autobiographical composition. The formality of autobiography shapes transsexual transition as plot, presenting the transsexual life as narrative *mythos*. All life events in the autobiographies seem to lead toward the *telos* of the sex-changed self. This gendered coherence is inextricable from the narrative coherence of the genre.

Many transsexual autobiographies make explicit the structuring effect of the genre on the life by drawing out a particular truism about autobiography as a voyage into the self. Writing the life, the trope evidences, inscribes it as a journey: a trajectory in which episodes lead toward a destination. The life written visibly and inevitably takes on this same progressive, connective, and destined pattern of the journey: departure, transition, and the home of reassignment. Most obviously among the autobiographies, Morris's *Conundrum* (fittingly, since the author is also a travel writer) transforms the trope of journeying into a theme for the life-writing. Morris presents transition as a mystical quest for the grail of the self: ordered, directed, and driven by the vision of an end. The use of "odyssey" as a title for a number of the autobiographies makes explicit how writing turns transition into a mythic voyage.[22] The "odyssey" is as much the writing as the life, for it is the writing that allows this scripted navigation into the life. One of the most recent transsexual personal accounts, Claudine Griggs's *Passage Through Trinidad: Journal of a Sex Change*, presents transition more prosaically through an account of an actual geographic trip required for surgery.[23] As Griggs's chapter titles succinctly evidence—"Decision," "Arrival," "Hospital," "Pain," "Routine," "Visitors," "Progress," "Freedom," "Anticipation," "Release," "West," "Home," "Aftermath"—writing the transsexual self through the literal journey nevertheless lends a diegetic, successive, and telic structure to transition, this frame inscribing transsexuality as schematic. Journeys, like narratives, have points of departure and destination, beginnings and ends; writing allows the transsexual to make connections, to trace "how I got here." The pervasiveness of the journey trope in transsexual writings, of this convention that draws attention to the self-conscious formality of the story, serves to remind us that we cannot assess transsexuality's linear plotting outside its stylistic frame of autobiography.

However, autobiography's structure is not that of simple linear progression. The narrative is founded on a temporal double movement. While structured as progression—developmental, moving toward a *telos*—the life in writing is always a retrospective reconstruction. Autobiography returns in order to re-present and in so doing, re-vise (rewrite and see again) the past. The subject's becoming through returning, the life's progression through revision of the past, is autobiography's structural sine qua non. It is in fact only retroactivity that bestows organization on the life story. Looking back as the conventional autobiographical omniscient narrator of his or her life, as the subject who knows the end of the story, the transsexual writes the life as directed. As Gusdorf states, life's unknownness, that quality of randomness, "cannot exist in a narrative of memories composed after the event by someone who knows the end of the story."[24]

The transsexual autobiography that we read is therefore the life as remembered by the envisioning, knowing "I." The entire life is filtered though the present moment of remembering: or in fact several different moments after the event—remembering in the life and in the writing. Stephanie Castle's term for moments in the autobiographies when the transsexual first realizes his or her gendered difference—the Joycean "epiphany"—suggests just this textualized, self-conscious quality of transsexual time in its autobiographical inscription.[25] An instant that takes its place in a sequence among other moments and thus transcends its own instantaneity, an epiphany is above all a narrative moment—when what it "epiphanizes" becomes clear. The "epiphany" in Morris's *Conundrum* illustrates this textualization of autobiographical narrative time. Morris claims to be able to fix her recognition of a transsexual self to a very precise instance when, as the three- or four-year-old James, she (as he) is "under the piano" his (her) mother is playing; it was then, Morris writes, that he (she) grasps "that [she/he] had been born into the wrong body, and should really be a girl" (3). But when does this moment really acquire this significance of absolute marker beginning the transsexual plot? While Morris may well have been aware of a deep-rooted sense of difference at the time of the experience, this difference does not become schematized as part of a transsexual narrative until that narrative is discovered and conceived—and this is surely not in the moment recounted, not by the young child. Indeed, we might venture that the episode does not properly acquire its full significance as origin story for the transsexual self until the moment of recounting, until it is assigned this place in the writing. It is as the framing vignette for *Conundrum* (the episode begins the autobiography, and in the final chapter we are told Morris is "under the piano still" [170]) that the memory becomes the scene that launches the transsexual plot. Meaning is conferred on the event most completely by this textual location. To remark the essential retroactivity of meaning in this way in the representation of the transsexual life does not invalidate Morris's claims for the scene. Rather, it underlines the extent to which, in the narrative we read, the life is absolutely and inevitably shaped by the moment of writing.

The life's directing by the autobiographer secure in knowing the end of his or her story, is, then, a generic feature of autobiography. Other forms of life-writing in which the subject writes without knowing the end of the story present the life as less product than process. Although journals and diaries are of course also a recounting of the past (writing can never be absolutely synchronized with the present moment of living), their dated entries fragment the life into an organization less linear and coherent, resemble life more closely as it is lived. Typically, if autobiographical retroactivity narrativizes the life, the continuous present of the journal creates life as open-ended, less schematic. It is fitting, therefore, that the two transsexual journals, Paul Hewitt's *A Self-Made Man: The Diary of a Man Born in a Woman's Body* and Jerry/Jerri McClain's *To Be a Woman* are accounts of the early stages of transition of, respectively, a female-to-male and a male-to-female.[26] In the present tense, in journal form, transsexual transitions appear not only a good deal less structured but in these instances, literally incomplete. By their own acknowledgment both Hewitt's and McClain's transitions remain incomplete by the end of each text (they are still waiting for surgery). While the form is surely chosen to fit the life (an unfinished form for an unfinished transition), it also in turn shapes (conforms to form) what we read of the life in these instances, presenting the transsexual narrative precisely as ongoing. The *bios* is thoroughly dependent on the representation.

The temporal "discontinuity" that Hausman finds in transsexual autobiography—the discontinuity "between the story of surgical sex change and the story of already being the other sex" (173)—between becoming and being, like the linearity of the transsexual plot cannot be understood apart from the temporal dynamics intrinsic to autobiographical form. There might seem to be a contradiction between the work of transsexual narrative—to document change: to say how I became a woman—and the transsexual's claim to already (truly) be a woman. Yet within the genre of autobiography this play between transformation and the continuity of the self, between conversion and identity, is not a disruptive paradox but a founding dynamic: a dynamic that in turn, as transsexuality is reliant on the autobiographical form, founds transsexuality. Conversion—along with confession, thoroughly embedded in autobiography's generic origins—is, we might say, autobiography's story of identity. For if the narrative of autobiography documents change (why deploy a form, after all, whose very purpose as diegesis is to trace the passage of time, if the subject does not change?), the *autos* of autobiography presumes identity, the continuity of the self, an "I" across time. Autobiography not only masters these splits between conversion and identity into a generic form; it necessitates them. Likewise transsexuality: its subject sex change of course, transsexuality is an archetypal conversion story; yet in conversion and change (transition) lies the key to transsexual identity.

What Hausman identifies as the "internal problematics" (142) "latent" (147) in transsexual autobiographies (the contradiction between always-already being and becoming) is, therefore, an overt structuring principle, not only of transsexual autobiography, not only classically, of all autobiography but of transsexual subjectivity. Even before the published autobiography, even before the subject's presentation to the clinician, autobiographical retroaction is at work in the subject's conception of his or her identity as transsexual. The repeated positing of a "true gender" *ab initio*, a recasting of the past to produce the present, propels the story of transsexual change; retroaction as much in the living as in the writing facilitates the subject's "progress" to and through transition. I have always/felt/behaved/looked (more) like a boy/girl; I have always been me. Martino captures how transsexual transformation is fueled by such a narrativization of subjectivity: "We, as sex-changed persons, are what we've always wanted to be" (270). The transsexual story, produced like every autobiography from the hindsight of the present moment but with transsexual subjectivity itself at stake in autobiographical retroaction, is that the subject become what, according to the subject's deepest conviction, s/he already truly was. In the case of transsexuality such becoming, it needs emphasizing, can only be accomplished through a circular revisioning of identity.

Given this positing of identity *ab initio*, in transsexual autobiography as in every conversion narrative, the "conversion" entails not so much a dramatic throwing off of a former self as a recasting of that past to make sense of and cohere—indeed, I am also arguing to constitute—the present one. It is in this light, as the necessary friction driving the autobiographical narrative and the transsexual transition interconnectedly, that we need to understand the tendency of transsexual autobiographers to posit an originally transgendered identity that often appears as a pre-transition psychic or embodied intersexuality. Intersexuality is a convention of transsexual autobiography, an effect of transsexuality's narrative form. The notion that I was already more like a boy than a girl, *that there was already something of the boy in me*, is a characteristic of transsexual autobiography as a body narrative. When Mark Rees's *Dear Sir or Madam: The Autobiography of a Female-to-Male Transsexual* opens with the young Rees as Brenda being asked whether he (as she) is a boy or a girl, Rees is representing his transsexual narrative as already plotted on his body: look, he says, my transsexuality was already corporeally legible to others; I have been me all along.[27] The device strives simultaneously toward coherence of narrative and body—to cohere the body with the narrative. The autobiographical self, as is its wont, suggests itself from the beginning as already there. The transsexual self simply follows form. Autobiography produces identity (sameness, singularity); transsexual autobiography, we should not be surprised, produces gender identity.

And herein (in narrative's intrinsic capacity to construct identity), surely, lies the lure of the genre of autobiography for the transsexual, a key reason why many transsexuals return to the narrative form after their diagnosis to write their lives. If autobiography in the clinician's office allows the subject to begin the transition, the published autobiographical narrative (through the revision of writing even more than the recursion of speech) allows the transsexual to integrate the self after transition: to make sense of a dramatic shift in sexed plots, to produce continuity in the face of change. Narrative *composes* the self. Conforming the life into narrative coheres both "lives" on either side of transition into an identity plot. This is not simply to remark autobiography as healing (although, particularly given the autobiographical requisite in the clinician's office, the therapeutic function of the return to narrative does need remarking) but autobiography as constitutive. Autobiography reconciles the subject to his or her past and in so doing allows a self to be instated in the present. In the case of Thompson, whose autobiography coauthored with his counselor literally doubles as psychotherapy (they write the book from his sessions), although he is unable to speak his life to the diagnosing psychiatrist, the act of returning in autobiography to write it has an explicitly integrating function that allows for this unspeakable—precisely the transsexual self—to be not only spoken but claimed as self. He now writes *as* a transsexual, the implication being that the passage of writing works through something of the trauma of that transsexual passage. "The remembering and the telling of his life's events" entailed in the book's production, his counselor/coauthor claims, "proved as cathartic as any therapy. At first his story came pouring out in a jumbled and fragmented fashion, but as we journeyed [again, the revisioning as voyage] through this life, the memory of events, feelings and conversations sharpened." In autobiography's process, Thompson "put[s] together the pieces of his fragmented life"; narrative has an explicitly cohering function.[28] Like surgery, autobiography heals the splits in plot into a transsexual identity; indeed, like and after surgery's re-membering of the body, the remembering of the life integrates and fills in for the absences of the narrative self. Autobiography melds together a body narrative in pieces. In short, for transsexual autobiographers, what Gusdorf describes as autobiography's "sin" of coherence may be quite explicitly a (second) salvation.

Inevitably, given the onomastic and pronominal shifts that are intrinsic to transsexual transition, transsexual autobiographies do contain some startlingly cracked gendered syntax as the subject narrates the transsexual movement: "A Little Boy Discovers Herself"; "A Girl's Journey to Manhood."[29] The transsexual autobiography, surely exceptionally among autobiographies, must change its autobiographical subject: from Barry to Caroline, from George to April, from Robert to Roberta, from Marie to Mario, from – to Raymond, the autobiography must represent two protagonists. Richards's *Second Serve* in fact heightens this difference by creating a dramatic framework out of the see-saw swing between its two gendered personae, Dick and Renée, as they vie for the part of protagonist, the "I" of the autobiography. One scene occurring before Dick's transition to Renée, yet when Renée is beginning to assert her will to existence, illustrates the dizzying effect in its inscription in language of the shifts in the transsexual plot—the difference this body makes to autobiographical narrative. The episode recounts the loss of Renée's virginity, her first sexual experience as a woman (but is it)?

The splits in perception—between how Renée desires to be seen and how she is seen; between this cross-dressed, male-embodied self of the past and the female-embodied "real" Renée writing now—multiply (and multiply gender) the autobiographical subject. Auditioning for a part in a drag show, Renée finds herself the object of desire on the part of the club owner. Renée wants to be seduced as a heterosexual woman but the club owner, Jimmy, a gay man, fancies Dick/dick in a dress. During the first movements of Renée's seduction, "I" recounts the scene as if it occurred to a third person, as if outside it—which, indeed, not identical with this cross-dressed Renée from a pretransition past, *she* is: "[Jimmy] stroked her thigh and feeling no resistance moved his hand higher. He ran his fingers between her legs. A warm flush suffused Renée's person, and she opened her legs a little. . . . All seemed to glow as she gazed at him and then felt his lips pressed urgently against hers" (73–74). As the seducer gets down to business, however, and Renée feels more secure in being desired as a woman, "I" is able to join in identification and take over Renée's part in the narrative, now speaking both for and with her: "Jimmy suggested we go upstairs. I agreed, and he led me to his room. When he removed his kimono he revealed a well-kept body, completely nude. I was still in my dress, and he came to me with another languorous kiss. I said I was a virgin" (74).

But as Jimmy undresses Renée and Dick—and crucially dick: for it is the body that makes the difference to the subject of transsexuality—threatens to disrupt the realization of Renée's (hetero)sexual fantasy, the narrative slips back into the third person: "Off came the dress, and with it went some of the dewiness of Renée's perspective. The bra was next and she began to feel much less secure. . . . Deprived of her accouterments, Renée began to fade, and Dick, who had been sent on vacation to parts unknown, came snapping back" (74). It is finally sex (body and act)—the sexed difference between that past self and the autobiographical self writing in the present—that brings Dick firmly back onto the stage and sends Renée along with the again disidentifying "I" scurrying off into the wings: "[Dick] didn't like what he found. He was taking a homosexual's penis in his mouth. Renée, however, was not completely gone, and it was she who insisted that Jimmy penetrate her face-to-face as a man would a woman. Jimmy, kindly agreed to this ungainly setup. Dick lay in absolute horror as he felt his anus invaded" (74) At the moment of penetration (from Renée's perspective, for Dick, penetration as a male by a homosexual), "I" who identifies in the present as a heterosexual woman can no longer keep up in the description the autobiographical identification or coherence: it is Dick's anus and not Renée's vagina (as of this moment in the plot's recounting "I" 's futural part) that receives Jimmy's penis. The split of the transsexual autobiographical subject—the difference between me then and me now in body—becomes starkly inscribed in Dick's different naming in the narrative.

But while the gendered referent of the "I" necessarily changes in transsexual autobiography as this scene so spectacularly captures, autobiographical form ensures the continuity of the subject as a signifier. Transsexual autobiography represents the transformation, but it also generates the crucial points of conversion to show how the transsexual splits are rejoined into a singular autobiographical subject. From Renée's signature on *Second Serve* and our equation of the signature with the narrator and protagonist of the autobiography, we know all along that there is really only one subject to the narrative; the autograph guarantees the subject's gender coherence. In *Second Serve* "I" does finally transfer its allegiance from Dick to Renée and this doubled subject homogenize itself as the narrative is brought up to the present. This "sex change" occurs not during sex reassignment surgery as we might expect, but at a richly signifying moment in the narrative; for while it may be somatic transformation that allows the transsexual to feel sex-changed, writing in the autobiographies may generate its own transitional moments (more symbolic, more in keeping with the flow of the story) to cohere the transsexual subject. Narrative enacts its own transitions. In *Second Serve* the primary moment of integration occurs on the transatlantic voyage Richards must make to Europe on h/er way to Casablanca for the surgery. Although Richards will return as Richard Raskind, unreassigned, dick/Dick intact, marry a woman, have a child, and attempt one more time to live as a man, it is on the crossing from New York to Genoa that Richards really "becomes" Renée, feels h/erself to be no longer acting a woman but to be one. She gives free rein to Renée, cross-dressing for the first time consistently, abandoning Dick's identity in New York: "As the *Michaelangelo* steamed through the quiet Mediterranean waters, I felt myself sinking more and more into the persona of Renée. It was not a role anymore. I felt myself to be a woman, and except for the much atrophied genitals between my legs I really was one" (222). Brilliantly punning on the words "passage" and "crossing," the narrative exuberantly spinning out the valences of the trope of journeying in which transsexuality and autobiography are both so invested so that transsexuality, autobiography, and the journey are all richly conjoined, Richards makes the ship a figure for her transition: "The Michaelangelo was my transitional vehicle" (219). The ship is a "transitional vehicle" in three senses: literally, according to the geographical trip; transsexually, in terms of the identity plot; and thus, autobiographically (the split of the "I" is cohered). In her representation of this entire "voyage" Richards underlines that a narrative sensibility drives the transition all along so that transsexuality appears as already narrative—"on the boat it was F. Scot Fitzgerald, in Italy it was Fellini" (246–247). If transition is always already narrativized—novelistic, cinematic—then how can we begin to read transsexuality outside of narrative's properties?

Indeed, for the transsexual even to discover the possibility of transsexuality—to transform it from private fantasy to realizable identity plot—takes place "in" narrative. To learn of transsexuality is to uncover transsexuality as a story and to refigure one's own life within the frame of that story. The autobiographies' description of how transsexuals come to name themselves transsexual graphically illustrates that self-knowledge as a transsexual requires such a narrativization. Self-naming in the autobiographies is typically an "instance" (but my point is that as simultaneously revisionary and visionary, as narrative it is never an instance) enabled by the reading of other transsexual narratives, sometimes newspapers, but often previous transsexual biographies or autobiographies. The media coverage of Christine Jorgensen's story in 1952 and her own autobiography of 1967 produced a narrative model for many; even the biography of the hapless Lili Elbe, another male-to-female who underwent unsuccessful reassignment in 1933 without hormone treatment (the surgeons attempted to implant ovarian tissue; she died soon after the procedure), galvanized transitions, for at least it suggested the right projected trajectory.[30] The reading of transsexual narratives allows for the recognition of one's own *bios* as a transsexual narrative. In *Mirror Image* Hunt describes how her reading of Morris's *Conundrum* motivates her to seek out hormones, the other transsexual a mirror image for Hunt to model herself on: "Morris had faced this dilemma and solved it, and given the courage and resolution, so could I. Morris had taken hormones and so could I.... Morris had gone to Dr. Harry Benjamin in New York, starting down the road that would end on the operating table, and I could do that to."[31] Previous transsexual autobiographies provide a narrative map: for the writing of the autobiography, of course, but also for the subject's self-construction as transsexual. The autobiographies have a central place in what Stone terms the "Obligatory Transsexual File"—the collection of newspaper clippings, articles, photographs, any text on transsexuality—that transsexuals amass to enable transition.[32] Recent transsexual autobiographies have even begun to display a consciousness of their self-help function, listing support group/medical help telephone numbers.[33] Transsexuality is thoroughly engineered by autobiographical narrative in this sense also: not only through the oral autobiography in the clinician's office, not only in the retroactive reconstruction of the life into a transsexual *bios* but through the reading of published narratives, the latter often engendering both the former. Again, this recycling of the transsexual narrative from life to text to life (from body to narrative to body again)—what we might think of as inter-transtextuality, both in the autobiographies and in the oral recounting—does not invalidate the transsexual's gender. Rather, given the dependence of transsexuality on narrative, given that transitions always requires that narrativization of the life, there is no other way in which the subject—indeed, surely the point is any subject—could come to naming, to realization of his or her categorical belonging except through some form of narrative.

Clinical narratives in their turn also come to play a role in the subject's mapping of a transsexual plot. The subject returns to the clinical definition in order to recognize his or her transsexuality for what it is. One of Richards's earliest moments of self-recognition derives from reading Richard von Krafft-Ebing's *Psychopathia Sexualis*, which she finds in her mother's (a psychiatrist) study; this nineteenth-century sexologist's case histories of sexual inversion initially mirror her own gendered displacement. In their very naming, published autobiographies are underwritten by the existence of the official medical discourse. "Diary of a Transsexual," "Autobiography of a Transsexual," "Story of a Transsexual": the subject derives his or her autobiographical license from that designation as a categorical subject. The transsexual is autobiographical subject (that is, writing overtly under the rubric of transsexuality) because s/he is medicodiscursive object. If to be a transsexual one must be an autobiographer, to be a published transsexual autobiographer one must have been subject to the diagnosis. On this count too, transsexual autobiography's conventions are formally in keeping with those of autobiography. Historicizing the origins of autobiography, Gusdorf states that the genre only emerges when the subject "seizes on himself for object" (a moment Gusdorf uses the discovery of the mirror—in the subject of history and the history of the subject—to emblematize).[34] When specified, Gusdorf's formulation explains how transsexual autobiography emerges at a homologous moment: when the transsexual autobiographer seizes on the self as a medicodiscursive object. Again, there is no stalling contradiction between this doubled location, between medical discourse and transsexual self-representation, since generically, within the narrative form, the autobiographer is by definition subject and object of his or her text, only an autobiographer because a readable subject for the other.

The clinician's preface attached to many of the autobiographies explicitly stages the transsexual's medical designation, working the clinical narrative formally into the autobiography. Like white abolitionists' prefaces to slave narratives, the clinician's preface "grants" the autobiographer a narrative voice, vouching both for its representationality (authenticity) and its representativeness (exemplarity). This is the true story of a slave, of a transsexual; this book has (is) a categorical life. "In this book," writes Harry Benjamin at the beginning of Christine Jorgensen's *A Personal Autobiography*, "Christine has written a document of great medical value. Her life story should forcefully support all those institutions and individuals who endorse and provide hormonal and surgical help for transsexuals." If the transsexual continues to derive authority (authorship) from the clinician in writing his or her narrative, the transsexual's autobiography, as a completed trajectory, a kind of transsexual fait accompli or case history, in turn affirms the success of the clinician's work. Indeed, the language of Benjamin's preface suggests a definitive contract between clinician and transsexual, a contract that the transsexual in writing her autobiography fulfills. Jorgensen's personal account is "long overdue," Benjamin writes, "owed" not only to self, family, and fellow transsexuals but "to science and the medical profession"; "[she] was *in duty bound* to supplement the technical report made by her Danish physicians . . . in 1953 with her own account of the inner and outer events in her still rather young life."[35] In writing her autobiography, the transsexual returns the favor of authorization, part of a reciprocity between clinician and subject that continues to take place through the conventions of autobiographical narrative.

With the same effect of legitimating the personal story through the medical narrative, other transsexual autobiographies ventriloquize these medicalizing voices within their narrative. Canary Conn's autobiography begins and ends with the author giving a talk at a medical symposium on transsexuality organized by her surgeon—she is his principal speaker, speaking (like Jorgensen for Benjamin) for him but also for herself through him. Still shaky and queasy from her surgery only a few days before, wheeled out into the auditorium in a wheelchair and bundled in blankets, Conn is markedly a patient and authority, exponent in both senses—not only on stage but also, in that the lecture opens the narrative, on page, for the reader.[36] The opening of *Mirror Image* employs an ingenious device for securing the transsexual's narrative subjectivity through and yet free from objectification from her medicodiscursive construction. Hunt begins with a long description of the sex reassignment surgery of another male-to-female transsexual, using the other as a mirror to reflect back into the text her image in reverse. While the other's anesthetized body is laid out on the operating table, her eyes bound closed with tape, Hunt watches the proceedings from within the operating theater. The other stands in for Hunt (Hunt reveals that she underwent the same procedure in the same location with the same surgeon only six months previously), medical object then in order that Hunt can be autobiographical subject now. Intercalating into the scene a history of transsexuality and vaginoplasty, Hunt like Conn masters the authoritative voice of the clinician (indeed, she defers her own story, the personal account, until chapter 4), medical discourse overtly providing the plinth for transsexual autobiography.

The autobiographer's interlocution with the clinical narrative is by no means always loyal, however, and other autobiographers use their personal histories not to authorize their account but to rewrite the clinician's and produce a better story for the self. The first sections of Richards's autobiography parodically replay the form of the clinical "case history": "If I sat down to write a case history of an imaginary transsexual, I could not come up with a more provocative set of circumstances than my childhood," Richards opens her narrative (5). This particular case history, we later learn in *Second Serve*, was supplied by her analyst during nineteen years of therapy. Freudian shrink Dr. Bak thinks Richards is really just "a nice Jewish boy from Queens" (164) who, like every other man, loves his penis and cross-dresses in order to assure himself that he has still got it. Breaking up Bak's diagnosis through a kind of narrative bricolage, using his story (but overreading it) to structure her narrative, Richards caricatures her mother, "Dr. Bishop," as the formidable phallic mother, seeking to compensate for not being the son her own father wanted by becoming more of a man than the men she scorns. In Richards's parodic replay, Dr. Bishop transforms her daughter into a son, naming her "Michael," and emasculates her son, Dick, inaugurating his cross-dressing by sending him to a Halloween party as a convincing pretty little girl: "when I was a girl, Mommy loved me" (16). Mommy produces a little boy as little girl. The plot of childhood in the autobiography turns precisely on key fetishistic tropes as the game of the "disappearing penis" that Michael plays on her brother, or as Dick the little boy snuggling up next to Dr. Bishop in bed in the mornings and then watching her dress, transforming herself from the "warm, soft" (7) Mommy to the austere Dr. Bishop: "Every morning I experienced my mother's naked body as she softly went through her cycle. The slight sag of her breasts, the shape and color of her nipples, the soft muff of dark fur between her legs, these were as familiar to me as any of her dark flannel suits" (20). The "life" is not a reproduction of Dr. Bak's case history, for Richards raids his psycho-sexual discourse precisely in order to break with it. She goes on (in her life and her life story) to transition, against Bak's prophecies of doom, to lose her penis and precisely not "miss" it. His case history (indeed, as with Benjamin's later) does not so much underwrite her autobiography as it would undermine it—that is, if she had not found the means to author her own plot (in both senses) differently. It is not insignificant that, as a star opthamological surgeon with her own medical texts in print Richards is herself a medical author. The difference between transsexual as clinical object and medical authority is already broken down, and the clinical definition appears more rescriptable.

In neat counterpoint to Richards's account, Martino, a transsexual who as a male nurse likewise has a medical insiderness, unravels a psychoanalytic account of female-to-male transgender—the little girl who won't give up her penis (both books interestingly suggest the psychoanalytic account of transsexuality in particular as in need of rewriting).[37] Like Richards, Martino enlists the official discourse to satirical effect. Tracing through his life an explicitly oedipal thread—his desire to be better than his father, to love his mother in a mode in which he sees his father as failing and even calling it such ("A bit of Oedipus, you think?" [28])—Martino ironizes the notion of a masculinity complex, using this narrative in order to fund the humor in his own account, in what would otherwise be too painful a story to read as it has been "a painful life to live, a painful story to write" (xi). When his second phalloplasty starts to go wrong, for example (the first has already been surgically removed as a failure) and the tip of his penis necrotizes, Martino must sit nightly in warm baths and "very slowly, cut away at the dead tissue" (262). In his return to it in writing, the trauma (physical, emotional) of the act—this literalization of the loss of the end of his desire—can be staved off for the sake of the reader with a joke *on* psychoanalysis: "Talk about castration complex!" (262). The humor works to keep us going past the trauma, and this most patronizing of clinical plots for the female-to-male is made ridiculous in its autobiographical literalization.

If the transsexual autobiographer perceives a need to establish authority either through or over the official medical discourse, it is precisely because the "pain" of the classic transsexual story—"scenes" of childhood cross-dressing and sometimes gruesome surgery—in its very telling threatens to subvert the transsexual as authorial subject and transform him or her into absolute other for the reader's horror and/or fascination. As in the clinician's office, in the published autobiography the subject faces the question of how to make the transsexual story readable: a task that again entails not simply making the life visible but making it processable. This may indeed require some revisioning on the part of the author, for the subject now addresses an audience, I suggest, that is more than likely drawn to reading in expectation precisely of such scenes. If transsexuals read the autobiographies for identification, the nontranssexual readership that sustains the market for these autobiographies is surely motivated primarily by fascination, an interest in the transsexual precisely as prodigious other. Ironically, transsexual autobiographies depend for their circulation on a certain degree of objectification of the transsexual, what we might call the tabloidization of transsexuality: the daytime talk shows, the supermarket tabloids, for which transsexuality is headline material. Particularly in their packaging, transsexual autobiographies may even explicitly court this readership by advertising their own prodigious status: "an extraordinary story," "an amazing account," "the life of an extraordinary woman." From this status as bizarre other the autobiographer must yet hew a coherently gendered authorial subjectivity: s/he must move from the extraordinariness of transsexuality as a cultural story to the act of self-justification always entailed in writing my story.

Nevertheless the autobiographer patently wants to be read not simply as a coherently gendered subject but as a transsexual. On this count the conventions of autobiography would appear to be fundamentally at odds with those of transsexuality. For if the highest ideal of transsexuality is to pass, and its antithesis is to be "read" (in the lingo when a transsexual is read, she has failed to pass, she is taken for what she wishes most strongly not to be), then autobiography allows the transsexual's reading. If somatic transition allows the transsexual to pass and blend in as nontranssexual, to be incorporated and not be read as transsexual as I suggested, autobiography undoes this passing and writes the body back out. While the purpose of transsexuality is to redesign the body so that one won't be able to "tell the difference" (the difference, that is, of transsexuality), the purpose of transsexual autobiography is to tell this difference. Transsexuality promises to make the transsexual unremarkable; autobiography re-insists in the face of this (this is autobiography's effect) on the subject's remarkability. Writing the narrative may indeed be a mechanism for working though the life; *publishing* it—putting the life in a public domain—is a different matter altogether. The paradox of transsexual autobiography surely rests here: not one between technology and intersexuality that compromises transsexuality but a paradox between passing as nontranssexual and writing as an autobiographer who wants to be read as transsexual.

What are we to make of the autobiographer's desire to be read as transsexual? I suggest that in publishing the narrative the transsexual is not concerned with getting readers to conform their lives to his or her own, with covering over transsexuality as Hausman insists, but on the contrary, with declaring and uncovering a transsexual history. For while sex reassignment surgery brings with it the chance of incorporation as a man or a woman, an unremarkability (a passing as real that should not be undervalued), becoming fully unremarkable requires the transsexual to renounce the remarkable history of transition—the very means to this unremarkability. The autobiographies are all written from a point posttransition precisely when the past self could be concealed, when passing makes possible the detachment of the transsexual past; surgery, on the surface, allows for an "amputation" (Robert Allen's surgical image for this detachment) of the pretransition past.[38] But although it can make the body seamless in its "new" sex, what history would this body have postreassignment? At the end of her autobiography Morris insists that the question posed to her so often—what does it feel like to be a woman after living so many years as a man?—is doubly unanswerable: both because of the felt experience of her transgendered identification (she never felt herself to be a man) and because of her radically foreshortened history as a woman. Neither history is really hers. To reconstitute her past—and what is a subject without a past, what, after all, an identity without a narrative?—she must write, therefore *as a transsexual*. In autobiography, transsexuals meticulously re-member that past. The body may have been subject to change, but the story is subject to preservation—to recording as transsexual autobiography. As Roberta Cowell's declaration at the end of her autobiography in fact can only serve to remind us—glancing at herself in the mirror before her first entrance to a ball as a woman, she thinks "[t]he past is forgotten"—the entire preceding narrative is evidence that the past is anything but forgotten.[39] Autobiography is very determinedly an act of remembering. In preserving in the autobiography a body of transsexual memory, in not performing the renunciation of a transsexual past, all transsexual autobiographers—by dint of their status *as* transsexual autobiographers—hold on to transsexuality as a subjectivity.

As well as allowing the transsexual to become a man or a woman in the clinician's office, autobiography, then, allows the transsexual to remain (very publicly) a transsexual. The autobiographical act on every count does not undercut but permits the realization of transsexual subjectivity—indeed, in a way not imagined by the medical narrative. Autobiography's conventions are both the means to passing through transsexuality and to passing back into it. There is, in the final instance, an exquisite tension in transsexual autobiography between body and narrative (the quest for gendered realness next to the refusal to cede one's history as a transsexual), a tension that doesn't stall but sustains the transsexual's capacity to write. Like Narcissus captured by the sight of his reflection, the transsexual in autobiography neither fully merges with nor moves away from the image of the changed self. The act of self-reflection both begins the metamorphosis and prevents the total mergence of past into present self that would mean the disappearance of this remarkable narrative.

Reading Back: Toward a Transsexual Canon

As she works to uncover the technology transsexuals putatively "cover over" in their autobiographies, Hausman's approach to transsexual autobiography as a suspect text uncannily mirrors that of the policing clinician who has gone before her: the critic catches us out in our duplicity again. Yet in weighing the evidence against us, Hausman and clinician fall short as narrative critics, for they fail to take into account the extent to which transsexuality is organized by the conventions of autobiography. The layers of concealment attributed to the disingenuous transsexual are none other than the layers of narrative itself: a layering that does not invalidate transsexual subjectivity but makes it possible. Although outside the domain of psychiatry and psychology specializing in transsexuality (no writer has worked in a sustained way with transsexual autobiographical accounts before her), Hausman admits that her purpose is in fact to work *against* transsexual accounts. Her agenda is openly to "subvert the official story put forth by transsexual autobiographers" (141). Given that transsexual autobiographies have been so unread in cultural theory, given that they hardly represent an official story in or beyond gender theory, it is not clear what is at stake in this urge to subvert, the desire to "work" the contradictions of transsexual representation and reveal the putatively latent story of transsexual autobiography before even its blatant story is known. Perhaps the preface to *Changing Sex* contains something of a clue.

Here, in her account of how she came to decide on the topic for her project, Hausman describes how she "fell into" writing about transsexuality "sideways," inadvertently," while tinkering with the idea of transvestism which was "kicking around feminist literary criticism at the time" (vii). In the library she discovered transsexualism: her response, "Now *that* was really fascinating" (vii). Incredibly, *Changing Sex* suggests this "fascination" with the subject of transsexuality from a point outside of it not simply as one location from which to explore transsexuality (and surely given transsexuality's entanglement in "fascination," this would require some explanation) but *the* authoritative site from which to speak. Particularly in the chapter on the autobiographies, the "critical reader" is set up in opposition to "the reader interested in verifying his or her gender confusion" (156) (i.e., surely, the transsexual). Whereas the gender-confused use transsexual autobiography to verify their gender confusion, critical readers (presumably having no gender confusion to verify) apparently get to see through to the internal problematics of these texts: as if transsexuals were not critical thinkers and readers; indeed, as if one couldn't be a transsexual and a critic at the same time. But—even assuming the discreteness of these identities in the first place—why assume in the second place that the critic can read more about sex and gender than the transsexual ? Much as she might use her writing to block it out, Hausman too has a gender, a gender and a body thoroughly embedded in her narrative, never divorced from her praxis of reading. Again in her preface (this is where *Changing Sex* reveals *its* "internal problematics"), Hausman writes that she was pregnant for most of the year she spent rewriting the book. Her personal concern at the time was that she might come to bear an unclearly sexed child: "I am perhaps one of few expectant mothers who worry that they will give birth to a hermaphrodite" (x). The autobiographical anecdote reveals more about her critical perspective than any theoretical moment in the text. Her preoccupation, that her body might contain a body that resembles too closely her object of study, makes crystal clear that she views the unclearly sexed body in her study with anxiety and alarm and that she locates her own body in a clean, unambivalently sexed location beyond this embodied sexed confusion. The horror in her fantasy of pregnancy derives from its breaking down—through the imaginary hermaphroditic child—her sustained antithesis between critic and transsexual, authority and object of study. Her fear is that she may herself via her "product" (book/child: here, the fear is that *there will be no difference between body and narrative*) come to reflect the object of her study, mirror image. No wonder the critical force of her perspective: her struggle to make sure that the watch-glass of the laboratory through which she views the transsexual as other does not become the plate-glass of the mirror in which she might see herself.

It is the omission of autobiographical narrative in the discussion of transsexuality that has led to a massive overvaluation of technology in the "construction" of the transsexual. Hausman's project suggests that it is technology and not narrative that "makes" the transsexual: we are authored by the medical technologies of plastic surgery, endocrinology, and the "idea of gender." But if autobiography is transsexuality's proffered symptom, the transsexual necessarily authors his or her own plot *before* s/he has access to technologies. I have made this argument ontogenetically, but it also needs to be made phylogenetically. As she fixes on technology as the marker of the transsexual subject, Hausman maintains that we cannot use the category of transsexual for "subjects exhibiting cross-sex behaviors prior to the technical capacity for sex reassignment" (117), that transsexuals did not appear until after sex change became possible. But Hausman—and to date, other critics—fail to read the narratives that subjects told to author themselves prior to the diagnosis of transsexuality. Even without the official discourse of sex change, the plot lines of nineteenth- and early twentieth-century transgendered subjects are remarkably consistent with those of contemporary transsexuals, the consistence and continuity of this narrative and its conventions the very factor that produced a medical discourse around transgender that led to the writing of a transsexual diagnosis in *DSM-III*. The diagnosis then stands for a recognition of the "trans-history" (with all the connotations we can give that coining) of trans narratives. Reading transsexual autobiography—and reading it back to form a canon of transsexual narratives—is not merely a critical exercise but a political enterprise. Indeed, narrative may be our keenest weapon in these skirmishes over transsexual representation. Narrative is a reflection, above all, of our capacity to represent ourselves.

> "Do you think I *could* be a man, supposing I thought very hard—or prayed, Father?"
> —Stephen Gordon, Radclyffe Hall, *The Well of Loneliness*

> "The negative sides to the book are just as interesting—why the need to be so male-dominated—the relinquishing of Mary for a safe heterosexual relationship? Should it be seen as the first 'invert' novel rather than lesbian? Should we describe it as a lesbian novel at all?"
> —Reader surveyed, Rebecca O'Rourke, *Reflecting on The Well of Loneliness*

> The dullness of the book is such that any indecency may lurk there—one simply can't keep one's eyes on the page.
> —Virginia Woolf, *Letters*

chapter 4

"Some Primitive Thing Conceived in a Turbulent Age of Transition": The Invert, *The Well of Loneliness*, and the Narrative Origins of Transsexuality

The Trials of a Lesbian Novel

Since the publication of Radclyffe Hall's *The Well of Loneliness* in 1928 its critics have generally agreed on one thing: that the sexual subject at the center of Hall's novel is lesbianism.[1] Even when the magistrate presiding at the novel's obscenity trial denounced its subject without naming it, his invective ("these horrible practices," "these two people living in filthy sin," "acts of the most horrible, unnatural and disgusting obscenity") left no doubt that he was talking about female homosexuality.[2] If Britain had pretended in the nineteenth century that sexual practices between women did not exist (and thus did not warrant prohibition), it could hardly continue to do once the trial had publicly prohibited *The Well*: "As a 'Modern Mother' protested, far from protecting those whose minds were 'open to immoral influences,' the ban on *The Well* had created such a ballyhoo that no young girl or boy could now 'remain ignorant of certain facts which ordinarily would never have come to their notice.'"[3] Broadcasting the unspeakable crime that it set out to censor, *The Well*'s trial crucially set in motion its history of being read as a lesbian novel.

The association of lesbianism with *The Well* has only intensified during the history of its reading: *The Well* has progressed from a lesbian novel, to the most well-known lesbian novel, to "*the* lesbian novel," as Jane Rule put it in 1976.[4] Yet as the last two decades of criticism since Rule's canonization show, this definitively lesbian novel has also become the definitively troublesome lesbian novel. *The Well* is *the* lesbian novel least reconciled to its lesbian status. Its very donnée defies a lesbian reading: its protagonist is unwaveringly male-identified, its plot dooms lesbian love as tragic and impossible. Depicting the lesbian as a woman who would be a straight man, perpetuating that most obvious of cultural stereotypes, *The Well* is, in effect, lesbianism's most famous representation *and* its most infamous misrepresentation. The novel's idealization of masculinity and heterosexuality has, not surprisingly, been considered to make it a bad representation of lesbianism: early lesbian-feminist readers Blanche Wiesen-Cook, Lillian Faderman, and Catharine Stimpson certainly thought the novel insufficiently lesbian. The heterosexual/masculine framework for *The Well* has been read to recuperate the novel as a historically accurate representation of lesbianism: Caroll Smith-Rosenberg and Esther Newton challenged the earlier lesbian-feminist rejection by situating the novel in its historical moment. Stephen's identifications have even been read to acclaim the novel a discursive reversal of these ideals: Sonja Ruehl and Jean Radford have seen *The Well* as transforming the cultural discourses that structure it, and Gillian Whitlock has read it as at least attempting this endeavor. Most recently Teresa de Lauretis has recruited its protagonist for a psychoanalytic theory of lesbian desire. But *The Well* has never been read for its blatant transgendered narrative, and Hall's novel has remained foundationally yoked to lesbianism.[5]

Yet subliminally, transgender has been the subject of criticism all along. As even the above lesbian readings suggest, transgender is *The Well*'s stumbling block, that which must be "worked" if the novel is to made sense of as lesbian. Why does Hall portray Stephen Gordon (in name, body, behavior, and ideals) as so morbidly masculine, on the scale of mannishness as less a manly lesbian than a man *manqué*? What is remarkable about previous critical work on the novel is how close it has come, in the same moment as claiming the novel's subject as lesbian, to performing that reading where Stephen is a woman who really would be a man: that is, where she is not lesbian but a female-to-male transsexual. While no critic has actually performed this reading, transsexuality has consistently encroached on lesbianism in readings of the novel. It as though the female-to-male transsexual has required a concerted displacement to the margins in order for the lesbian to remain center stage of the novel's interpretations. Sandra Gilbert and Susan Gubar, for instance, note the transsexual possibilities of *The Well* only to suggest that transsexuality serves as the medium for lesbianism: Hall was struggling "with a sense of lesbianism as tragic transsexuality."[6] They argue that transsexuality represents in part a means for Hall to convey the specific isolation of the lesbian artist in the absence of a community of women, and in part, analogously to other modernist "sexchanges," a "metaphor" for the general gender anomie that followed World War I. Esther Newton also invokes transsexuality in the novel as a lesbian signifier. Although Newton's essay represents the most sustained attempt to explicate the transgendered plot of *The Well*—and, exceptionally, recognizes transgender as a "real" experience—it similarly recoups the cross-gendered scheme for lesbianism. Transgender is lesbianism's historically situated erotic drag: Hall "uses cross-dressing and gender reversal to symbolize lesbian sexuality;" her heroine is a "lesbian in male body drag"—as "a mannish lesbian," a precursor of the lesbian butch and emphatically not transsexual.[7] In both essays the implication is that lesbianism is the true transhistorical subject, while the transgendered paradigm is the culturally contingent investiture for this subject.

Critics have anchored this reading of *The Well* as lesbian novel through similarly sublimating transgender into homosexuality in the discourse that provides Hall with her transgendered design: the sexological discourse of sexual inversion. In spite of the fact that *The Well* explicitly and exclusively identifies its protagonist an invert—it is notable that nowhere does *the* lesbian novel use the category "lesbian"—criticism has made a categorical slide from invert to lesbian. Rightly tracing Hall's debt to nineteenth-century sexologists, critics have wrongly reduced sexual inversion to homosexuality. Across the board of history inversion has been understood as an attempt by the medical establishment to describe homosexual desire, an attempt that, because it preceded psychoanalysis's separation of sexuality from gender, egregiously failed. If inversion's discursive moment imbricated gender and sexuality and naturalized gender roles, the argument has been: how else to think homosexuality except through this transgendered scheme in which women who desired women wanted to be men and men who desired men to be women? George Chauncey's reasoning has provided a touchstone: "The Victorian assertion of male sexual aggressiveness and denial of female sexual interest established the logical framework for the earliest medical inquiry into sexual deviance, and determined the manner in which researchers defined it.... In the Victorian system, therefore, a complete inversion or reversal of a woman's sexual character was required for her to act as a lesbian; she had literally to become man-like in her sexual desire."[8] Inversion has been rendered synonymous with the "medicalization of homosexuality," and the masculinized female inverts and feminized male inverts who crowd sexological works and find their fictionalized representative in Stephen Gordon have been read as really homosexual, their sexual inversion—that is their transgendering—as merely symptomizing homosexuality. Again, the assumption is of transgender as a figure for homosexuality, of transgender as homosexuality's heterocentric construct. Indeed, in the constructionist work foundational not only of this approach to sexology but arguably of lesbian and gay historiography as a whole, Foucault's *The History of Sexuality*, transgender serves as the homosexual subject's discursive threshold: inversion is said to mark homosexuality's origins as a category or "a species."[9] It is from this historical narrative of sexual inversion as homosexuality's origin that literary criticism has taken its cue, reading transgender in *The Well* as a sign—whether loyal or parodic, regressive or transgressive, transgender nevertheless remains an archetypal homosexual sign—for lesbianism.[10]

My contention in this chapter is, interconnectedly, with the homosexual reading of inversion and with the lesbian reading of *The Well*, with context as much as text; for the sublimation of transgender in the one has enabled its sublimation in the other. In configuring inversion as a metaphor for homosexuality, we have left out what sexual inversion in sexology and in Hall's novel are most literally about: that is gender inversion, cross-gender identity. Through sexual inversion sexologists sought to describe not homosexuality but a broad transgendered condition of which same-sex desire was but one symptom, and not vice versa. The lesbian and gay critique of sexology has sometimes acknowledged this, and that as a consequence there is substantive gendered matter in inversion that exceeds homosexual identity. Chauncey for instance concedes that sexual inversion "did not denote the same conceptual phenomenon as homosexuality" but "referred to a broad range of deviant gender behavior, of which homosexual desire was only a logical but indistinct aspect."[11]

Nevertheless, same-sex desire has continued to dominate "deviant gender behavior" in the work uncovering the invert. It has done so, I suggest, because in pursuing the sexology as a construction of homosexuality premise, we have focused overly on the theoretical passages in sexological texts. Reading the invert as the sexologists' constructed effect, we have examined in detail the sexologists' analyses but have not looked at how inverts constructed themselves. Contained in the form of case histories, the narratives of inverts, the stories of their individual lives, make up the bulk of and basis for sexology's theories, yet they are typically treated as peripheral to the theory rather than its foundational material. For a sexual historiography intent on reconstituting the invert as subject, the case histories are key; for it is here that inverts make their most sustained appearance as subjects. The value of those case histories that present the invert autobiographically is particularly significant, for they evidence that subjects could conceive of themselves as transgendered, that inverts identified themselves through cross-gender paradigms. When read via personal narratives in case histories, transgender in sexual inversion cannot be reduced to the sexologists' figure for homosexuality but must be seen for some inverts as the grounds for a transgendered identity.

For a transsexual historiography in particular, the transgendered case histories in sexology are foundational: they reveal inverts, to varying degrees, identifying with, appearing as, living as, and sometimes seeking out the surgical means to aid a transition to the "other" sex. Sexology provided the narrative setting for the transgendered subject to become medicalized. Without this medicalization of transgendered narratives, gender deviance would not have been hitched to the medical technology that "cures" the transsexual through sex change. To become transsexual, to make that somatic transition from gender deviant to sex-changed, the transgendered narrative needed to become diagnosable. Sexology provided the discursive space for medicalizing and diagnosing transgendered narratives in the form of the case history; and, in fact, through the case history the diagnosis of inversion can be shown to have relied, like transsexuality, on a dialogics of narrative between clinician and subject: if among inverts number the first transsexual autobiographers, among sexologists number their first "readers." From the perspective of transsexual history—in contrast to homosexual history—sexology can be seen to have been powerfully enabling and productive. Inversion's case histories crucially propelled the transgendered subject—through narrative—toward transsexuality.

Written historically and formally after the case histories of inversion, modeled on their plots, *The Well* is not only thematically but concretely caught up in the inception of transsexual subjectivity. Published on the very horizon of the discursive transition from inversion to transsexuality, *The Well* in its turn also provided something of a narrative map for transitioning transsexuals. Read in situ, as a fictional consequence of inversion's case histories, *The Well* comes into focus as not only not a lesbian novel, not only our first and most canonical transsexual novel, but a narrative that itself contributed to the formalization of transsexual subjectivity.

Reading Inversion: The Sexological Case History

In 1864 a female subject wrote to German sexologist Carl Westphal that s/he had felt like a man since childhood, had spent much of h/er life in mental institutions, and was now actively seeking medical help: "Ich . . . möchte gern ein mann sein" (I would like to be a man). Westphal diagnosed h/er under his specific category for sexual inversion, "die konträre Sexualempfindung" (contrary sexual feelings). Through the nineteenth century, h/er case was recognized as one of the first descriptions of female inversion; in the twentieth century, h/er case has been recast as a founding moment for medical research into female-to-male transsexuality.[12] Recycled from harbinger of inversion to harbinger of transsexuality, Westphal's case encapsulates how inversion's narratives have formed a kind of palimpsest for transsexuality. For twentieth-century sexologists inversion represents not an outdated misrepresentation of homosexuality but a useful first draft of the transsexual diagnosis. The case histories of inversion—the narrative product of modern medicine's first attempt to describe transgender—appear to offer up the very stuff of transsexuality: the expression of being differently gendered; the recounting of a plot that pulls toward being the other sex; even sometimes the articulated desire to change sex. In the project of establishing transsexuality as a condition that has not simply come into being as a consequence of available technology (a project that has been key for justifying the radical intervention of contemporary transsexual treatment), sexology's case histories have been invaluable. They reveal transsexual desire preceding its clinical moment of definition; they document that the desire to change sex existed before it was diagnosed as transsexual.

Of most value to the project of reading transsexuality back through inversion are cases which describe the transgendered subject as having undergone some form of sex transition; in these cases the transsexual plot is not merely desired, it is realized. Incredibly, as much as half a century before transsexuality was officially named as such, transgendered subjects used medical science to reconfigure their sex. As endocrinology was still in its early stages—at the time of sexology's recording of these cases it was only in the process of discovering sex hormones—the earliest sex change subjects could only turn to plastic surgery (itself a new science) in their quest to cross the borders of somatic sex.[13] Magnus Hirschfeld's 1922 report describes a female who had obtained a bilateral mastectomy to masculinize h/er body; and a German sexological journal at the end of a decade published the case of a female who had undergone genital masculinization, remarkably as early as 1882.[14] Through sexology, sex-reconfigured subjects make their first appearance in the late nineteenth and early twentieth centuries—well before the development of sex change technology as such.

Because they precede the medical scripting of the transsexual plot and the technology that would allow this plot's more successful realization, such cases were, not surprisingly, exceptional. Yet whether inverts were actually surgically reconfigured or not, the conception of inversion as an embodied cross-gendered condition structured transsexing anyway into the very category of the invert. In that s/he was considered congenitally intersexed, the invert was already sited somatically between the sexes. Positing the invert's embodiment of transgender, sexology created the conceptual space to record those sex-changed subjects in the first place; that inversion was an embodied category allowed such subjects to appear exemplary inverts. Sex change then might be seen simply to have carried inversion to its logical extension.

Projecting inversion as transgender onto the body, sexologists at first sought to diagnose inverts via their bodies. The specific corporeal text they "read" underscores that inversion was first and foremost a transgendered condition. Inversion's somatic markers were essentially cross-sexed characteristics. Any embodiment of gender difference, any degree of what was considered an erring from the sexed norm, was an indicator of sexual inversion. Richard von Krafft-Ebing notes as the physical signs of "viraginity" in a female invert a "deep voice, manly gait [and] small mammae" (s/he "makes the impression of a man in woman's clothes"). Havelock Ellis likewise finds in his female subjects transgendered symptoms of inversion ranging from "slight" hirsutism of the body and face, to more "genuine approximations to the masculine type" in which "the muscles tend to be everywhere firm, with a comparative absence of soft connective tissue," to genitalia which are "more or less undeveloped."[15] Effectively corporealizing inversion, sexologists practiced a kind of transgendered anthropometry. They sought to correlate sexed intermediacy to cross-gender identity in the bodies of their patients. The assumption (the hope of sexologist as clinician) was that the inverted body would render up its own identity narrative.

As a sexual *psycho*pathology, however (sexology both begins modern psychiatry and spurs the development of psychoanalysis), inversion was an illness not so much of the body as of the mind. Embodied but innate, inversion was not inevitably legible on the body's surface. The substantive material for diagnosing inversion lay, therefore, not in corporeal markers but in the subject's speech. The expression of cross-gendered difference, the production of a cross-gendered narrative came to signify sexual inversion. It is upon the basis of h/er expression of desire for sex change that Westphal's subject was diagnosed as inverted and may be reclassified as transsexual. Narrative constitutes the critical point of overlap between inversion and transsexuality. As much as transsexuality, inversion takes autobiography as its primary symptom. This shared symptomization in autobiographical narrative is the factor that has allowed current sexologists to read transsexuality back through inversion's narratives, even in those cases where somatic sex change did not take place. As historian of sexuality Vern Bullough suggests in a seminal essay similarly arguing for the existence of transsexuality before the diagnosis, it is because "Individuals of the past often expressed themselves in ways similar to today's preoperative transsexuals" that we can document transsexual subjectivity in the nineteenth century.[16] In the history of the transsexual, both as a discursive and individual subject, sex change is not the diagnostic indicator of the transsexual subject but its "cure," not its cause but its outcome. Before transsexuality's emergence as such, inversion operated similarly as a body narrative, with the subject's narrative standing in for what the body of the invert could not speak.

In fact, for the sexologist, the body of the invert was by definition an unreliable text, for the invert's body failed to speak its subject's true gender. Krafft-Ebing's "man in woman's clothes" suggests a woman who but for the mistake of her body would have been, should have been, a man: h/er body misrepresents the subject's authentic self. In its earliest formulation even before its pathologizing in sexology, inversion is represented as a corporeal mistake, a cross-gendered condition caused by a deceptive body. In this configuration of the material body as a mistake, the definitive transsexual split between sex and gender, between outer body and inner identity, is opened up. Most notably, Karl Heinrich Ulrichs writing in 1860s Germany described his own male inversion as an authentic womanly identification belied by a male corporeal surround: "Sunt mihi barba maris, artus, corpusque virile;/His inclusa quidem: sed sum maneoque puella" ("Have I a masculine beard and manly limbs and body;/Yes, confined by these: but I am and remain a woman").[17] As we have seen, Ulrichs's formula of the "wrong body" will recur identically as the popular trope for transsexuality a century later in transsexual accounts, as will his image "anima muliebris in copore virili inclusa" (the soul of a woman enclosed in a man's body).[18] The bodily experience of inversion is described with exactly the same body image formula as transsexuality. The production of transgender through such bodily figures evoked—and, as they entered a medical setting, crucially came to symptomize—the internal gendered difference, the dis-embodiment, constituting first inversion, then transsexuality.

Although he is considered one of the first advocates of same-sex desire, Ulrichs's description of inversion effectively begins the mapping of transgender as an identity in the modern West. While deriving from Plato's category of "urning," his network of inverted subjects—the *"mannling(e)"* and *"weibling(e)"* (the masculine and feminine) "urning" and "urningin"—in fact represents a codification of transgender identity.[19] "Urnings" are arranged according to the degree of transgendered split between soma and gender; it is this split—the difference of transgender and not homosexuality—that Ulrichs sought to calibrate. Translating Ulrichs's scheme into a medical frame, Krafft-Ebing's *Psychopathia Sexualis* similarly measures not homosexuality but transgender: again, the precise split between sex and gender. Krafft-Ebing's "antipathic" or "inverted sexual instinct" organizes inverts according to the presence of cross-gender in varying pathological "degrees": "in the milder cases, there is simple hermaphroditism; in more pronounced cases, only homosexual feeling and instinct, but limited to the sexual life; in still more complete cases, the whole psychical personality, and even the bodily sensations, are transformed so as to correspond with the sexual inversion; and in complete cases, the physical form is correspondingly altered" (188). While homosexuality is certainly denoted in Krafft-Ebing's scheme, crucially substantiating the transgendered subject of inversion, it accounts for only one of a number of characteristics of inversion.

In the translation of inversion from identity to pathology, of Ulrichs's tropology to a systematized typology of disease, narrative proved the key instrument. Through the form of the case history sexologists such as Krafft-Ebing were able to typify and specify the various "degrees" or characteristics of inversion. The personal narrative, rewritten into case history, provided the clinician with the pathognomonic signs of inversion. The case history created the textual space for the clinician not only to record but to perform the diagnosis, for the "disease" manifested itself above all in figures of speech. If "[n]arrative is indispensable to diagnosis," as Julia Epstein argues in her study of the emergence of the form of the case history, nowhere is this truer than in the context of the emergence of transsexuality through inversion; for here the subject's autobiography must re-present a body that fails to present its subject's "true" gender.[20] The case history's purpose was to uncover in the subject's autobiography, both in the clinician's office and then again in the pages of the sexological text, inversion as a pathological condition. It is via the case history in sexology, then, that autobiography came to be *the* vehicle for the medicalization of transgender identity.

Since many of inversion's narratives reached the sexologist already written as autobiographical accounts, the reading of autobiography often took place in a quite material sense. And as their case histories often reproduce them apparently in full, sexologists seemed to have considered these autobiographical narratives as already possessing the documentary value and the pathological texture of the case history, as if the subject's narrative evidenced quite clearly the subject's disease. Many of the fullest autobiographical accounts in sexology are also the most transgendered. This correspondence suggests that the more transgendered the subject, the more self-evident for the sexologist his or her inversion and thus the less need for the sexologist's intervention: in other words, the more evidence *for us* that inversion *was* transgender. The longest invert autobiography in Krafft-Ebing's *Psychopathia Sexualis* (case 108), for example, is a fantastic account of a Hungarian male who feels as though h/e has already undergone a sex change. With a clinical exactness—as a physician himself the invert comes to Krafft-Ebing self-diagnosed, having written h/is own case history—the subject writes of inhabiting an imaginary, sentient female surround at odds with h/is physical body: "I feel like a woman in a man's form; and even though I am often sensible of the man's form, yet it is always in a feminine sense. Thus, for example, I feel the penis as clitoris; the urethra as urethra and vaginal orifice . . . the scrotum as *labia majora*; in short, I always feel the vulva" (301–302). H/is narrative meticulously locates inversion not in homosexual desire—importantly, there is nothing homosexual about his sexual practice—but precisely in h/is embodied experience of transgender, the physical feeling of being a woman. This embodied transgender identification structures h/is heterosexual practice. During coitus with his female partner, h/e inverts genital morphologies, imagining h/imself to have a vagina penetrated by the penis of the (other) woman. H/is desire even prefigures the transsexual plot of surgical transformation: "I am sure that I should not have shrunk from the castration-knife, could I thus have attained my desire" (294). In formulating the diagnosis and reading the invert, the sexologist responds to the narrative's dominant motif: Krafft-Ebing here uses the term *"transmutio sexus,"* a change of sex (311). Because the function of the autobiographical narrative of inversion was to inscribe the subject's symptom, the sexologist's production of a diagnosis was above all a case of explication de texte. In the most evident transgendered narratives the explanation required was minimal.[21]

As with that of transsexuality our reading of sexology has been undergirded by assumptions about how interpretative authority worked in this medicalized setting. The critique of sexology as a misconstruction of homosexuality assumes that the transgendered narratives recounted in the case histories are the products of the sexologist's master narrative, that the avowed transgendered identifications of the invert are the internalizations of the sexologists' discourse. With Foucault's concept of "reverse discourse," the subject is at best a respondent. Inverts appear as not the authors of their own inverted plots but the products—indeed, insofar as they are *really* homosexual and not transgendered, the fictional products—of a larger medicodiscursive design: hence, surely, the cursory reading that inverts' actual narratives have so far received. Yet because sexologists relied on autobiographical narratives for producing their diagnosis, it can be seen that inverts were not the simple effects of this discourse but rather that the transgendered pull of their autobiographies infused and determined the transgendered design of sexology. Krafft-Ebing's case 164 dramatizes neatly how the invert's narrative could precede and shape the sexologist's diagnosis. In this case, that of a transgendered female who "felt towards other women as a man does" and "bewailed the fact that she was not born a man," Krafft-Ebing paraphrases what was clearly the subject's own prior diagnosis of h/erself: " 'Her genitals could not be right.'" Surely originally "*my* genitals cannot be right," the invert's expression of transgendered wrong embodiment has plainly authorized (decided and provided the terms of) the sexologist's transgendered analysis: Krafft-Ebing diagnoses this case simply as one of "masculinity." As this case illustrates, the exchange between clinician and patient is a good deal more dialogic than has been made out, the sexologist's diagnosis here quite literally a citation of the preceding autobiographical narrative. The "discourse" of inversion, its transgendered paradigms, can be seen to have been absolutely dependent upon the subjects' articulations and identifications. Thus the importance of reading the narratives of inverts carefully in order to reconstitute these identifications.[22]

It is fitting, therefore, that the invert's case history in *Psychopathia Sexualis* that reads as most convincingly transgendered is based on the formal autobiography of a professional author. The transgendered narrative of the invert here appears distinctly self-authored, the clinician emphatically an unintended (or at least unspecified) reader. Though a note refers us to another sexologist for "the expert medical opinion of this case" (416 n. 1), for his own rendition Krafft-Ebing has "gleaned the ... facts" from "the autobiography of this man-woman," the female invert Count Sandor V, a.k.a. the Countess Sarolta V (417). Sarolta/Sandor's case, like Krafft-Ebing's Hungarian doctor, poses a substantial challenge to the equation of inversion with homosexuality. As its subject never lived as a woman and was clearly profoundly sex-dysphoric, this case also reads as one of the most persuasive female-to-male transsexual narratives in sexology. Born female, raised and educated as a boy, Sarolta became Sandor and lived full-time as a man (hence I refer to him as such). He married twice, frequented brothels, and took lovers on the side. In spite of this evidently profuse desire for women, "Sandi" balked at mutual sexual relations. While loving the female body of the other, he maintained his own female genitals as untouchable zones both for the other and—a key sign that this untouchability was caused by something singularly more deep-rooted than the fear of discovery that Krafft-Ebing himself suggests as reason—for himself: "She knows nothing of solitary or mutual onanism. Such a thing seemed very disgusting to her, and not conducive to manliness" (424). As we have seen, this rejection of bodily sex (suggested also by the fact of his having found menstruation "a thing repugnant to her masculine consciousness and feeling" [424]), is a poignant indicator of transsexual agnosia. In one of the earliest attempts to delineate female-to-male transsexuality Ira Pauly writes that this refusal of sex via sexuality is one of the key points on which the transsexual's narrative diverges from the lesbian's: the transsexual "avoids potentially pleasurable stimulation, either through masturbation or in her homosexual relations, because it confronts her with her own female anatomy. This is typical of female transsexualism and distinguishes it in some ways from homosexuality."[23] As characteristic of a transsexual narrative where dysphoria stems from the body of the subject, in place of his deceptive body as a female invert Sandor sought to realize an imaginary male one, padding the front of his trousers with handkerchiefs and gloves, substituting this soft penile prosthesis for a hard one ("a stocking stuffed with oakum as a priapus" [425]) in sexual encounters. Though his sexual practice is ostensibly same-sex, given the profound degree of cross-gendered identification, behavior, and appearance conveyed in his case, his narrative cannot be classified as such without erasing the very logic of its transsexual design.[24]

Sexologists were apparently quite aware of the deictic power of personal narrative in the case history, its capacity to articulate directly the transgendered design of sexual inversion. Following Krafft-Ebing with his definitive work on sexual inversion in 1897, Havelock Ellis openly abandoned his predecessor's attempt at typologizing inversion. Instead of chasing each case with diagnosis, Ellis acts as the case histories' editor, explicitly allowing them to speak for themselves: "It has seemed best to me to attempt no classification at all" (235). This tactic is significant for formally handing authorial control of inversion's story to the subject. Ellis trusts that his subjects can convey their inversion most powerfully in their own words—as he introduces History 39, "the narrative is given in her own words" (235). That History 39 is the most cogent female-to-male transgendered self-narrative in *Sexual Inversion* is again no coincidence. The more pronounced the speaker's inversion, the more transgendered his or her identification and the less supplementation was deemed necessary by the sexologist to explain or gloss the condition.

As with Krafft-Ebing's Sandor, Ellis's D spins out a thematically coherent transgendered narrative. S/he begins with childhood feelings of gendered difference and a poignant description of the invert's sense of h/er body as a mistake: "Ever since I can remember anything at all, I could never think of myself as a girl. . . . When I was 5 or 6 years old I began to say to myself that whatever anyone said, If I was not a boy at any rate I was not a girl. This has been my unchanged conviction all through my life. When I was little, nothing ever made me doubt it, in spite of external appearance. I regarded the conformation of my body as a mysterious accident" (235). Each episode in h/er narrative substantiates her nonbelonging in womanhood. Sent to an all-girls' boarding school in an attempt to "turn [h/er] into a young lady," s/he creates for h/erself a world of male identification, a complex set of rescue dreams in which s/he plays male liberator: "I was always the prince or the pirate, rescuing beauty in distress or killing the unworthy" (239). Underscoring her difference from the homosexual, feelings of attraction toward women only serve to make D more conscious of the gap between sex and gender, the "hiatus . . . between my bodily structure and my feelings" (241). As a woman (unlike Sandor, D does not live as a man), s/he is unable to act on h/er desire for women and explains this "lack" by referring back to her body: "There was something that I simply lacked; that I never doubted. Curiously enough, I thought that the ultimate explanation might be that there were men's minds in women's bodies" (241). Indeed, D can only imagine romantic or sexual relations with women by refiguring h/erself as a man: "I admired [women] and when I was tired and worried I often thought how easily, if I had been a man, I could have married and settled down with one or the other. . . . I always imagined myself as a man loving a woman" (242). But the disjuncture between the felt reality of the imaginary and the fraudulence of physical reality remains too powerful and painful for such fantasies to become practicable: "What I felt with my mind and what I felt with my body always seemed at this time apart" (242); "My life was a sham; I was an actor never off the boards. I had to play at being something I was not from morning til night" (243). In closing s/he affirms h/er identification with men and h/er difference from women ("I always feel that I am not one of them" [243]). In its account of this identification and h/er repudiation of h/er own bodily sex (to the point where s/he cannot undertake sexual relations), h/er narrative, like Sandor's, reads as axiomatically transsexual. Transgender is not only patently not a symptom of her same-sex desire, it stalls any practice of same-sex desire.

Ellis reveals that the "largest number" of his case histories were written as autobiographies by inverted subjects either anonymously or with authors known to him (91). Of the latter, Ellis states that he has often supplemented the original narrative as his relationship with the author has developed. While we can know neither the extent nor the effect of Ellis's "fill[ing] in" (he sutures his "editorial" work with the original narrative), it is evident that as the autobiographical narrative authorized the sexologist's diagnosis, it was in turn authorized by the sexologist (91). Inverts, like transsexuals, could *read* their way into an identity plot. In Ellis's History 38 the female invert's string of transgendered childhood moments—making everyone call h/er "John"; urinating through a tube; "shame and anger" over menstruation—draws its narrative cohesion retroactively from a moment of self-discovery via what must have been another case history in sexology (231): "About this time I read a book where a girl was represented as saying she had a 'boy's soul in a girl's body.' The applicability of this to myself struck me at once" (232). In this case the invert uses sexology (another invert's narrative), in particular that famous "wrong body" trope of inversion, to authorize—that is both to organize and validate—h/er own narrative mnemonics. The speaking subject is by no means passive in relation to the discursive identity, a vessel to be "filled" by the sexologist's content of inversion. Like the transsexual s/he makes the connection to the other text, actively borrows the transgendered design for h/er own story, in turn shapes the sexologist's narrative, and, in this sense, authors or constructs h/er self through the available intertexts, sexological or otherwise. To represent the invert as the sexologist's constructed effect does nothing to convey the complex intertextuality and mutuality of this exchange.

For Ellis as much as for contemporary readers of sexology, the question of authority—to what extent the subject is the author of inversion's story—is the ultimate determinant of the case history's validity and the authenticity of inversion. Startlingly, Ellis reveals that the assumption that undergirds our critique of sexology (that the subject's narrative was a product of the sexologists' preexistent identity plots) was already in circulation at his time of writing. First suggesting a link between this assumption and general historical suspicions about the essential unreliability of the speech of sexual others ("Many years ago we used to be told that inverts are such lying and deceitful degenerates that it was impossible to place reliance on anything they said. It was also usual to say that when they wrote autobiographical accounts of themselves they merely sought to mold them in the fashion of those published by Krafft-Ebing" [89]), Ellis goes on to argue that it is precisely his subjects' familiarity with past accounts—the very fact of the case histories' intertextuality—that ensures their narratives' authenticity. Far from encouraging the subject to plagiarize from other cases and reproduce inversion as a homogenous narrative, the availability of previous accounts enables the breakup of any such narrative as it might have been written by the expert under his classificatory scheme. The more narratives read and written, in other words, the more ways of telling the story of inversion became possible: "there is no doubt that inverts have frequently been stimulated to set down the narrative of their own experiences through reading those written by others. But the stimulation has, as often as not, lain in the fact that their own experiences have seemed different, not that they have seemed identical" (90). The sexologist's text—here Ellis is referring specifically to *Psychopathia Sexualis* but presumably he foresees the possibility of this occurring with his own *Sexual Inversion*—functions as a vehicle for the inverts' self-creation (both in the life and in the autobiography). Precisely because he believes inverts make not only good authors but good readers, Ellis finds his subjects' speech to be sufficiently trustworthy to enable him, as expert/author, to refrain from analysis.

The agreement among historiographers of inversion is that, following Ellis's *Sexual Inversion*, the category "invert" began to disappear from medical literature and that by the 1900s it was beginning to be replaced by that of "homosexual." What has not been noted is the extent to which the disappearance of the invert is correlated with a dramatic devaluation of the psychopathological subject's narrative as evidence. In Freudian psychoanalysis—the central vehicle of these shifts—sexual inversion appears as myth, sexology's false construction of homosexuality: "The mystery of homosexuality is therefore by no means so simple as it is commonly depicted in popular expositions, e.g., a feminine personality which therefore has to love a man, is unhappily attached to a male body; or a masculine personality, irresistibly attracted by women, is unfortunately cemented to a female body . . . the supposition that nature in a freakish mood created a 'third sex' falls to the ground."[25] While transgender continues to have a place in psychoanalysis, it is refigured by Freud from gender identities into phantasmatic and momentary sexual identifications: pit stops on the way to the development of *sexual* identities. The narrative of sexual psychopathology does not simply turn from sexual inversion to sexual object-choice; it refigures this inversion as (makes it into a figure for) sexual object-choice. In one instance—with sex change here explicitly a metaphor—transgender is used to figure the moment of a female subject's homosexual becoming. Of the girl's exchange of her father as love-object for her mother, Freud writes: "*She changed into a man*, and took her mother in the place of her father as love-object."[26] (It is surely in Freud that the lesbian and gay reading of sexual inversion as a metaphor for homosexuality takes root.) Simultaneous with these discursive shifts from transgender to homosexuality, from sexology to psychoanalysis, and from the body to the unconscious, the patient's speech becomes a suspicious text. It is no longer what it seems, a reliable account, but is to be decoded as much for what it does not say as for what it does. The role of author-ity, of who gets to decide meaning, is markedly switched back to doctor as the psychoanalyst does the work of interpretation. Especially when it is articulated by the subject, the transgendered narrative is no longer self-evident but abstruse, pointing back to a story not told by the unconscious. In his most overtly transgendered case Freud reads at the root of Schreber's narrative of imagined sex change not transgender but a repressed homosexuality: in Schreber's autobiography transgender figures—by *not* figuring—a refused homosexuality.[27] It might be said that the story of inversion disappeared because medical practitioners stopped listening. Psychoanalysis had its own story to tell.

In a striking illustration of the intersection of sexology and psychoanalysis Ellis's *Sexual Inversion* briefly critiques psychoanalysis's mode of reading—its tendency to reauthor the patient's personal narrative. Ellis mounts a defense of the subject's account as "reliable"(88) and "frank" (90). Writing in the tradition of Krafft-Ebing but contemporaneously with Freud, on the cusp of these transitions, Ellis is himself ambivalent, however, about the relation between sexual inversion and homosexuality. While ostensibly distinguishing between homosexuality and inversion ("Sexual inversion, as here understood, means sexual instinct turned by inborn constitutional abnormality toward persons of the same sex" [1]), Ellis locates inversion under the umbrella of homosexuality ("It is thus a narrower term than homosexuality" [1]) in a way that prefigures Freud's subsuming of sexual inversion into homosexuality. Straddling two discourses, the sexological and the psychoanalytic, Ellis retains the somatic essentialized component of inversion and the validation of its personal accounts but paves the way for the disappearance of the distinct narrative of the invert. Lesbian and gay criticism has considered Freud's isolation of sexual object-choice and the disappearance a progression: it meant the capacity to think homosexuality apart from gender. From the point of view of transsexual/transgender criticism, however, the substitution of the sexual invert with the homosexual in the early twentieth century signifies a massive discursive loss: it meant a loss of medicine's capacity to transcribe (and thus diagnose) transgender, a loss of the recording of transgendered narratives.

The fact that sexology did record transgendered subjectivity is inseparable from its approach to personal narrative. If psychoanalysis read the personal narrative of transgender as replete with metaphors for the unconscious (or unconscious metaphors), sexology took the personal narrative of transgender literally. In her discussion of psychoanalysis's practice of reading its first narratives, those of hysterics—a body narrative if ever there was one—Mary Jacobus has suggested that "[w]hat the analyst learns from the hysteric's misreading is how to be a good (that is, a metaphoric) reader; how to disembody the text and discover what the picture covers."[28] The question of what constitutes a "good reading," both in the context of inversion/transsexuality and in this critical context (not mid-eighties poststructuralist feminism striving to denaturalize women's bodies but late-nineties emergent transsexual theory striving to embody theory's transgendered metaphors), probably could not be more different. For the transsexual, being diagnosed, being read, turns precisely on a reader willing to move in the other direction against the very disembodying metaphoric dynamics of reading. It was because they literalized transgender, because they read it so corporeally, that sexology's case histories of inversion were able to begin the medicalization of transgender that would prove crucial for the later materialization of the transsexual subject.

The Transsexual in Between

Although gender inversion will not become a diagnosable medical condition again until transsexuality, there is a crucial intervening period between the disappearance of the invert in the 1900s and the writing of the transsexual diagnosis in 1949. Despite the fact that transgender did not prominently occupy medicodiscursive identities, key events in transgender and transsexual history are concentrated here. The first sex change cases appear in 1922 and 1928/29, recorded within sexology but now specifically tagged "transvestism"; we have shifted to the category under which the first renowned transsexual, Christine Jorgensen, will later be diagnosed.[29] More seminally, the first transsexual to complete a full transition with surgery and hormones combined—thus the first fully technologically sex-changed transsexual—Michael Dillon, born female, transformed to male did so during this period.[30] How did this first transition occur in the absence of diagnostic categories?

A transsexual, a doctor, and an author, Dillon left something of a narrativization of his transition. His 1946 publication, *Self: A Study in*

Ethics and Endocrinology (as its title suggests an eclectic mix of moral philosophizing and hormonal theories), contains a chapter that represents what is surely the first medicolegal treatise on transsexuality.[31] Using a rationale that will be much echoed by later clinicians, Dillon argues for the right of transsexuals to hormonal and surgical sex reassignment: "Surely, where the mind cannot be made to fit the body, the body should be made to fit, approximately, at any rate to the mind" (53). As transsexuality would not be coined until three years later, however, Dillon must make this argument without naming the transsexual. Working in the absences of medical terminology, in between inversion and transsexuality, Dillon has no choice but to follow psychoanalysis's story of sexuality and name the transsexual "homosexual" (this pivotal chapter is entitled "Homosexuality"). His task then entails distinguishing the homosexual who wishes to change sex from the homosexual who doesn't—that is, the transsexual from the homosexual. He performs this by differentiating homosexual and transsexual gender plots, in particular by distinguishing their relations to transgender realness. Where the homosexual—or to set up Dillon's nomenclature, the "effeminate" male and the "mannish" female homosexual—may well perform the other sex, the transsexual—the "feminine" male and the "masculine" female homosexual—yearns to become it (44). Where the "effeminate" or "mannish" homosexual cultivates an incongruity between sex and gender, the "feminine" or "masculine" homosexual seeks to resolve it: "Where the one imitates and acquires, the other seems to develop naturally along the lines of the other sex" (50). Post-Judith Butler, we might understand Dillon's distinction between homosexuality and transsexuality as between gender performativity and gender ontology. While Butler's project is to call this distinction into question, for Dillon there could not have been more at stake in sustaining the differences between replaying gender as a figure for same-sex desire and the desire to be literally resexed. What was at stake prior to transsexuality in discourse was precisely Dillon's capacity to call himself a man and distinguish himself from the mannish lesbian. Only through this distinction could he validate his sex change and lay claim to maleness.

So convinced is Dillon by his own distinctions between "masculine"/"feminine" and "mannish"/"effeminate" homosexuals that, once he has established the gendered realness of "feminine" and "masculine" homosexuals (i.e., transsexuals)—their true identity as the "other" sex—he refers to them by inserting the category "homosexual" into querying quotation marks (54). The typography suggests his own sense of the inappropriateness and provisionality of the category "homosexual" for the transsexual subjects it denotes. Moreover, his antitheses between homosexuality and transsexuality overtly confer on the transsexual subject a transgendered naturalness set against the homosexual's transgendered artifice. The very modifiers he uses suggest this difference: "effeminacy" and "mannishness" connote an ersatz relation to gender realness next to "feminine" and "masculine." Unlike Dillon's homosexual his transsexual pulls inexorably toward becoming real-ly sexed: toward, quite simply, being. The masculine/feminine homosexual is marked by a clear-cut transgendered plot from the beginning, a plot that appears naturally to fit that of the "other" sex: "The pretty curly-headed boy with pink complexion . . . objects to fights, to mud and dirt and to sports, and . . . prefers his sister's doll. . . . The girl, on the other hand, lean and wiry, scorns dolls and girls' games, likes to play Indians and soldiers, and is ever ready for some risky adventure or a fight" (50). Dillon's exemplary transsexual subject then gives voice to his/her difference, shaping his/her life into a transgendered narrative and thereby offering up that classic symptom of his/her difference: "Invariably the cry is 'I have always felt as if I were a girl,' or alternatively from the girl comes the cry: 'I always felt as if I were a man.' In these instances the body may approximate in essentials to one sex, male or female, but the personality is wholly peculiar to the opposite one" (50–51). Although Dillon might employ homosexuality in his terminology therefore, his delineation of transsexuality through coherent transgender plots and, crucially, the symptomization of transsexuality in the subject's narrativization of this plot, paradigmatically returns to the symptomatology of sexual inversion and prefigures that of the transsexual diagnosis. Dillon's use of endocrinology as the explanatory narrative for these gendered differences in lieu of the psychoanalytic/psychological theory then dominant further reinforces his affiliation to sexology. It recalls—or rather updates—the "glandular" theories of sexual inversion popular with sexologists: the correlation of sexual inversion to internal secretions.[32]

That Dillon's deployment of sexology to articulate transsexual subjectivity remains oblique only—that he does not draw on sexology's categories of inversion explicitly—is a sure sign that by the time of his writing sexual inversion has been outmoded as a discourse. Yet Dillon's more indirect connection between transsexuality and inversion produces an intertextual moment far richer and more gratifying for our purposes. For it is to *The Well of Loneliness* that the first fully sex-changed transsexual turns for an illustration of the masculine female "homosexual." While Dillon might name the transsexual a homosexual and not an invert, it is the invert in *The Well* that exemplifies his model transsexual subject:

> Some years ago Radclyffe Hall published a novel entitled *The Well of Loneliness*. It was a penetrating title and the story was concerned with this subject, the life of a girl of this type, her difficulties and the attitude of others towards her. Had the book been handled with more restraint, it might have done much as a popular novel towards bringing about an understanding of the situation; but unfortunately, as it was, it was banned as soon as published. (51)

In the absence of inversion's case histories, *The Well* stands in as an inverted case history and stands, precisely in this guise, for a transsexual narrative. Since Dillon read *The Well* as a transsexual novel, identifying his own "masculine homosexuality" with that of the fictional Stephen Gordon's, it is arguable that *The Well*, as the fiction of a female invert, helped actuate Dillon's own transsexual life-plot, its narrative motivating or supporting the first full bodily transsexual transition. *The Well*'s narrative perhaps filled in for that discursive absence of transgender. Dillon evidently believed that *The Well* had all the makings of a representative transsexual text, its potential to bring about the kind of enlightenment toward transsexuality his own book attempts some eighteen years later thwarted only by its banning. But how did Dillon arrive at this reading? What interpretative grounds did he have for finding a transsexual plot in *The Well*? Having established the significance of transsexuality for its discursive context, it is to the text that we may now turn.

Dreaming Flesh: The Transsexual in *The Well*

Written three decades after the category of sexual inversion had begun to be displaced by homosexuality and, moreover, after Hall's key sexological influence, Havelock Ellis, had himself rendered the terms "homosexuality" and "sexual inversion" interchangeable, *The Well*'s exclusive and categorical return to sexual inversion appears all the more deliberate. As with Dillon's resistance to all things "psych-" for explaining transsexuality, Hall's eschewal of the more current theories of psychoanalysis for sexology needs to be understood historically as a rejection of the conceptual supremacy of the axis of sexuality over gender and, concomitantly, of homosexuality over transgender. That Hall skipped over psychoanalysis not out of unfamiliarity but, rather, out of a belief in its inutility for her project is evidenced by the one reference to psychoanalysis that appears in *The Well*. Warning her that her unsociability is becoming "unwholesome," that master of irony standing out in this very unironic novel, Jonathan Brockett, tells Stephen: "You'll be bagging a shell like a hermit crab or growing hairs on your chin or a wart on your nose, or worse still a complex. You might even take to a few nasty habits towards middlelife—better read Ferenczi!" (301). Brockett's allusion to Freud's disciple Sandor Ferenczi reveals that Hall not only knew psychoanalysis, s/he knew enough to be able to reference and ironize it. With a stroke she flattens psychoanalysis into superstitious nonsense: the psychoanalytic notion of the complex is comparable to an absurd popular myth about the effects of social isolation. *The Well* not only refuses psychoanalysis, via Brockett's remark, it makes a point of showing that it refuses to take it seriously.

Critics who accept Hall's turn to sexology as deliberate nevertheless read it as strategic, namely, as Hall's attempt to undermine the stigmatization of homosexuality by transforming the conception of same-sex desire from sinful choice to innate condition. As Ruehl writes, sexology is Hall's "deliberate political intervention" into the representation of lesbianism.[33] But if it was Hall's intent to tell a politically transformative story of female homosexuality, she did not need sexual inversion to do so. There were other more positive representations of lesbianism available at the time of her writing, representations, moreover, less likely to rile the censors and thus more likely to reach her reading public. Martha Vicinus suggests Natalie Barney's "hedonistic lesbianism" and Renée Vivien's "self-created tragedy" as possible alternatives.[34] Indeed, vitally for our reading of the subject in this novel, just as she signals her awareness of psychoanalytic alternatives, Hall indicates her familiarity with at least one of these models by embodying Natalie Barney in *The Well*'s Valérie Seymour: a charming, feminine figure whom Catharine Stimpson identifies as a much more worthy representation of lesbianism, a much better lesbian, than the novel's congenitally masculine protagonist. And rightly so; for the whole point of Valérie and her queer circle in Paris is to set off the difference of Stephen's plot, to elucidate how Stephen stands apart, a misfit even here. Even though inversion inflects the bodies of these others—Brockett's fluttering "white soft-skinned hands of a woman"(333),

Pat's "ankles ... too strong and too heavy for those of a female" (353)—the Paris section underscores that Stephen's inversion is by far the most "pronounced" (356). Like sexology's most pronounced cases, like Dillon's masculine female "homosexual," it is not to the lesbian but the transsexual that Stephen corresponds. Hall's use of sexology is not a turn (whether strategic or inadvertent) to homosexuality but a turn away from it, to a condition unambiguously transgendered and embodied.

Hall patently wished her readers to remark *The Well*'s investment in sexology and to factor it into our reading of the novel. She worked hard to persuade Ellis to write the commentary on the novel that appeared as its preface. Not content with presenting it simply as her fictional account of an invert, Hall wanted *The Well* authenticated by this man whom she regarded as "the greatest living authority on the tragical problem of sexual inversion"—authorized as realistic, feasible if not factual: as if Stephen's narrative could itself stand as an inverted case history.[35] And indeed, with Ellis thus positioned as introducing it, *The Well* does formally resemble a case history, the framing device recalling Ellis's role as editor and authorizer of his own case histories. Within the body of the novel Hall's two citations of Ulrichs and Krafft-Ebing have a similar effect of authorizing Stephen's narrative as inverted case history. In the first instance Stephen's father, Sir Philip, uses a copy of Ulrichs to decode a portrait of Stephen with her mother. Making marginal notes in the sexologist's work, he turns from written to visual text, as if the former's narrative enables him to read the body that he sees in the latter—"that indefinable quality in Stephen that made her look wrong in the clothes she was wearing as though she and they had no right to each other, but above all no right to Anna" (23). In the second instance Stephen reads herself through a copy of Krafft-Ebing similarly annotated by her father. Unlocking her father's "special book case" ("as she slipped the key into the lock and turned it, the action seemed curiously automatic"), like Ellis's inverted reader of sexology, she finds the key to her difference in its pages: "Krafft-Ebing—she had never heard of that author before. All the same she opened the battered old book, then she looked more closely, for there on its margins were notes in her father's small, scholarly hand and she saw her own name appeared in those notes" (207). In both episodes the paternal annotations locate the fictional Stephen in the referential sexological text; Hall is suggesting that Stephen's difference can be diagnosed via its authority, her narrative read as exemplary sexological case.[36]

The fact that Stephen does not change sex does not obstruct a transsexual reading of the novel. As I have been arguing all along, it is the life-plot rather than actual somatic sex change that symptomizes the transsexual. In order to achieve the diagnosis necessary to access the medical technology to change sex, one must recount a transsexual narrative; the subject is necessarily a transsexual before changing sex. Thus Esther Newton's quick dismissal of the applicability of transsexual to Stephen by delimiting the category to those "who actually have had surgery to alter their bodies" places the sex-changed corporeal cart before the transsexual narrative horse, we might say.[37] Since narrative not body is the diagnostic indicator of transsexuality, in fact in returning to the transgendered patterns of inversion's case histories, *The Well* clearly reproduces this diagnostic indicator of transsexuality. *The Well*'s narrative closely echoes the transgendered plots of the case histories. Stephen's childhood reproduces, for instance, many of the details from Krafft-Ebing's case Sandor/Sarolta. Like Sandor, Stephen is born to an aristocratic family, raised and educated as a boy by a sympathetic father. Like Sandor, Stephen is drawn toward the archetypically masculine sports of the nineteenth century: fencing, horse-riding (she insists on riding astride like a man), and hunting. Her childhood describes a life-plot that, as Dillon would say "develop[s] naturally along the lines of the other sex." And like Krafft-Ebing's female inverts, Stephen's transgendered difference is inscribed as a plot on her body, and her plot in turn is driven by her somatic difference. Stephen exceeds femaleness (in the portrait above, Anna's beauty, "so perfect a thing, so completely reassuring," serves to bring into relief Stephen's gendered otherness [23]), yet falls short of maleness. Stephen resembles ("dare[s] to resemble" [203]), yet crucially fails to reproduce her father: she is "a caricature of Sir Philip; a blemished, unworthy, maimed reproduction" (11)—(at once, too and not adequately) strong, tall, narrow-hipped, broad-shouldered, large-handed, cleft-chinned, big-jawed. This masculinized body, this legibly transgendered body of the female invert, launches Stephen's trajectory into a "no-man's land of sex" (77).

Even before Stephen's birth, however, the transsexual plot is outlined, in the Gordons' certainty of a son and their naming him Stephen. Their retaining this name sets up the grammar upon which the entire plot of *The Well* is predicated: Stephen should have been male. Stephen's relation to maleness is repeatedly framed as a "should have been," the conditional perfect of the modal auxiliary (what ought to have been—

the mood of transsexual loss) returning at key moments to remind us of the sexed absence that undergirds her story. Lady Anna remembers looking at the Malvern hills, "great with the child who should have been her son" (93). Stephen envies Martin Hallam's life, "a man's life, the life that should have been hers" (100). She longs to fight in the war, the war that should have been hers to fight. The narrative's pathos, taking up the sexed regret of the case histories (as in Krafft-Ebing's case: "she bewailed the fact that she was not born a man"), stems from this mood, the inexorability of this failed-sexed imperative. A narrative of what should have been, paradoxically driven forward by regret for what might have been, *The Well* takes place in an equivocal space of transsexual regret for a past that never was.

This nostalgia over a maleness that has failed to materialize produces in the novel images of bodily lack for Stephen, the lack of the female-to-male transsexual. The male body that should have been haunts descriptions of Stephen's actual body, a phantom morphology in the text. We have the sense that something—something material—is missing. Stephen suffers "some great sense of loss, some great sense of incompleteness" (101); she is "defrauded" (12, 163), her body "maimed" (104), "maimed and insufferable" (217), and "sorely afflicted" (217); she feels "bodily dejection" (140), she is a "genius . . . in the chains of the flesh, a fine spirit subject to physical bondage" (217). The implication is that, as a female who ought to have been a man, Stephen is incomplete. No moment conveys this sense of Stephen's corporeal incompleteness, her wrong embodiment, more poignantly than the novel's mirror scene, a scene that knits into *The Well* the trope of contemporary transsexual narratives:

> That night she stared at herself in the glass; and even as she did so she hated her body with its muscular shoulders, its small compact breasts, and its slender flanks of an athlete. All her life she must drag this body of hers like a monstrous fetter imposed on her spirit. This strangely ardent yet sterile body that must worship yet never be worshipped in return by the creature of its adoration. She longed to maim it, for it made her feel cruel; it was so white, so strong and so self-sufficient; yet withal so poor and unhappy a thing that her eyes filled with tears and her hate turned to pity. She began to grieve over it, touching her breasts with pitiful fingers, stroking her shoulders, letting her hands slip along her straight thighs—Oh, poor and most desolate body! (187–188)

Teresa de Lauretis has recently suggested this mirror scene as a figure for lesbian desire. She argues that what Stephen wants to see in the mirror is a more feminine body: "The body she desires, not only in [her lover] but also autoerotically for herself, the body she can make love to and mourns for, is a feminine, female body."[38] But the mirror scene is not a moment of sexual perversion—the perverse desire of the mannish lesbian—but of sexual *inversion*; the inverted body of the pretransition female-to-male transsexual is caught and split by the mirror. Far from being a representation of masturbatory pleasure as de Lauretis suggests, the mirror scene captures a corporeal alienation powerful enough to produce in the subject the desire to maim her body. Ironically, it is the "maimed" state of Stephen's maleness—what's missing, what's not there—that produces in Stephen the desire to maim it further. The mirror scene stems from Stephen's failure to *be* male. It reflects not her "phallic self-sufficiency," but its antithesis: inadequacy, lack, in a projected image of maleness.[39] Masculinized through lifting weights and fencing ("its muscular shoulders . . . its slender flanks of an athlete"), her body yet remains a legibly female body ("its small compact breasts"). Masculine yet female, it is the transgendered ambivalence, the very gendered doubleness caught by the mirror, that Stephen hates, and the thrice repetition of "yet" in the short passage underscores precisely this ambivalence. "[Y]et . . . yet . . . yet": the syntax (itself a doubling back, a nostalgic return) casts a catena of regret back to the male soma that "should have been."

It is notable that for de Lauretis to recoup the scene for a fetishistic theory of lesbian desire, the critic must perform some disavowals and substitutions of her own. First, to claim it as a scene of masturbatory pleasure she must read past that final sentence, "Oh, poor and most desolate body!" to harness the phrase "this bitter loving" from a sentence in the subsequent paragraph in order to claim *this* moment as one of a bitter loving, of disavowed masturbatory pleasure: "Stephen in front of the mirror, 'touching her breasts with pitiful fingers, stroking her shoulders, letting her hands slip along her straight thighs . . . (and if we might fantasize along with the text, watching in the mirror her hands move downward on her body) even unto this bitter loving.'"[40] Second, to claim the scene as a figure for lesbian desire de Lauretis must remove the scene from its sexological context and read it through the psychoanalytic paradigm that Hall opted against. To take note of that all-important cri de coeur at the end of this paragraph, in which the narrative joins most fully with Stephen's bodily abjection, and to read the scene in the context of the anguish over wrong embodiment in sexual inversion's case histories—to read this body in its narrative, then—is surely to be struck with the absolute unpleasure that infuses the entire passage.

The "frame" of the mirror scene, the context in which the passage occurs (mentioned by de Lauretis but, again, crucially not factored into her reading), works to affirm this syntax. The episode takes place toward the end of Stephen's affair with Angela Crossby, when Stephen senses she is being usurped by the "real" man, Roger Antrim. Feeling herself "no match for the "calm, self-assured, insolent and triumphant" (188) Roger whose "right to be perfectly natural" (44) she has envied since a child, Stephen resorts to the only potent tool she does have—money—to try to buy Angela's love with gifts. It is at the end of one day of such desperate shopping that Stephen returns home to enact the scene before the mirror. In confirmation of Stephen's fears, Angela herself has already suggested Stephen's not being a man as the reason for their failing relationship:" 'If you were a man—' She stopped abruptly, and burst into uncontrollable weeping" (177). Like all of her erotic investments in the novel, Stephen's relationship with Angela stalls precisely on this syntax of the failure of the present indicative: quite simply, the failure to be. If like Ellis's D, Stephen can only imagine herself "as a man loving a woman"—as she says to her mother of Angela, "If I loved her the way a man loves a woman, it's because I can't feel that I am a woman. All my life I've never felt like a woman, and you know it" (204)—the mirror scene reveals the shattering of this illusion and the reality of her failure to be a real man.

While the split between her gendered imaginary and sexed reality is captured graphically by the mirror scene, this transsexual difference has been structured into the narrative from the beginning. As a child Stephen initially experiences herself as identical to the masculine image she projects, the male body image she experiences. When dressed as a boy, in response to the observation that she "look[s] exactly like a boy," Stephen insists that she *is* a boy: "Yes, of course I'm a boy. . . . I must be a boy, 'cause I feel exactly like one" (16). As she discovers to her frustration, however, neither looking like nor feeling like constitute being. When she dresses up and acts like Nelson, it is "only pretending or playing" (38); "being a girl spoilt everything—even Nelson" (33). Performing boyness only serves to drive home not being a boy, to bring into relief the discrepancy between being and seeming. Performing gender for Stephen does not defuse but enunciates the power of gender ontology, a failure to be real.[41] Stephen "dressing up" reveals the pathos of her lack of realness: "she was conscious of feeling all wrong, because she longed to be someone quite real, instead of just Stephen pretending to be Nelson. In a quick fit of anger she would go to the cupboard, and getting out her dolls would begin to torment them. She had always despised the idiotic creatures which, however, arrived with each Christmas and birthday" (17).

The split between seeming and being, between reflection and self-conception, causes Stephen to turn against what she is. Not being "real" leads to an enraged acting out against the feminine—in this scene, symbolized by the dolls, which are more real in their artificial gendering than Stephen will ever be. As strongly as she identifies with the masculine/father, the feminine/mother constitutes the site of a violent disidentification in the novel. This rage against the feminine—a rage in which the narrative partakes by prolonging Stephen's alienation from her mother—should be understood as a displacement of Stephen's rage over her female body, over her ontological sex. In this instance the dolls refer obliquely to what she is (female) and isn't (in alignment with the feminine). Precisely because there is no affirmation or loving of the feminine in herself, the feminine is not treated with the fetishistic disavowal de Lauretis suggests. Rather, at root of the desire to torment the feminine is Stephen's very unambivalent repudiation of her female corporeality. This rejection of femaleness is clearly what drives Stephen to direct her frustrations toward a dress with which her mother has sought to refeminize her in the following scene, the feminine here doubled up in the conjunction of dress and mother:

> She wrenched off the dress and hurled it from her, longing intensely to rend it, to hurt it, longing to hurt herself in the process, yet filled all the while with that sense of injustice. But this mood changed abruptly to one of self pity; she wanted to sit down and weep over Stephen; on a sudden impulse she wanted to pray over Stephen as though she were someone apart, yet terribly personal in her trouble. Going over to the dress she smoothed it out slowly; it seemed to have acquired an enormous importance; it seemed to have acquired the importance of prayer, the poor, crumpled thing lying crushed and dejected. (72)

The slippage in the first sentence between dress and self ("longing intensely . . . to hurt it, longing to hurt herself in the process") clarifies that Stephen's desire to "rend" or "hurt" the dress symptomizes her desire to rend or hurt her own body. The dress functions metonymically for the female body, and the desire to hurt the former at once reveals and sublimates the desire to hurt the latter. Preceding the mirror scene, this dress passage closely foreshadows that scene's description of Stephen's desire to maim her body. In the mirror scene Stephen is undressed, her desire like her body naked, her rage not displaced onto an object. But both passages track the same emotional shift from rage to pity; and in both Stephen's pity is aroused for her body/dress as if for an other, "as though she were someone apart": "Oh poor and most desolate body"; "the poor crumpled thing lying crushed and dejected." The female body is alien, horribly dislocated from self. In the gap between the morphology of her masculine body image and her duplicitous material female body, Stephen's alienation is engendered, and transgendered.

Unlike transsexuals with access to technology Stephen does not get beyond her mirror stage. There are no subsequent mirror scenes in the novel to dramatize integration, and her bodily alienation remains frozen in the plot. Yet in spite of sustaining this anguish over Stephen's disembodiment as a female invert, *The Well* does offer one moment of bodily healing, deferring Stephen's somatic refiguration from the real of *The Well*'s plot to a dream. That it is the sole dream, a phantasmagoric narrative embedded in this otherwise realistic novel, makes it especially significant, yet it has received no previous critical attention. The dream occurs during Stephen's childhood love for the housemaid Collins. It is sparked and framed by the "housemaid's knee" episode, in which Collins's knee has swollen with fluid as a result of polishing floors. In her infatuation with the housemaid Stephen desires this swelling to be transferred from Collins to herself so that she can undergo the "'orrible operation" that Collins fears (17). It is in the midst of her prayers for this fleshly transference that Stephen slips into the dream:

> "Please, Jesus, give me a housemaid's knee instead of Collins—do, *do*, Lord Jesus. Please Jesus, I would like to bear all Collins' pain the way You did. . . . I would like to wash Collins in my blood, Lord Jesus—and I would like very much to be a Saviour to Collins—I love her, and I want to be hurt like You were. . . . Please give me a knee that's all full of water." . . .
>
> This petition she repeated until she fell asleep to dream that in some queer way she was Jesus and that Collins was kneeling and kissing her hand, because she, Stephen, had managed to cure her by cutting her knee with a bone paper-knife and grafting it on to her own. The dream

was a mixture of rapture and discomfort, and it stayed quite a long time with Stephen. (18)

Like the dreams told Ellis by his female invert, D, Stephen's dream follows the plot of the rescue fantasy: she occupies the place of subject, ostensibly saving her beloved from bodily harm.[42] The dream is shot through with erotic charge; indeed, it is aroused by what is surely the most sexual scene in this very unsexual novel. Collins exposes her swollen knee for the young Stephen to touch:

> They were standing alone in the spacious night-nursery, where Collins was limply making the bed. It was one of those rare and delicious occasions when Stephen could converse with her goddess undisturbed, for the nurse had gone out to post a letter. Collins rolled down a coarse woollen stocking and displayed the afflicted member; it was blotchy and swollen and far from attractive, but Stephen's eyes filled with quick anxious tears as she touched the knee with her finger. (17)

The syntax of the dream originates in this prior real moment. Stephen's observation—her perception governs both the scene and the dream representation—of the bodily debasement of Collins as she "limply" makes the bed is signified in the dream by Collins in a kneeling posture. Most significantly, Collins's revelation and Stephen's touching of her "afflicted member" are responsible for the shift in Stephen's subsequent dream identification from Jesus ("she was Jesus") to Collins, of Stephen's final positioning herself in the place of Collins by grafting Collins's swelling onto herself.

These identificatory shifts in the syntax of the dream are crucial for through them Stephen takes on for herself both the afflicted body and the healing of this body. Within this fantasy of healing via substitution Stephen's own "afflicted member"—the maimed and defrauded body of the mirror and dress scenes—becomes the knot of the dream. Her own body is displaced onto and rescued through the beloved's. In rescuing the woman and establishing her difference, Stephen effectively rescues herself from her own womanhood. The chain of substitution (Stephen = Jesus = Collins) is suggested in the syntactic confusion in the description. Subjects and objects are ambiguous; pronouns quickly lose their referents and properties are left unspecified. It is clear that Collins is kneeling and Stephen is curing. Yet whose knee is being cut and what part of the body is receiving the grafted swelling (her own what?) remains wonderfully obscure. Might not this ambiguity allow the dream to stand as a transsexual fantasy of flesh grafted from one part of the body to heal the female invert's own "afflicted member"? Particularly given its thematic skin substance and its moment of writing only ten years before the first female-to-male phalloplasty was performed on Dillon, the dream resonates powerfully as a reassignment dream, a fantastic prefiguring of the healing possibilities of surgical grafting of the flesh. Cutting through the flesh with a bone paper-knife (the tissue as bloodless and pliant as paper, the body as rearrangeable as text), *The Well*'s dream of transferable flesh omits the as yet unrealized details of surgical intervention, passes over the surgery by placing it in the past tense ("*had* managed to cure her"). The moment of surgery has already occurred; the flesh has already been transplanted; the healing has been performed. The dream in *The Well*—Stephen's transsexual body narrative embedded in the novel—takes the plot of transsexuality phantasmagorically to its "natural" conclusion of somatic transformation.

The dream additionally elucidates how Stephen's transsexual lack, her failure to transition, structures her relationships in the plot, the way in which her erotic investment is directed consistently by her desire for some form of "hetero" relation to the socially debased feminine other. As subservient, both socially and physically, the kneeling Collins provides a literalized template for Stephen's later erotic interests. These both fall short of her own landed gentry status. Angela Crossby is stigmatized in at least three ways—by her louche past, as an American, and as the wife of a nouveau Birmingham trader. Mary Llwellyn is poor, orphaned, uneducated, and simply too Welsh to be English. These class differences between herself and her love-object stand in, work as a substitute, for the sexed differences that she, Stephen (and the narrative) imagines should have existed. Social opposition takes the place of "natural" sexed opposition, as Stephen's repeated investment in the déclassée other struggles to reenact the healing of her own dismembered body that she fantasizes Collins's "ample" body can afford her (13).[43]

Yet in the real of the plot this class substitution, the "love of a good woman," if you will, proves inadequate, the difference insufficient to make up for Stephen's lack. If the narrative of the dream allows for the healing of the maimed body of the invert through a form of surgical grafting from the housemaid, the plot fails to realize this healing through the series of socially inferior female lovers. As in the most transgendered of case histories the bodies of Stephen's lovers plainly fail to compensate the invert's wounded body. Her "lesbian" relations are infamously unsuccessful. The plot repeats Stephen losing the woman to the real man three times—a triple triangulation in which Stephen is uncoupled, always the odd one out. She first loses Collins to the footman; then Angela to Roger Antrim; and finally, as the novel ends, Stephen herself pushes Mary to Martin Hallam. It is this repeated failure of lesbian relations more than any other feature that thwarts the attempt to read the novel as lesbian. The difference between butch lesbian and transsexual is most pronounced here, in this refusal of desire. While female-to-male transsexuals appear to share many similarities with lesbian butches, Newton writes, the key or "most impressive difference is the rejection or acceptance of homosexual identity."[44] Thus, even according to Newton's own criterion *The Well* is not a butch text, for the novel patently allows no representational space for the "lesbian" love-object. Stephen is left at the end of the novel as once again lacking in respect toward real men.

Other critics reading the novel as lesbian have rightly found this failure to sustain an erotic connection between women a problem for a lesbian reading of the novel. For Stimpson such "structural logic" renders *The Well* a "narrative of damnation" of lesbianism;[45] Radford and Whitlock see it as the novel's investment in heterosexual romance; and Ruehl reads it as depicting lesbianism as sterile and barren. Even de Lauretis reads Stephen's sacrifice of Mary finally as "a repudiation of lesbianism as such."[46] Concurring with lesbian critics most fully on this point, I believe that we need finally to acknowledge what the novel affirms in this very repudiation of lesbianism. That Stephen gives up Mary to Martin Hallam in spite of Mary's devotion to her indicates that the invert functions not as a figure for lesbianism—a lure or a construct—but precisely as its refusal. Through her passing over Mary (both passing over her and passing her over to Martin), Stephen affirms her identification with the heterosexual man. More powerfully than any moment in the novel—and certainly more troublingly for the transsexual critic recuperating *The Well* as a transsexual novel—this act highlights her disidentification with women and locates her in a masculinist economy in which women are to be exchanged (given up/sacrificed/courted).

Transitional Ages

In her discussion of the points of overlap between the identities of lesbian and female-to-male transsexual Gayle Rubin speculates on the transsexual potential of lesbians in history: "It is interesting to ponder what . . . lesbian forbears might be considered transsexuals; if testosterone had been available, some would undoubtedly have seized the opportunity to take it."[47] Although Rubin makes no reference to Hall or *The Well*, the sole photograph in her essay is of Hall in 1936: at her most passing—profiled unsmiling in suit and tie, one hand straightening her lapel, the other rigidly holding a cigarette, cropped hair slicked back—Hall appears like an incarnation of this speculation. If the narratives of homosexuality and transsexuality are entwined as Rubin's essay indicates, the writing of transsexual history will surely depend upon performing retroactive readings of figures and texts that have been central to the lesbian and gay canon.

Nineteenth-century sexology represents a particularly entangled moment in the history of sexual and gender subjects. Categories were defined and rapidly refined, the invert—"that primitive thing conceived in a turbulent age of transition" (49), as Hall describes Stephen—proliferating into the identities of homosexual, sadomasochist, transvestite, fetishist, cross-dresser, intersexual, bisexual, and transsexual. But as the governess Puddle's remark to Stephen cautions—"you're unexplained as yet—you've not got your niche in creation" (153)—simply because the transsexual had not yet been named or fully explained does not mean that transsexual experiences did not exist or that transsexual stories were not related under another rubric; or, as illustrated so effectively by Dillon's case, that transsexuals didn't continue to exist even when the invert disappeared off the discursive map. In a cogent and refreshing critique of the construction theory of homosexuality, Terry Castle demonstrates how literature can provide evidence of "lesbian self-awareness well before the so-called invention of the lesbian around 1900."[48] If lesbian and gay historiography needs to think back over texts written before the putative construction of homosexuality as Castle's work suggests, transgender studies (particularly now, at its moment of inception) ought to consider how much more is at stake in not taking the invention hypothesis too literally with regard to the transsexual—especially since the derogation of transsexuality has turned on this axle of transsexuals as not the authors of our own narratives. The value of sexology's case histories and of *The Well* is in intervening in this representation and demonstrating otherwise: that not only did transsexual desires and sex-changed subjects exist prior to medical terminology but the stories inverts told brought forth the medical narrative of transsexuality.

That the transsexual novel has proven so deeply disturbing and troublesome in the lesbian canon—the most "obscene" novel for criticism too—makes perfect sense. In recasting Hall's novel as transsexual, we can see that our dogged attempts to read it as lesbian in spite of its narrative have been a case of trying to fit a square peg into a round hole. But in this failure to reconcile *The Well* to a lesbian context lies the novel's value for a transsexual canon: for it is those narratives that don't quite fit, which exceed or resist their homosexual location that (perhaps like transsexuals themselves) might find belonging in a transsexual context.

At the trial of *The Well* in November 1928 Virginia Woolf was mulling over similar concerns about the relations between identity and narrative, substance and form: "What is the difference between the subject & the treatment?"[49] Woolf's question was especially pertinent because her own *Orlando* had been published but one month before *The Well*'s trial, and had not only escaped the obscenity law but met with critical acclaim; this in spite of the fact that, with its dedication to and photographs of the renowned sapphist Vita Sackville West and its sex change, *Orlando* is surely the more sexually illicit book.[50] While critical tendency has attributed the different fates of these novels to their different aesthetic treatment of the same lesbian subject—*Orlando*'s comedy versus *The Well*'s "aggressively polemical stance"[51]—Woolf's question at the trial suggests the very difficulty in making this distinction between aesthetics and subject, narrative and identity; it suggests, I think, an intricacy of treatment and subject, of body and narrative. If the histories of these two novels, *Orlando* and *The Well*, have been so antithetical, not only in 1928 but in their subsequent critical history (again, *Orlando* feted where *The Well* has met with disapprobation, at best ambivalence), it is because at root in each novel is a different subject. For in spite of its fantastic sex change *Orlando* is emphatically not about transsexuality. Indeed, *Orlando* is not about the sexed body at all but the cultural vicissitudes of gender. As h/er narrative propels h/er through four centuries of history, Orlando is free to move beyond h/er body—quite queerly, to break through the limits of the flesh; *The Well*'s protagonist, by contrast, remains as trapped in her sexually inverted moment as she is in her body.[52] That it was *Orlando* and not *The Well* that was adapted for postmodern cinema is hardly surprising: because it is not embedded in medical discourse, because it is ultimately the queerer text, it is *Orlando* that makes the better transition to contemporary configurations of gender fluidity.[53] Imprisoned in her sex, caught in her narrative, embedded in her moment, Stephen is barred from the frisson of sexuality and the resolution of the couple and—as a consequence—the embrace of contemporary queer representation that result from Orlando's easy androgyny.

In our own fin de siècle age of transition, in which *Orlando* resurfaces as film—the contemporary transgender moment—transsexuality and homosexuality become complexly re-enmeshed. The parallels between *The Well* and the transgendered narrative of my next chapter, Leslie Feinberg's *Stone Butch Blues*, between their masculine protagonists and their respective struggles with female embodiment in the world are powerful, and the texts are worthy of juxtaposition.[54] Yet even though *Stone Butch Blues* is the text that contains the technologically enabled somatic transition and explicitly draws on the plot of sex change, it is by far the less unambivalent transsexual narrative of the two. The protagonist's journey in *Stone Butch Blues* is structured on an ambivalence in relation to transsexuality, taking her through somatic transition and back again; her narrative traces a return from the maleness for which Stephen only longs as an end. It is this difference of ambivalence, a wavering around transition—or rather a transformation of transition into a new identity—that characterizes contemporary transgender. That lesbian and transsexual are reconfigured into a new subject, that they prove not quite as irreconcilable as they do in Hall, is what distinguishes Feinberg's transgendered story. The transgendered story is the transsexual's story, only not quite.

> Home is the natural destination of any homeless person.... A homeless life has no storyline.
> —Lars Eighner, *Travels with Lizbeth: Three Years on the Road and on the Streets*

> Keep Ithaka always in your mind.
> Arriving there is what you're destined for. —C. P. Cavafy, "Ithaka"

> Strange to be exiled from your own sex to borders that will never be home.
> —Leslie Feinberg, *Stone Butch Blues*

> Traitors to our sex, or spies and explorers across the boundaries of what is man, what is woman?
> —Minnie Bruce Pratt, *S/he*

chapter 5

No Place Like Home: Transgender and Trans-Genre in Leslie Feinberg's *Stone Butch Blues*

The Transgender Moment

In the summer of 1994 a group of transsexuals and their supporters set up camp opposite the lesbian-feminist Michigan Womyn's Music Festival. Since 1991, when Nancy Burkholder was escorted off the land after coming out as a postoperative male-to-female transsexual, the festival's insistence on originary female sex as the qualifying home grounds for gendered membership, its "womyn-born-womyn-only" entrance policy, had been used openly to exclude transsexual women. A facet of what Gayle Rubin describes as the "xenophobia" of lesbian culture toward transsexuals, such metaphoric territorializing of gender and literal territorializations of physical space have often gone hand in hand.[1] Most infamously, Janice Raymond's *The Transsexual Empire: The Making of the She-Male* represents male-to-female transsexuals as agents of a medical empire sent out to colonize women's community and somatic home: not natives to an originary femaleness but latecomers, aliens, and thus not bona fide women.[2] The image of the transsexual as outsider appeared to naturalize the literal exclusion of transsexuals from lesbian spaces such as Michigan. Because it was correspondingly catachrestic, the transsexual intervention of 1994, "Camp Trans," was richly appropriate. Simultaneously asking for transsexuals to be allowed entry to the festival land and questioning the festival's definition of woman, the activists challenged both physical and identity territorializing. The mere presence of transsexuals on the borders of the festival posed a profoundly theoretical question about the symbolic borders of gender: the question, where did the "real" festival end and the other begin? also meant, what exactly are the limits of authentic womanhood?

Published first in 1979, *The Transsexual Empire* was reissued the same year as Camp Trans took place. While it would be nicely ironic if the reissue of this polemic against transsexuality could be shown to have catalyzed Camp Trans, *The Transsexual Empire*'s 1994 addendum, the "New Introduction on Transgender" with its critique of "the politics of transgenderism," evidences that "trans" and "politics" had already been conjoined, that the new "transactivism" that Camp Trans symbolized was already underway.[3] Indeed, the work that first brought "trans" and politics together, Sandy Stone's "The 'Empire' Strikes Back: A Post-transsexual Manifesto," appeared as early as 1991. (As the first part of its title suggests, Stone's essay was a riposte to *The Transsexual Empire*, which had singled Stone out as archetypal male-to-female transsexual lesbian-feminist marauder. Raymond may still be seen to have fueled the developments she opposed). Stone's essay provides what has become the crux of the transgender movement, and its effects were visibly at work in Camp Trans. Namely, Stone argues, if the ideal of transsexuality is to pass, and its antithesis to be read, a trans politics requires an inversion of these practices; for in passing and assimilating as nontranssexual, transsexuals effectively fail to challenge representations such as Raymond's that allow the transsexual no literal or figurative space as subjects: "It is difficult to generate a counterdiscourse if one is programmed to disappear."[4] In order to counter this discursive erasure, Stone suggests the transsexual trade in passing as a woman or a man and—punning on the textual terminology of reading—that s/he read and write him/herself into existence as a transsexual. In spite of the echo Stone's posttranssexuality is not a mere restatement of transsexual autobiographers' desire to be read as transsexual. Juxtaposed with her critique of their conventional narratives—indeed with this manifesto drawn out of a critique of their conventional narratives—the difference of Stone's "post" prefix becomes clear. As the coinage suggests posttranssexuality pushes past a conventional narrative of transsexuality, displacing passing altogether and reading transsexual history back out to unfound the very gendered integrity transsexual autobiographies seek to establish. Most significantly, Stone hopes that, in being read, transsexuals might come to constitute a gender-disruptive "*genre*—a set of embodied texts whose potential for productive disruption of structured sexualities and spectra of desire has yet to be explored."[5]

It was in its production of a gender-disruptive, legibly transsexual subject position that Camp Trans seemed to fulfill Stone's posttranssexual vision. Trading passing for reading out their pasts, transsexual activists staked a subjectivity and a politics not by insisting on transsexual belonging within sex/gender borders (but we *are* real women) but by challenging the criteria used to make up those borders (what is a real woman?). One transsexual, originally sexed female but now embodied as a man (thus satisfying the festival's requirement of natal femaleness but looking nothing like a woman), asked if the festival policy allowed him entry; another self-identified transsexual man born with male and female genitalia asked if the policy meant that "only half of [him] could come in."[6] In revealing these sexed crossings, Camp Trans in practice, like Stone's posttranssexuality in theory, encapsulated the new transgendered politics. The intent of narrating trans was not simply to instate transsexuality as subject position but to unsettle gender's stable grounds.

One commentator legendizes Camp Trans into the founding of a political movement: "a Stonewall for the rest of us."[7] In her analogy of Camp Trans to the queer movement's originary moment lies the key to transgender's difference from transsexuality, the reason why Stone's "post"-transsexuality needs to be understood as a configuration of transgender rather than a simple extension of transsexuality. If, as I have argued, the embrace of transgender constituted the threshold between lesbian/gay and queer in the early nineties, the transgender movement has in turn entailed an attempt to queer transsexuality. Stone's enlistment of Judith Butler's *Gender Trouble* to produce the transsexual as a gender-troubling figure makes clear this genealogy back to queer. Coming out; pride in marginality; a politics that deconstructs identity: many of transgender's tenets *are* queer. As transgendered or posttranssexual, the transsexual claims that queer place in the borders: gender troubler now oppositional gender outlaw. If passing is intrinsic to transsexuality, in the transgender movement passing has become a marker of cultural abjection. "The fundamental building block of the whole [transgender] movement," as one community figure is cited in a landmark report on transgender, "is the willingness of transgender folk to put themselves out there and be visible."[8] Leaving the haven of assimilation achieved in transsexual passing, the queer/posttranssexual/transgendered transsexual comes out and creates home in the transgendered community. This is the significance of transgender's trade-in of passing for being read: the comfort of genetic-sexed belonging for the platform of a political subjectivity.

According to queer models therefore, transgender has radically questioned transsexuality's body narrative, calling for an overturning of many of its features. The transactivist group Transexual Menace is campaigning to have the diagnosis "Gender Identity Disorder" removed entirely from the *Diagnostic and Statistical Manual of Mental Disorders*. "Gender Euphoria NOT Gender Dysphoria": its slogans invert the pathologizing of transgender, offering pride in queer difference as an alternative to the psychiatric story.[9] The closure of most of the gender clinics in the United States in the 1980s (in large part an effect of professional research that questioned the efficacy of the narrative of sex change) has already loosened transsexuality's medical strictures.[10] There are fewer demands that the transsexual fit a conventional narrative in order to get treatment as the categories "nonoperative" or "nonsurgery" transsexual gain credence in the medical community.[11] Concomitantly, the need, even the desire to head toward recognizably sexed homes (male *or* female, man *or* woman) can no longer be assumed. Vitally named by these new medical labels along with "transgendered," subjects are transitioning partially, intermediately—for instance, taking hormones to reconfigure their secondary sex and choosing to retain their genital sex. Alongside these discursive and somatic shifts, inspiring and reflecting them, new forms of transsexual expression are emerging: new narratives for new bodies and identities. Most prominently, Kate Bornstein's *Gender Outlaw: On Men, Women, and the Rest of Us* opposes transsexuality's telic narrative structure (that it has a gendered outcome) precisely as it rewrites the telic structure of conventional autobiographical narrative. Our first "postmodern" transsexual (thus posttranssexual) autobiography, *Gender Outlaw* fragments continuous and connective narrative into deliberately disjointed vignettes. Bornstein doesn't so much narrativize her transsexual life as (a performance artist) she performs it, acting out—without integrating into a singular stable gendered identity—its parts: "My identity as a transsexual lesbian . . . [is]

based on collage. You know—a little bit from here, a little bit from there? Sort of a cut-and-paste thing. And that's the style of this book. It's a transgendered style, I suppose."[12]

Yet even as the style of transgender cuts and pastes bits and pieces of queer to produce a troubling performativity, the very fact of transgender's naming—a transgender studies, a transgendered movement, a transgendered subject, and so on—still marks transgender's irreducibility to these queer correlates. Most obviously, as the term "transgender" suggests, this irreducibility pivots on the category of gender and an approach to transgender as the grounds of an identity. The event often considered, with Michigan, to have crystallized the transgendered movement clarifies transgender's distinction from queer discourse on this axis: in December 1993 a young female-embodied subject who passed as a man without the aid of hormones or surgery was killed in Humboldt, Nebraska, on discovery as a female. While the murder of Brandon Teena was in itself deeply disturbing (another transitional body "erased" off the discursive map), it was the representation of Teena in the press as a cross-dressing lesbian that channeled anger into politically mobilizing action. That mainstream and gay press alike used female pronouns for Teena, although Teena had lived as a man and articulated his desire for sex reassignment surgery, was experienced by many as a second erasure of the subject. Donna Minkowitz's article, "Love Hurts. Brandon Teena Was a Woman Who Lived and Loved as a Man. She Was Killed For Carrying It Off" (the title of which encapsulates the author's stance on Teena's "true identity" as a woman: "the wonder boychick," "the handsomest butch item in history—not just good-looking but arrogant, audacious, cocky—everything they, and I, look for in lovers"), for example, spurred a seminal incident: the forming of the first transactivist group, Transexual Menace, whose members gathered to protest outside the offices of New York's *Village Voice*.[13] The protesters alleged a queer cooption of a trans story in Minkowitz's reading: what had happened to the trans plot in her lesbian retelling? If Camp Trans represented transgender as a queering of transsexuality, the Teena case complicated this queer affiliation, suggesting that transgender was not only irreducible to but on occasion needed deliberately to be separated from a generic queerness. Moreover, Teena's death demonstrated the limited capacity of the transitional subject as "gender outlaw" to change gender conventions. Like Venus, the outlaw was himself subject to outlawing, murdered precisely because of his outlaw status before he could even change himself.

The etymological history of the term "transgender" certainly reveals the threads of transgender connecting to and separating from queerness as much as from transsexuality. "Transgenderist," from which "transgender" derives, was coined in the late 1980s to describe a male subject with a commitment to living as a woman more substantial than that denoted by "transvestite" or "cross-dresser."[14] The terms available for a committed cross-gendered identity—"transsexual" and that personification of queer, "drag queen"—did not capture the specificity wanted for a trans*gendered* identity. In contradistinction to the transsexual, the transgenderist crossed the lines of gender but not those of sex; in contradistinction to the drag queen, the transgenderist's feminine gender expression was not intrinsically bound up with a homosexual identity nor could its livedness be made sense of through drag's performativity. As much a rescription of queer performativity as transsexual narratives, then, transgender emerged steering a careful path between transsexuality's investment in the materiality of sex and a queer refiguration of gender into sexuality. What complicates the task of specifying transgender apart from queerness and transsexuality, however, is that the threads of difference between these projects and subjects are rewoven in the second sense in which "transgender" has come to be used, often (confusingly) concurrently with the first. "Transgender" now also functions as a container term, one that refers not only to transgenderists but to those subjects from whom it was originally invented to distinguish transgenderists: transsexuals and drag queens, transvestites and cross-dressers, along with butches and intersexuals and any subject who "trans-es" sex or gender boundaries. This collective sense underlies the coalitionary politics of transgender, assembling into a movement subjects previously dispersed if not assimilated in straight and queer worlds. In sum, if it was specification that allowed its naming in the first place and this umbrella sense that has enabled the affiliations of transgender, at the heart of transgender's project lies a contradictory dynamic in relation to queerness and transsexuality: both differentiating against and inclusive of them. From this bipart history of the term it makes sense to assume that "transgender" needs to be read in relation to, but not reduced to, transsexual and queer narratives.

This chapter examines the emergence of transgender on the fault lines and tensions between transsexual and queer. As Camp Trans and the Teena/Minkowitz case suggest, the relations between these projects often get played out in debates about narrative and territory—debates that create narratives about territory: about what it means to cross gender or sex, to share or distinguish identity space, to establish, differentiate, and affiliate plots and movements. Within this project, home may prove a powerful organizing trope. If the drive of conventional transsexual narratives is nostalgically toward home—identity, belonging in the body and in the world—and that of queer performativity away from it—resisting domestication, upturning the grounds of identity politics—then transgender would seem to contain important ambivalences about home and territory, belonging and political affiliation. To explore these ambivalences, I turn to a figure also at the Camp Trans protest, one whose configuration of body, desire, and identification perhaps most concretely challenged the festival's entrance policy. A female-born subject who has masculinized hir body with testosterone and a double mastectomy, thus often passing as a man in the world, and yet who broke off hormone treatment and now locates in hir work as a "transgendered lesbian," Leslie Feinberg uniquely embodies transgender ambivalence. Minnie Bruce Pratt's slashed pronoun for Feinberg, her partner—"s/he"—and Feinberg's own use of this form and the third person "hir" provide an index to the remarkable difference Feinberg poses, in body and language, not only to conventional gender, sex, and sexual narratives but to both transsexuality and queerness.[15] Feinberg's own writings and hir life create transgender out of interstices. Overlapping, intersecting, but ultimately marking out a specific location apart from both transsexuality and a generic queerness, Feinberg's *Stone Butch Blues: A Novel*—a text that for many represented the voice of the new transgendered movement—heads toward liminality on all fronts; yet idiosyncratically and poignantly *Stone Butch Blues* makes of liminality a transgendered home.[16] Most significantly for thinking about the future of affiliations in and around the emergence of transgender, Feinberg recognizes a crucial irony about home: although home is a place we make up, recognizing its fictionality only fuels its mythic lure. Specifying our locations even while we question the grounds for our distinctions may provide the very mobilizing force for a transgendered movement.

A Dislocated Subject and the Dream of a Transgendered Community

"Autobiographies of those who might have been transsexuals, but did not become so," remarks Bryan Tully with palpable regret for this absence of what he imagines would be a textual wrench in the machine of transsexual reproduction through autobiography, "are not usually written."[17]

Stone Butch Blues is the exception, the story of a transsexual who turned back; or, rather, of a subject who, like Feinberg himself, halts her transition through surgery and hormones to found an embodied transgendered subjectivity. Although not a transsexual autobiography, *Stone Butch Blues* does not abandon but refigures the conventions of transsexual autobiographies: like the subjects of transsexual narratives Feinberg's protagonist remakes her body with hormones and surgery; unlike transsexual autobiographers she refuses the refuge of fully becoming the other sex and the closure promised by the transsexual plot. Jess Goldberg chooses instead an incoherently sexed body in an uneasy borderland between man and woman in which she fails to pass as either. Her decision to start and to stop transitioning, to live an embodied transgender and not transsexuality, is informed at all points by a longing for home. It is her repeated displacement from and desire for home that leads her to, and then diverts her from, the transsexual plot.

Jess overtly disidentifies with transsexuality, rejecting that famous rhetorical formula she admits she received from TV—"I don't feel like a man trapped in a woman's body. I just feel trapped" (158–159). Yet like the transsexual's, her narrative is driven by her sense of not being at home in the sexed body. The identity Jess does embrace, that of the stone butch or the "he-she," denotes this bodily displacement. The stone butch experiences her female body as that which is most *unheimlich* in herself: as with the transsexual the body that should be home is foreign, the familiar felt as most strange. Conventionally, the "stoneness" of the stone butch lies in her sexual untouchability, an untouchability that is the very basis for her sexuality. Stone butch may well constitute the critical difference between female-to-male transsexual and lesbian butch. The transsexual's transgendering lies in his actualized rejection of sex; the touchable lesbian butch's is at all points contained in her sexuality. *Stone* butch is a strikingly "rigid" gender identity, yet this rigidity is "softened" and the stone butch's female sex made livable by her sexual practice. The touch of Jess's lovers never moves above her thigh. Like the transsexual she fears feeling a sex she cannot own. But the dildo she straps on to make love enables her to displace internal female bodily sex to an imaginary male projection without the need for genital surgical intervention. Sex, as Jess's first lover tells her, "[h]er mouth . . . very near my cock, . . . 'is an act of sweet imagination' ": " 'If you're going to fuck me with this,' she said, stroking it, 'then I want you to feel it' " (71). For Jess the "lesbian" "dildo" never is one; it is always felt as a "cock" in a profound sense, a part of her stone-butch body. Thus her sexuality sustains her gender displacement and her gender displacement transforms the meaning of her desire: her stone butch masculinity transgenders the symmetry of same-sex sexuality. If, as Rubin has argued, "the boundaries between the categories of butch lesbian and female-to-male transsexual are permeable," no narrative subject "permeates" more fully than Feinberg's Jess Goldberg, a stone butch who refigures her sex, crossing and recrossing those boundaries.[18]

While gendered contradiction has played a key role in making visible queer pride, Feinberg's stone butch filters this contradiction through shame, conveying it as an acute discomfort, an affect to be resolved. Shame is a profound grappling with the self's location in the world—the feeling of being out of place, of not being at home in a given situation, combined with the desire to be at home. "No other affect" writes psychologist of shame Gershen Kaufman "is more central to identity formation.... Answers to the questions, 'Who am I?' and "Where do I belong?' are forged in the crucible of shame."[19] At root in gender identity disorder is a shame that has rightly been described as "existential": gender dysphoric shame develops not from what one does but from who one is.[20] Born of the self watching the self, shame reflects a split in the subject. In the split, gender-dysphoric subject shame is felt specifically over the body; and perhaps body image and shame are generally intimately related. Shame is most often expressed somatically—blushing, lowered face; and shame is often thought to originate in a consciousness of genitals.[21] In Feinberg and in lesbian folklore the stone butch remains at least partially clothed when making love because of her shame over her female parts. Her sense is of a mismatch between her masculine desire and her female sex; her unspeakable wish is to bring these into alignment. That she does not speak this wish where the female-to-male transsexual does is an indicator that the stone butch, unlike the transsexual, finds a way (I am suggesting her stone sexuality, that act of sweet imagination) to manage the split, to balance in a refigurative desire the difference between material body and body image.

The account of Jess's childhood and early adult life is steeped in an almost insufferable shame. Jess repeatedly claims to be out of touch with her feelings, unable to express them, yet she frequently articulates feeling shame. Although the social reading of Jess's gendered difference (from her own body in conjunction with her difference from others around her), of her not belonging in a recognizable gendered place, inscribes this sense of shame, the recurring question of Jess's life—"[a]re you a boy or a girl?" (16)—reveals that Jess's gendered difference is already corporeally legible to those around her and in fact invites this reading. Like transsexual autobiography *Stone Butch Blues* suggests transgender as a core gender identity helplessly writ large on a body, not produced by a culturally determined way of looking but, rather—especially in its accounts of Jess's alignment with nature in childhood—natural: "Nature held me close and seemed to find no fault with me" (17).[22] Yet as a transgendered text *Stone Butch Blues* is suitably ambivalent about the course of shame's production. While representing the subject's gender difference as natural, the narrative makes clear that the experience of this difference is filtered through cultural constructions of gender. Others' anxieties raised by her ambivalence as a child and an adult generate and are seen as rationalizing the sexual violence against Jess, a sexual violence that in a circular fashion reinscribes her shame. In the first instance Jess is stripped down and locked in a coal bin by a gang of neighborhood boys: " 'Let's see how you tinkle,' one of the boys said as he knocked me down and two of the others struggled to pull off my pants and my underpants. I was filled with horror. I couldn't make them stop. The shame of being half-naked before them—the important half—took all the steam out of me" (18). Shame is the naked transgendered body on public display. That "half" is important for it reveals Jess's sexed difference both from the boys and from what she herself appears not to be. Similarly, on both subsequent occasions when she is raped, first by schoolboys and then by the police, and when men urinate on her bed in the psychiatric ward, the sexual violence against Jess is both caused by and reinforces her difference, her "unnaturalness." These incidents centralize and subjugate Jess's body, exacerbating her shame over its abjection and her identificatory distance from it. During the second rape, for instance, Jess displaces the real event and leaves her body behind by focusing on an imaginary place, a desert surrounded by mountains. This "place" will increasingly become a lure, symbolizing a natural home and an escape from the persecution and unbelonging she faces in the real world.

Shame fuels her desire to get out—out of the body and out of the world that stigmatizes her body. But it is only once the discrepancy between feeling and being is inflected through the cultural insistence on belonging, on continuity between body and identity, that the subject even makes sense of not belonging as shame. The feeling of not being at home in the body unreconciled with the desire to be at home only becomes shameful in a world that normalizes being in place. Next to her "normal" feminine sister whose "dream was a felt skirt and an appliqué poodle and rhinestone-studded plastic shoes," Jess feels out of place and longs to belong: "I wished I could find a way to be good. Shame suffocated me" (19). Likewise, her failure to fit in to charm school serves to highlight her "shameful differences" (23). And while working in the bindery, Jess fears starting the round of singing, ashamed of the difference her voice will make among the native women workers: "I realized I felt ashamed of my own voice" (79). In childhood the shaming of difference is reinforced by Jess's mother who confesses her own shame over Jess's refusal to wear a dress to temple. And this in spite of the narrative making clear that a 1950s upstate New York blue-collar town renders all kind of difference shameful—in the Goldbergs' case, their working-class Jewishness: *Shabbas* candles are lit behind closed curtains, an ethnic and religious difference that, like Jess's different desires, is shamed into secrecy. Jess claims, "Everyone in my family knew about shame" (19). But unlike Jess's gender-dysphoric shame, her family's shame about nonbelonging does not originate in or increase the abjection of the body.

If the concepts of being at home and not being at home in one's sexed body take on meaning in a culture that emphasizes identity belonging, Jess's change of context—her move to Buffalo to seek out a place as a stone butch within its butch/femme community—represents an attempt to change the meaning of her ambivalence. And, temporarily, she succeeds: in this space her gendered difference is her passport to belonging. Correlatively, shame is generalized, structured into the community. In Feinberg's representation of its 1950s/1960s working-class manifestation, butch/femme code *expects* stone butches to conceal the femaleness of their bodies, bind their breasts, wear men's clothes, and remain untouchable in bed. At moments the community even manages to invert the values of the dominant culture that shames them, resulting in scenes, such as Butch Ro's funeral, which are among the most powerful in the text. At the funeral shame lies in the "burly, big-shouldered he-shes who carried their womanhood in work-roughened hands" wearing dresses ("outdated, white, frilly, lace, low-cut, plain"); it lies in their *not* concealing their sex: "Wearing dresses was an excruciating humiliation for them. . . . This clothing degraded their spirit, ridiculed who they were" (117). Nevertheless, the home offered by this community ultimately proves transitory and, in the seventies, Jess finds herself again displaced. The end of the

Vietnam War brings men back to their jobs in Buffalo, putting Jess and the other butches out of work in the plants and factories. Lesbian feminism rewrites butch/femme erotics as heterosexual/sexist role play, coming to replace Jess's community in the bars with evenly gendered, middle-class lesbian couples, performing acts of exclusion that were part of the real historical process of reshaping and redefining the lesbian community as feminist. While the transgendered texture of the butch/femme community housed and valued the gendered contradiction and bodily shame in the figure of the stone butch, the new lesbian-feminist ideology has no place for the non-woman-identified woman.

As it describes this historical shift, the narrative underlines how Jess's identification as a stone butch profoundly dislocates her from the category "woman." When her femme lover, Theresa, begins to identify as a lesbian feminist, herself finding no bar between femme and lesbian feminist, Jess as a butch proves unable to take on either modifier, lesbian or feminist. Theresa shows Jess a campaign poster of two naked embracing women, bearing the legend "Sisterhood—make it real" (138). In visceral reaction perhaps to their very nakedness (their "lesbian" likeness, the shamelessness of their unclothed female bodies touching), Jess claims not to "feel [the women's movement] so much . . . [m]aybe cause I'm a butch" (138). Rejecting Theresa's suggestion that "Butches need women's liberation, too" and that as butch Jess *is* a woman (138), Jess steadfastly insists on her transgendered difference: " 'No I'm not,' I yelled back at her. 'I'm a he-she. That's different' " (147). As cultural feminism validates femaleness and seeks to tone down the gender "difference" of the lesbian from other women (the lesbian becomes archetypal "womyn," in that new signifier emptied out of any trace of the masculine), Jess correspondingly finds herself once more not at home, out of place.

It is this social unbelonging that Jess represents as the manifest reason for her decision to begin hormone treatment. Jess externalizes her transition, suggesting that passing as a man is the only thing for a stone butch to do at this historical crossroads when "real" men and "real" women became dominant in her public and private cultural picture. Somatic transition would appear to be an economic, a social, but not a psychic necessity. And, certainly, more than transsexual texts, *Stone Butch Blues* demonstrates cogently the cultural significance of passing: how the stone butch's taking hormones to pass is a passing up the ladder of social acceptability—importantly, not so much from female to male as from queer-looking butch to clean-cut straight young man. Yet in this attention to cultural locatedness lies the crucial tension in the transgendered plot of this text. For as it naturalizes Jess's transgendered difference, *Stone Butch Blues* naturalizes the transition that embodies this difference; it represents passing for Jess as a coming home to her body: a resolution of bodily shame. In its description of her transition the narrative suggests that Jess's move away from femaleness is emphatically not a case of a "lesbian's" or a "woman's" going under cover as a man to escape stigmatization but part of one stone butch's attempt to embody her transgender. Passing for Jess (in spite of how the plot turns out) is emphatically not a woman's or a lesbian's passing phase. Elsewhere, in hir history of transgender, Feinberg argues that to understand the specificity of transgender identity, we must read the transgendered "gender expression" behind such passages and challenge the pervasive notion that (here female-to-male) transgendered identities are simply a "disguise" for women's or lesbian's stigmatization: "I just don't believe that the debate about why 'women pass as men' can be understood only in the light of women's, or of lesbian and gay, oppression. It has to be viewed in the context of trans history in order be make sense."[23] *Stone Butch Blues* makes the same case in fiction. It requires us to understand Jess's transition as part of her transgendered identity, in the context of her "transhistory."

Complicating Jess's own social rationale for her transition, then, Feinberg reveals that through transition Jess becomes reconciled to her body. Jess takes great pleasure in the physical changes she undergoes, hormones and surgery creating a body more appropriately hers. This conception of transition brings *Stone Butch Blues* into close alignment with transsexual narratives. It is fitting, therefore, that Feinberg conveys Jess's increasing pleasure and relief in transition most evidently in a mirror scene. In this scene of reconciliation to the body Feinberg's transgendered narrative intersects most visibly with the transsexual's:

> As I brushed my teeth, I glanced in the mirror and had to look a second time. Beard stubble roughed my cheeks. My face looked slimmer and more angular. I stripped off my T-shirt and my BVD's. My body was lean and hard. My hips had melted away. I could actually see muscles in my thighs and arms I never knew I had.... I took a hot soapy shower, enjoying the feel of my hands on my skin. It had been so long since I'd been at home in my body. (171)

In contrast to the body-concealing strategies of herself as female-embodied stone butch (painful breast-binding, wearing suits), Jess on hormones stands before the mirror unclothed and without shame: not only now able to look but to touch and find pleasure in her nakedness. This reconciliation to her naked sex stems from her being no longer a naked female. The hormones have masculinized that femaleness. The narrative's metaphorizing of transition as a coming home, the notion of transition as somatic repatriation, underscores that femaleness is a foreign land and masculinization a journey toward home; Jess describes her double mastectomy similarly as "a gift to myself, a coming home to my body" (224). And as Jess comes home in her body, she not surprisingly also finds a niche in the world. She discovers for the first time an unambivalent place to get her hair cut, a place to go to the bathroom without trepidation. She becomes acceptable to the world: in short, culturally locatable.

The question *Stone Butch Blues* poses, then, is why Jess does not continue in her transition. If Jess achieves such happiness at being at home in her body, why does she stop taking the hormones? Why does she give up the protection and security provided her in passing as a man for the dangerous intermediacy of the gender-ambivalent? For while her lowered voice, her masculinized facial structure, and her body without breasts remain irreversible effects of female-to-male somatic transitioning, coming off testosterone does refeminize her, restarting her period, thinning her beard, widening her hips, and softening her face somewhat—"blending gender characteristics" (224). In direct correlation to this embodied intermediacy Jess finds herself once more out of place in the world, the cycle of violence against her resparked by her visible difference: after her move to New York City, she is stared at, beaten up, chased, fired, taunted. In effect, in ending hormone treatment, Jess ends up in the world in a place of neither-nor/both, her cultural unbelonging literalized by her being unable to ride her Norton motorbike into Canada with her driving license listing her sex as female. Why this return or doubling back in and of the narrative into this zone of dangerous intermediacy? This is the crucial turning point, for it is here that the transgendered story splits off most dramatically from the transsexual plot.

The difference of this transgendered narrative—both from a transsexual and a queer trajectory—the reasons for Jess's unique decision, can be explained through Jess's unique experience of passing. For the transsexual, passing is becoming, a step toward home, a relief and a release: it aligns inner gender identity with social identity; one is "taken" in the world for who one feels oneself to be. In the queer deployment of transgender, passing is conversely identity's unbecoming: passing deontologizes sex and gender, the "doing" of gender profoundly destabilizing the reality of an "is." Although passing for Jess keeps separate the feeling of being gendered from the world's perception of this gendering (Jess is what she feels, not—as in much queer theory—what she seems), in distinction to transsexual narratives, passing ultimately reopens in Jess a painful split between inner and social identity that undoes the initial relief the hormones brought. If, in beginning hormone treatment, Jess states, "the hormones are like the looking glass for me. If I pass through it, my world could open up," half-way through the mirror, it is *Jess* (her gender/sex split) and not her world that opens up (151). In passing as a man, Jess realizes that *being* a man is not-home but in fact "borders that will never be home" (11).

The split that passing brings on in Jess is captured in—what else?—a series of mirror scenes, their similarity with and difference from those in transsexual narratives (like but not quite) articulating the specificity of the transgendered narrative. Jess sees reflected in the mirror not what the subject of transsexual narratives sees, the not-me; before her transition Jess invariably sees herself, a transgendered woman looking back at a transgendered woman. As a child cross-dressing in her father's suit, Jess sees reflected not a man but an "uncatalogued" woman (not pictured in *Sears*), the transgendered woman she expects to become. After giving herself her first shot of testosterone, Jess reassures herself that in the mirror she still sees "me, looking back at me" (164). Even after having sex with Annie, a heterosexual woman who takes her (in both senses) as a man, while trading dildo for sock in her BVDS (hard on and off again) in Annie's bathroom, Jess sees "me looking back at me" in the bathroom mirror (192). During this, the most schizophrenic moment in the text ("She put her hand gently between my thighs and squeezed the sock. 'I got a lot of pleasure out of this tonight, she said' "[192]), when what Jess passes for is most divorced from what she feels herself to be, the mirror makes clear that Jess has maintained to herself while passing as a man the stability of her identity *as a masculine woman*, that transgendered ambivalence—"It's one thing for the magician to reveal the art of illusion. It's another thing to tell a straight woman that the man she slept with was a woman" (195). What Jess sees in the mirror is now notably gendered—not simply me looking back at me—yet this gendering is clearly not male although neither it is unambiguously female; it is instead a transgendering. Passing for Jess has involved the production of an illusion—a projection, not a reflection—of being a man; it is not a stage in the process to becoming one as it is in transsexual narratives. Yet now in contradistinction to queer theory's version of transgender, it is Jess's inner (trans)gender identity that determines her sense of herself not her passing, her "performance"—sexual and social—as a man. The masquerade does not constitute her identity; it is simply that: a masquerade concealing her sense of her real self. It is this distinction on both sides that determines her transgendered trajectory in between.

Once Jess reaches the point where her passing is so successful that she no longer sees "me looking back at me" in the mirror, once the contradiction between what she appears to be and what she feels herself to be has reopened (this time on the other side), Jess decides to end her testosterone injections. Jess's "me" after her experience with hormones turns out to be the space of gendered contradiction and ambiguity, neither woman nor man but in fact both. In describing the moment of her return Jess displays the peculiar splitting—the "double consciousness" (as she quotes Du Bois)[24]—engendered by passing:

> I drew one cc of hormones into a syringe, lifted it above my naked thigh—and then paused. My arm felt restrained by an unseen hand. No matter how I tried I could not sink that needle into my quadriceps as I'd done hundreds of times before. I stood up and looked in the bathroom mirror. The depth of sadness in my eyes frightened me. I lathered my morning beard stubble, scraped it clean with a razor, and splashed cold water on my face. The stubble still felt rough. As much as I loved my beard as part of my body, I felt trapped behind it. What I saw reflected in the mirror was not a man, but I couldn't recognize the he-she. My face no longer revealed the contrasts of my gender. I could see my passing self, but even I could no longer see the more complicated me beneath my surface. . . . I hadn't just believed that passing would hide me. I hoped that it would allow me to express the part of myself that didn't seem to be woman. I didn't get to explore being a he-she though. I simply became a he—a man without a past.
>
> Who was I now—woman or man? . . . What if the real me could emerge, changed by the journey? Who would I be? . . . I searched the apartment for a cigarette, but as I picked up the pack I watched my hand crush it. (221–222)

The gendered contradiction in Jess in this scene is at its most powerful. Not only does Jess for the first time in the narrative not recognize her reflected self in the mirror, the "real me" now concealed "beneath my [reflected] surface," a mask of passing, her bodily gestures contest each other in a complex embodiment of this split subjectivity. Watching herself crush the pack even though she had wanted a cigarette, unable to inject the testosterone in spite of habit (restrained by a seemingly external force), Jess experiences her desires as multiple and contradictory: a sign of this double consciousness that passing has installed, a disjunction between psyche and body again. In these careful details Feinberg demonstrates how Jess's body negates itself to a point of stasis, necessitating the end of her transsexual trajectory: after this she can go no further. The moment is the embodiment of negation in Jess's story.

What has been negated in Jess's passing are "the contrasts of [Jess's sense of her] gender," her embodied gendered difference, her transgendered ambivalence: above all, her stone butch self. Always bringing with it some loss of the past, floating the subject only in the present or shrouding him or her in a fictionalized past, passing in Jess necessitates a concealment of her transgendered history: Jess simply became "a he, a man without a past." As a subject who continues to identify as a transgendered woman in the present, Jess remains bound to her actual past. She chooses to keep with her and to make visible—to make consistently readable—the strange familiarity, the ambivalence and liminality of the transgendered, sex-reconfigured stone butch: "No matter how painful it was to be a he-she, I wondered what kind of courage was required to leave the sex you'd always known" (95). Holding off from the transsexual's future destination of integral sex, in not passing on, Jess in effect locates identity in the passage itself. Her "real me" can emerge only at this point in her transition: she is "herself" only after her experience with hormones and surgery has somatically transgendered her, but only before they have transsexed her. Trading in passing as a man for being read as a he-she—or rather making the knot of contradiction between passing and being read into the grounds for her transgendered identity—Jess ends up passing neither as man nor woman *and* being read as both. She makes the fantastic transformation, the intermediate space of crossing, her lived reality.

Passing might bring Jess home to her body, but assimilating as a man means the loss of specific community. Yet the transgendered intermediacy she ends up embodying hardly provides Jess with a haven in the world. In effect, if Jess trades in a sexed home to prevent the disappearance of her transgendered past into the larger culture, this desire for a culturally specific home leaves her visibly transgendered body with no place like home in the world: no sexed home to which it would seem to belong. The final chapter of *Stone Butch Blues* seems to want to resolve Jess's sustained cultural unbelonging and to provide the text with some kind of narrative resolution: it is with the question of where Jess might find a community home that *Stone Butch Blues* closes. The chapter begins with Jess's return to the lesbian and gay community, her taking the mike at a lesbian and gay rally in New York City, and her emergence from the subway stairs at Christopher Street symbolizing her reemergence in the lesbian and gay world. At the rally Jess speaks her transgendered history, coming out with the self passing has concealed: "I'm not a gay man. . . . I'm a butch, a he-she" (296). Reading her body back out, Jess's autobiographical act represents her attempt to find a home in queerness, where the concept of home, as she suggests to her lesbian and gay audience, might be loosened to allow for affiliations across difference, where the "we [might be] bigger" (296). Yet this real place of the West Village and the acceptance that Jess receives here from lesbians and gays is displaced by the location with which the text closes: the mythic transgendered place of Jess's final dream. This dream echoes two preceding dreams; read together as a staggered narrative within the text, the dreams stage the fantasy of finding a specifically transgendered home not defined or contained by the queer space symbolized in the West Village.[25]

The first is a daydream that Jess produces during her rape by the police. It figures Jess alone and apparently lost in the desert, heading toward mountains, "seeking sanctuary" (63). The second dream occurs immediately before Jess's decision to transition. The landscape is still mythic, now a deserted town from which Jess is walking away, looking, significantly, for people. Following a trail of smoke to a hut in a clearing in a forest, Jess finds inside the drag queens Justine, Peaches, and Georgetta, the butches Al and Edwin, and Jess's mentor, Rocco, who had taken hormones and had breast surgery before her. While in the real of her narrative at this point Jess has not begun to transition, in her dream, her body is already transformed: "I touched my own face. I felt the rough stubble of beard. I ran my hand across the flat of my chest. I felt happy in my body, comfortable among friends" (142). On waking, Jess describes her sense of her relation to the people in the dream: "I felt like I belonged with them, you know?" (142). She specifies a different configuration of gender as the criterion for belonging among the characters of her dream: "But in the dream it wasn't about being gay. It was about being a man or a woman," claiming, "I didn't feel like a woman or a man, and I liked how I was different"(143).

In the third and final dream Jess returns to the hut in the field, discovering a circle of people inside. Now it is clear that it is transgenderism that links these people, that forms the ring: "There were people who were different like me inside. We could all see our reflections in the faces of those who sat in this circle. I looked around. It was hard to say who was a woman, who was a man. Their faces radiated a different kind of beauty than I'd grown up seeing celebrated on television or in magazines" (300). Haunting this space are the Dineh women who, in raising Jess as a child, gave her a ring as a mythic signifier of her difference. The ring was taken from her during the police rape, the incident that precipitated the first dream of being lost in the desert. In the final dream Jess finds the ring. The woman/man who beckons Jess shows her how the ring as object is now refigured in the circle of transgendered people surrounding her. The final dream neatly returns what was taken from her during the first dream, this belonging now serving as a recovery of that loss. Looking around the circle, Jess is urged by her guide to acknowledge that the circle of people around her is as "real" as the ring.

In this recovery of the ring as community Jess's dreams chart the finding of a home in transgender. This home is not only more bounded and more specific than the real queer community of the West Village but has different criteria for belonging. Whereas in the queer community Jess's gender matters—" 'Good for you, sister,' she whispered in my ear. No one had ever called me that before"—in the transgendered space of her dreams, the question of what she is, "woman or man?" must remain, precisely, a question (297). Belonging here is the reward for gendered unbelonging elsewhere, the grounds for home in this transgendered space the sustained ambivalence between passing and being read. If the queer space of Christopher Street is a kind of community stopgap, then the text suggests that her "real" home is this transgendered space—as of the moment only representable in her dreams. Insofar as the figure of home stands for the concept of community, *Stone Butch Blues* in its final pages suggests the importance of holding out for a community based on the specific differences of transgender—differences in trans history and embodiment. "Transgendered people," writes Feinberg in the earliest collective sense of transgender, which is simultaneously an attempt to distinguish it from a generic queerness, are not "the cusp of the lesbian and gay community. In reality the two huge communities are like circles that only partially overlap"[26] Moving from the West Village to the transgendered home of her dreams, Jess crosses the overlap to locate in the circle organized around her specific difference on the other side: as of the moment fictional but, precisely because of that, a lure.

Generic Displacements: Fictional Autobiography

As Jess is a sex that, in the most literal sense, is not one, so *Stone Butch Blues* is a transsexual autobiography that in every sense is not one. That is, not only is *Stone Butch Blues* not a transsexual story, it is also not autobiography. Or rather, it is not *quite* one, for *Stone Butch Blues* presents itself as fictional autobiography on two levels. It is a first-person narrative fiction, a fictional character's autobiography; and it is a novel that, when the details of both trajectories are juxtaposed, appears to be outlined on Feinberg's own life, the author's autobiography in fictionalized form. Like Jess Goldberg, Feinberg grew up differently gendered and working-class Jewish in the fifties, came out as butch in the butch/femme community in Buffalo, worked in the factories until they closed in the seventies when s/he began testosterone treatment in order to pass as a man. And like Jess, Feinberg came off testosterone after four years, feeling trapped in her passing, never identifying comfortably as a man; s/he moved to New York to become a prominent speaker in the lesbian, gay, and transgender communities (a move that might be thought symbolized in *Stone Butch Blues* with Jess's arrival and speech at the Christopher Street rally).[27] The basic outline of the narratives—the fictional one of *Stone Butch Blues* and the real one of Feinberg's life—would thus appear to be the same. Yet if the lives of transgendered author and narrator are similar, the text's fictional frame prevents us from reading them as identical. In its narrative surround, *Stone Butch Blues* insists on its fictional status. The subtitle of *Stone Butch Blues*, "A Novel," and the inside cover disclaimer ("This is a work of fiction. Any similarity between characters and people, dead or alive, is a coincidence") fix the text's status as fiction (n. p.). Moreover, although the narrative is written in the autobiographical first person, in not giving her narrator-protagonist hir own name, Feinberg further grounds the text in fiction. The life recounted is manifestly not that of the real author, Leslie Feinberg, but that of the fictional character, Jess Goldberg.

Feinberg's comments on *Stone Butch Blues* similarly suggest an ambivalence over the text's generic status. In response to my paralleling the narrative of *Stone Butch Blues* and hir own life, Feinberg underlines the text's status as fiction:

> *Stone Butch Blues* is a total and complete work of fiction. It's in no way a version of my own life. It's certainly fair to say that the protagonist and I both grew up Jewish and differently gendered in Buffalo. I certainly drew on my knowledge of what industries and avenues were open or closed to a trans individual over a period of 4 decades. And the parallel of Jess Goldberg speaking at a rally is an interpretive one and therefore fair enough. But the emotional and situational path, transgender path choices and consciousness of the character is a work of fiction.[28]

The narrative draws on Feinberg's knowledge; but the work is a total and complete work of fiction, in no way a version of the author's life. Yet in a previous interview Feinberg suggests *Stone Butch Blues* as "a very thinly disguised *autobiography*."[29] As thinly disguised autobiography the fiction *would* then appear to be based on the life—but the life "disguised" as fiction.

What are we to make of the ambivalence in and around *Stone Butch Blues* regarding the text's generic status? Critically, in the above interview, even when Feinberg suggests *Stone Butch Blues* as autobiography, s/he carefully underlines the fictional framework for the narrative: the autobiography is disguised as fiction. She never suggests, in other words, that *Stone Butch Blues* is clearly *not* fiction. Juxtaposed, her comments on the genre of *Stone Butch Blues* do not produce a contradiction so much as a sustained ambivalence between genres. This ambivalence in and around *Stone Butch Blues* over genre constructs the text as a form between fiction and autobiography, a trans- or intergeneric space. As Leigh Gilmore writes of the similar intermediate generic space of autobiographical fiction (fictional autobiography's mirror image, the emphasis in this category falling on fiction with autobiography as the qualifier), this intergeneric form between fiction and autobiography "is situated at a boundary and calls attention to its hybrid form by lacking a distinct generic name."[30] Reading *Stone Butch Blues* via feminist autobiography criticism's important work on the significance of the correspondence between gender and genre, we might say that in recounting the alternative trajectory of hir transgendered subject, Feinberg produces an alternative generic form—a trans-genre: a text as between genres as its subject is between genders.[31] What is remarkably, indeed satisfyingly identical in Feinberg's response to gender and genre is this calling attention to hybridity on both counts: the author's resistance to going home to either side of either boundary, hir positioning of hir protagonist's gendered subjectivity and her text's generic form symmetrically in between. Beyond the critical pleasure to be reaped from this mirroring between transgender and transgenre, what is the practical significance of the transgendered text's occupying such an equivocal generic position? How do we read such a transgeneric text?

In the same interview in which s/he describes *Stone Butch Blues* as "thinly disguised autobiography," Feinberg hirself connects hir genre choice to the transgendered subject's gendered choice. S/he analogizes hir autobiography's thin fictional disguise with the transgendered subject's lack of disguise—that is, the generic form with the transgendered subject's incapacity to pass safely, the fact that the transgendered subject, like the autobiography, may be read through. Paraphrasing Dorothy Allison (whose fiction is also "thinly disguised autobiography"), Feinberg describes fiction as "less than autobiography but more than lies":

> [U]sing fiction gives you the ability to tell a very painful story that's filled with all the shame of growing up different in this society. I felt, by telling it autobiographically, that I would pull back in a lot of places. I also felt, as transgendered people, that we're always being told who we are, either physically or emotionally—strip or be stripped, you know? There's a way that we get dehumanized. "Let's see your body. We'll find out who you are. Let's hear what your innermost thoughts and feelings [are]." I feel we've each found our own boundaries of dignity which we will not go beyond; that we deserve. I really felt that by fictionalizing the story, that I would be able to tell more of the truth; be more brutally honest than I would if I were telling my own story.[32]

Weighing fiction against autobiography ("less than ... but more than"), Feinberg suggests that the genres might be distinguished on a kind of scale of truth. Fiction is less factual than autobiography but truer, for truth and facts are not identical in hir usage. While this may appear the old adage that fiction is truer than fact, Feinberg enlists it only to refigure it. S/he claims she chose fiction as the frame because of fiction's concealing or disguising effect. Concealing the facts allows hir to recount "more of the truth." To spin out the striking image that extends hir figure for *Stone Butch Blues* as a "thinly disguised autobiography," fiction clothes the naked body narrative of the transgendered subject in a kind of truth while autobiography strips it down to the facts and in the process strips off the truth. Autobiography seeks to "find out who you are," to reveal the naked facts of the subject; fiction conceals enough of the facts so that the truth can be read.

Feinberg's description of autobiography's generic effect as stripping the subject down to the facts echoes the work of the pre-Stonewall police within the plot of *Stone Butch Blues* and needs to be understood in this context. The police strip down Jess and other butches in the name of a law that insists that they must be wearing at least three items of "correctly gendered" clothing. Although the police's stripping of the transgendered subject is always the threshold to greater physical and sexual violence and humiliation, the removal of clothes is represented in and of itself as a violent act and shaming act: "The cops picked out the most stone butch of them all to destroy with humiliation, a woman everyone said 'wore a raincoat in the shower.' We heard they stripped her, slow, in front of everyone in the bar, and laughed at her trying to cover up her nakedness. Later she went mad, they said. Later she hung herself" (8). The police's stripping attempts to refeminize the butch, to reveal (more to the subject than to her onlookers) the "true sex" (the facts of her body) of the transgendered subject: "The cops dragged Al in just after Mona left. She was in pretty bad shape. Her shirt was partly open and her pants zipper was down. Her binder was gone, leaving her large breasts free" (35). But stripping her strips her of her "true" transgendered difference, for once the "facts" of her body are seen to be just the same, the stone butch without clothes is no longer visually different from other women. With Jess, as the cops strip her before they rape her, their sexual violence is an attempt to enforce on the transgendered butch the indisputable fact of her femaleness against their maleness, her essential and antithetical bodily difference from them. They treat her transgendered subjectivity as superficial, a comic, removable covering: "One of the cops loosened my tie. As he ripped open my new dress shirt, the sky blue buttons bounced and rolled across the floor. He pulled up my T-shirt, exposing my breasts. . . . As one cop pulled off my trousers, I tried to calm the spasms in my stomach so I wouldn't choke on my own vomit. 'Aw, ain't that cute, BVD's' " (62).

Given the desubjectivizing effect that stripping has within the plot of *Stone Butch Blues*, Feinberg's analogy for generic form—autobiography strips the transgendered narrative down to the naked facts—suggests autobiography's capacity to reveal the facts of the subject without the "disguise" of some fictional layer as powerfully violent, invasive, and fundamentally desubjectivizing of the author. Autobiography may lessen the "truth" of the transgendered subject in its very revelation of the facts. If a key reason why nontranssexuals read transsexual autobiography is to get at the facts of the transsexual's body/narrative, and if, as we have seen, the reader's desire for the facts of transsexual autobiography does tend to have the effect of a desubjectivizing "interrogation," Feinberg's metaphor suggests fiction as a tactical means for the transgendered writer to deflect such fascination with the literal. Fiction interposes a distance between the potentially policing reader and the transgendered author, skewing the relation of identity between Feinberg and her narrator protagonist. Within *Stone Butch Blues* Theresa's act of placing clean white underwear out for her raped stone butch lover in its repetition takes on the significance of an act of healing, the BVD's restoring Jess's true transgender identity, reclothing her after her stripping to the facts of her sex. Like the femme's act, fiction would appear to offer the protection of a truth that heals and clothes the greater difference of the transgendered subject. A "thin disguise," the fictional dimension of *Stone Butch Blues* thwarts the transparency, the naked literalism that characterizes the scene of reading autobiography (the book = the life): a literalism that would otherwise be redoubled when the scene involves reading that even more exceptional specimen, the transgendered subject.

Stone Butch Blues's investment in fiction prevents us from pinning the facts of the transgendered subject Jess to Feinberg. Not only can we not legitimately and accurately read a "novel" as a reproduction of Feinberg's life, we cannot demand (as we tend to think we can from ostensibly less mediated autobiography—although I have of course questioned this) that it reproduce reality. A novel is fiction: not the facts but explicitly a representation. Although she ostensibly accepts *Stone Butch Blues*'s self-description as a novel, in her reissued *The Transsexual Empire* Raymond makes the mistake of not reading *Stone Butch Blues* as enough of a fiction. She criticizes *Stone Butch Blues* for "fail[ing] to extend [its] personal insight into a political analysis of gender," for failing to reflect what she is convinced is the truth of gender: that men are male and women are (antithetically) female. What Raymond wants from *Stone Butch Blues* is a plot in which Jess doesn't transform herself "*from being woman-identified to being other-identified*," in which Jess doesn't transition and "disavow . . . her own womanhood" by crossing to the polarized other side, manhood.[33] Of course it is precisely this polarization of gender difference—this "fact" of gender as originally and inevitably equivalent to a binary of sex—that Feinberg's transgendered intermediacy reveals as fictional. Raymond's desire for a mimetic reproduction of this cultural given can only seem a "bad" reading of *Stone Butch Blues* as a "novel": a failure to engage with the narrative that Feinberg has actually written that throws these given "truths" into question.

Nevertheless, the fictional disguise of *Stone Butch Blues* is "thin." Thus, at the same time as we acknowledge it as fiction, inevitably we *do* attribute to the text a dimension of the literal that we do to all autobiography—although without rendering the text identical to autobiography. This attribution comes in part from the presence of autobiographical features in *Stone Butch Blues*. Much of the enormous power of this narrative resides in the credibility and strength of its first-person narrative form, in the capacity of Jess's voice to authenticate transgender experience. The other contributing factor to the autobiographical texture of the "novel" is the trajectory of the life itself. Jess's story is so extraordinary and exceptional, how could it *not* in *some* way be "a life"? It is precisely because the "transgender path" of Jess is unique, that *Stone Butch Blues* "reads like" autobiography. As the only representation so far of this experience (whether read as the story of a transsexual who turned back or of a stone butch who pushed on), *Stone Butch Blues* wields a powerful representational and representative force that is hard to resist. Feinberg hirself has encountered the effects of hir writing's force: s/he receives letters from readers addressed to the characters in the novel for hir as author to deliver.[34] In other words, even when readers concede that the protagonist is not the author (duly noting the difference of proper names), they continue to believe in the real-life existence of the "fictional" characters, displacing this reality from Feinberg to people Feinberg must have known—displacing, that is, autobiography into biography. While we cannot fix the story to a particular life, therefore, Feinberg's interweaving of the autobiographical form into hir fiction encourages us to read *Stone Butch Blues* as truthful, authentic, authoritative, and—on some level—indexical of its subject: all of the values we expect from autobiography (although of course, as good readers who recognize autobiography as representation we also claim no longer to have those expectations).

Stone Butch Blues wears its translucent guise of fiction in subtle, clever ways. Most important, although Feinberg does not assign hir protagonist-narrator hir own name, the name s/he does give encourages us to question the difference and partially read through the "novel" to a fictional autobiographical narrative. In the ambivalent gendering of the first name (Jess) and the implicit Jewishness of the last (Goldberg), the narrator-protagonist's proper name resembles the authorial signature. Jess Goldberg repeats Leslie Feinberg not differently or identically but similarly. According to Philippe Lejeune's first formulation of the "autobiographical pact," identity between author's and narrator-protagonist's name is the primary requisite of autobiography. Lejeune argues that even if, as would seem to be the case with Feinberg, the basic plot of the story with reference to other texts may be shown to be the same as the author's life, if the authorial and narrator-protagonist's names are different, the text cannot be categorized as autobiography. While he acknowledges that a fiction written as if it were autobiography is no different internally from autobiography (both are first-person narratives in which the narrator is the protagonist), the absence of identity between the proper names inside and outside the cover will radically change the way in which we approach the text—that is, we will read it as fiction instead of autobiography. Autobiography cannot involve degrees of truth or identity: "it is all or nothing"; identity equals absolute truth, nonidentity equals fiction; the genres are antithetical.[35] In his chart laying out how the difference or identity between author's and narrator-protagonist's names formulaically determines the genres of fiction and autobiography and the reader's approach to the text (reading according to the autobiographical or the fictional pact), Lejeune blacks out the square for the case in which the story appears to be based on the author's life but the narrator-protagonist's name is not identical to the author's. He allows no place for fictional autobiography, for the trans-genred text. There would thus seem to be no place for telling one's story without baring all.

Yet, as Lejeune was to realize in his virtuoso return nearly a decade later to this 1973 essay, his chart ends up demonstrating precisely "the existence of ambiguities and degrees" involved in genre.[36] The blackened spaces in the chart lay bare to Lejeune's reader his exclusion, and this absent supplement challenges not only the comprehensivity and accuracy of his theory but its very premise: the binary of fiction/autobiography. Feinberg's *Stone Butch Blues* is such a supplemental text. It disturbs both Lejeune's initial absolute generic distinctions and his concomitant conceptualization of identity structured through difference. The proper name in *Stone Butch Blues* functions according to neither identity nor difference but to resemblance. The narrator-protagonist's name is clearly a "bad" pseudonym for the author's: it reveals more than it conceals the relation. A "thin disguise" it calls for us to read through the apparent fiction, to assume that the text has some form of autobiographical body. At the same time, however, the nonidentity, this relation of resemblance, prevents us from closing the autobiographical pact and reading protagonist and author as identical, from reading the story as fact.

Feinberg's acknowledgments further destabilize the split between autobiographical and fictional contracts, complicating the subtitle's and the inside cover's declaration of the text's fictionality. They reveal a relation of resemblance between Feinberg's life and the text: "There were times, surrounded by bashers, when I thought I would not live long enough to explain my own life. There were moments when I feared I would not be allowed to live long enough to finish writing this book" (n. p.). In part because of the meaning of the statements and in part because "my own life" and "this book" occupy identical positions in each sentence—the syntax of which is almost (not quite) identical—it is strongly implied that "this book" is the explanation of "my own life," that the two are interchangeable. The packaging or context of the narrative (authorial signature and narrator-protagonist's name, text's subtitle, inside disclaimer, and acknowledgments) provides a contradictory picture about the text's generic belonging; it discourages the reader from taking a certain either/or stance. Even the front and rear cover photographs create this effect of ambivalence, of generic irreducibility. The faces they represent obviously "belong" to the same person: as written under the rear cover photograph is a blurb about Feinberg's life, they belong clearly to Feinberg. Yet although the inside publication information page states that the illustration on the front cover is a photograph, this photograph has been colored and retouched so that its photographic realness is concealed and it looks more like a drawing. Mirroring the narrator-protagonist's name, then, the cover photograph is apparently fictionalized yet simultaneously reveals a relation of resemblance between fictional subject and real author that subverts both absolute fictionality and absolute autobiographic realness.[37]

More than any other literary genre autobiography, like the transgendered subject, raises anxieties in the "reader" about genre, about belonging. What is "it"? How shall we categorize "it"? "Are you a boy or a girl?" Paul de Man famously concludes that "the distinction between fiction and autobiography is not an either/or polarity but . . . undecidable." Autobiography "is not a genre or a mode, but a figure of reading."[38] This figure de Man names prosopopoeia: literally, a face-making. Our reading of autobiography embodies and disembodies the human form (autobiography suggests presence and yet absence). The narrative re-presents, and veils the absence of, the absent body. "One's name . . . is made as intelligible as a face. [Autobiography] deals with the giving and taking away of faces, with face and deface, *figure*, figuration and disfiguration."[39] As a mechanism that allows the reader to constitute the "face" of the transgendered subject while preventing him or her from pinning the facts to a designated body (splaying the body of this "rare" butterfly for our collection), the genre of *Stone Butch Blues* is finally undecidable. The generic figure of the transgendered narrative mimics that of transgender, repeats Jess's relation to gender. This figure is resemblance: like, but not quite; on both counts a resistance to reinforcing categorical identity. The text refuses full autobiographical or fictional belonging as Jess refuses full transsexual becoming: the either/or of genre and gender—fiction or autobiography, woman or man—remains either an unmade choice or a both. *Stone Butch Blues* passes as fiction in the same way that Jess finally passes as a man: neither really does, both intentionally fall short, both refuse full cover.

In practice the figure of resemblance does not mean that we read *Stone Butch Blues* as neither fiction nor autobiography. Rupturing the conventions of genre as s/he ruptures those of gender, bypassing the interdiction on mixing pronounced by the "laws" of both, Feinberg holds out to the reader a fictional autobiographical pact in which we, if we want, can have it both ways.[40] While the text with its aura of autobiography has the capacity to speak the truth for an emergent community, to represent a subject, in its fictional disguise we are made aware of the complexities entailed in this act of representation: the problem of revealing the "facts" of transgender. Not only are not all transgendered subjects represented by *Stone Butch Blues*, neither can they speak or be heard to the same degree, in relation both to each and other autobiographical subjects. The fact that Feinberg refrains from fully signing Lejeune's autobiographical contract in her narrator-protagonist's proper name conveys that, for the transgendered even more than for the transsexual subject, autobiography, owning one's story, is not so clearly an option. Given the generic unbelonging of the transgendered story, its not-quite difference, how would *Stone Butch Blues* have announced itself as autobiography: "Not (quite) a Transsexual Autobiography"? As transgendered, the text could hardly have circulated as transsexual autobiography. Nor could it have joined the ranks of lesbian autobiography. *Stone Butch Blues* is not simply—indeed, I have argued, not even—a lesbian story. In the story of transgender Feinberg's transgenre makes clear that not all autobiographers *can* sign the autobiographical contract.

By the same token Feinberg also highlights and challenges the assumption that the author can *only* sign the autobiographical contract: that is, the belief that s/he could not produce anything other than autobiography. S/he suggests that the fixing of *Stone Butch Blues* as fact, as simply autobiography, is thoroughly bound up with another set of binary assumptions—those concerning class: "an elitist bias has been revealed to me by some who have conveyed their assumption that a blue-collar person, who lacks extended formal education, could not possibly write about anything except their own life."[41] To read *Stone Butch Blues* as simply autobiography is to perpetuate the fiction that the working-class author can *only* tell hir story, that is that s/he cannot craft anew but can only mechanically reproduce. If the apparent "nakedness" of autobiography (its revelation of the facts) signifies to the reader "working-class" and the layers of the imaginary in fiction that distance the real signify "educated," *Stone Butch Blues*'s fictional autobiography stymies yet another pair of categorical absolutes, neither embracing "educated" to jettison "working-class" nor allowing the reader to remain unchallenged in his or her assumptions of an uncreative working class. This neither/nor of Feinberg's style provides an index to hir unique approach to hir audience and is one of the key effects of hir transgeneric mode. Hir continued crossing of the personal story and theoretical truths about the complex embodiment of sex and gender has made hir the author, surely, who has most managed to reach audiences typically treated as distinct: academic and "community." Feinberg continues this crossover style in *Transgender Warriors: Making History From Joan of Arc to Ru Paul*. Here s/he unfurls the history of transgender though the frame of hir own personal discovery of transgender history, making the historical narrative accessible through hir own story. Transgenre is again a deliberate attempt to bring "theory," through the story, to a larger readership. Feinberg's comments on *Stone Butch Blues* illuminate reaching a larger unaddressed audience as the goal of this stylistic crossing: "I had read a great deal of gender theory that I felt was so abstracted from human experience that it did not speak to or about my life and the lives of other trans people. I wanted to contribute my voice to the discussion of gender theory in a way that was accessible, particularly to working class readers."[42]

Feinberg *has* written one explicitly autobiographical text, in which s/he *does* come out as transsexual. Published in 1980, the pamphlet is entitled *Journal of a Transsexual*, even though Feinberg tells us in this text that s/he left the sex change program s/he was in and came off hormones in 1974. The pamphlet represents a day in the (extremely violent) life of a *non-passing* female-to-male: the violence and bathroom trouble the narrator recounts in hir experiences are products of hir being read as gender-ambivalent, neither a "real" man nor a "real" woman. Contradictions abound not only sexually but, as in *Stone Butch Blues*, textually. While entitled *Journal of a Transsexual*, the pamphlet is published under what is evidently Feinberg's female name, Diane L. Feinberg. The title of the text and the authorial signature enact gendered contradiction, further refusing any degree of passing. In the text of the pamphlet Feinberg figures moments when s/he passes as a man as *losing ground*. S/he finds it harder to be read (hir desire *is* to be read) as a masculine woman in the winter when hir body is concealed under heavy clothing than in the summer when hir gender-ambivalent body is exposed: "In winter, once I'm covered by a coat, I could argue that I'm a woman 'til I'm blue in the face. It gets me nowhere. In winter I lose ground. Territory liberated in the summer is often overturned by bigotry in the winter.... As long as I do not argue that I'm a woman, I am treated more like a human being."[43] Being read is equivalent to liberating territory, making new space; passing to losing ground.

That Feinberg claims here to be a transsexual and a woman emphasizes trans as an ongoing process: not as a necessarily transitional state prior to the resolution of gender ambiguity but an identity site—a categorical home—in which the contradictions of the somatic and psychic, both within each and against the other, are sustained but sustained painfully and complexly. Reclaiming transitioning to the status of identity, *Journal of a Transsexual* captures with precision how this subject's demands to have hir body's narrative read make hir a threatening (and threatened) figure, keen enough—both desirous and brave enough—to keep moving through, at the very same time as s/he creates home in, the unstable grounds of gender ambivalence.

Transgender and Transsexual Locations: The Politics of Home

At the end of the millennium such gender ambivalence has come to trope this very moment of historical turning. As Rita Felski notes, the transsexual/transgenderist has been elected by contemporary theory to figure our century's favorite ends: the end of history, and of course the end of sexual difference. S/he, as we might say, has become a "semiotically dense emblem in the rhetoric of fin de millennium," his/her sex transition easing us through this epochal transition.[44] Constructing trans into the very "fin" of the millennium, postmodernism has challenged the key binaries of modernist identity grand narratives by idealizing the middle ground—the "/" or transition itself. But as it is the purpose of Felski's essay to argue, this promotion of trans comes at a price: the use of the trans figure to erode the borders between male and female, sex and gender, past order and future disorder, blurs local differences between embodied subjects and their variegated narratives; it leaves unattended differences that continue to matter on either side of the slash. For example, Felski writes, "Baudrillard's elevation [of transsexuality] to the status of universal signifier ('we are all transsexuals') subverts established distinctions between male and female, normal and deviant, real and fake, but at the risk of homogenizing differences that matter politically: the differences between women and men, the difference between those who occasionally play with the trope of transsexuality and those others for whom it is a matter of life and death."[45]

The differences between women and men, those who play with transsexuality figuratively and those who live it in the flesh—the differences, in other words, of sex—continue to matter politically for feminists above all. For reasons consistent with its methodological focus and continuity, most feminism continues to recognize sexual difference as crucially structuring of the world: a difference that has not been transfigured so much as obfuscated by work that declares its end.[46] If transgender locates in an interstitial space between sexes and transsexuality remains invested in the sexed body as home, is this differing approach to sexual division a way of distinguishing between transgender and transsexuality: a distinction that would then seem to bring transgender into closer affiliation with queer theory on the one hand and transsexuality with feminism on the other? That Felski's essay itself does not distinguish between transgendered and transsexual certainly suggests the need for their distinction. Her own non-differentiation serves to illuminate part of the problem she critiques: the theoretical assumption of trans as trope has overridden even the difference between trans trajectories. The value of Felski's essay (what should make it a landmark for emergent transgender studies) is precisely to suggest this universalization of trans as reason for the existence of transgender studies at the end of the millennium. It indicates why it is crucial that, as transgender studies makes its specifications, it needs to steer clear of reinscribing transition as the grand signifier of a generalized, disembodied, nonreferential transgression—how we need to avoid scuttling our differences as we navigate them on a transcendental *différance*.

The remarkable transitions in and within Feinberg's life and work—the fact that, as s/he shows, transsexuals can chose not to pass and indeed fail to pass; that transgenderists can decide to pass or find it difficult not to pass; that transsexuals may remain nonoperative under the diagnosis; and that self-identified transgenderists can reconfigure their bodies surgically with or without the diagnosis—are key to this project. Feinberg's complication of the significance of transition prevents a simple distinction between transsexuality and transgender that would consolidate those binaries of contemporary theory by aligning transgender and transsexuality with them: deliteralizing/literalizing; transgressive/reinscriptive. (This is crucial when we recall that these binaries stall the specifying of such narratives in the first place.) The problem in the representation of transgender's significance for transsexuality in cultural theory thus far has been precisely this tendency to be neat, the urge to avoid the ambivalent overlap with transsexuality that I have suggested is transgender. For if by its detractors transgender is typically folded back into transsexuality (Raymond, for instance, reads transgender as "a repackaging of the old gender roles" she criticized in transsexuality),[47] transgender's defenders can end up inadvertently erasing the specificity of transgender and transsexuality to similar effect—ironically even while they dramatize the absolute difference of these projects.

In her essay "Transcending and Transgendering: Male-to-Female Transsexuals, Dichotomy, and Diversity," for example, Ann Bolin contrasts transsexuality's conventional binary gendered past with the promise of a brave new transgendered binary-free future. Where "[t]en years ago ... transsexualism supported the binary gender schema," "[t]he transgenderist harbors great potential either to deactivate gender or to create in the future the possibility of 'supernumerary' genders as social categories no longer based on biology."[48] As Bolin's title suggests, transgender comes to stand quite precisely for diversity, transsexuality for dichotomy. In other words, transgender gets to play the postmodern second term (deliteralizing, transgressive) that puts in question transsexuality's outdated modernism (literalizing, reinscriptive) simply by following it. This form of differentiation in effect serves to specify neither transsexuality nor transgender. First, reading transsexuality as history ignores the ways in which transsexuality is very much an ongoing narrative (vide the most recent autobiographies); it does nothing for transsexuality's *presence* to read transgender as transsexuality's putative demise. Second, rendering transgender a symbol for a postmodern future does nothing to show how transgender has been historically embodied and lived by transgendered subjects (vide Feinberg). Such chrono-troping of transgender renders transgender equivalent to this moment that surely—as a moment (post-postmodernism? after the "fin" of the millennium?)—must pass. Will we not then be left to discard transgender in looking for the next transgressive thing? In sum it seems clear that for transgender studies to concretize these trajectories in the midst of theory's universalization of trans, transgender's relation to transsexuality cannot be explained with so neat and evolutionary a narrative.

Six years after its formulation, Stone's posttranssexuality—though key for spurring transgender as a movement—with its suggestion of an "after" to transsexuality for these reasons appears more troubling. Even though a "post" prefix is supposed to signify an interrogation into rather than a simple negation of what follows, implicit in "post" is always the notion of a throwing off, a departure from, and some element of dismissal of, its suffix. (Consider, for instance, postfeminism, which Stone unfortunately invokes as companion piece to posttranssexuality.) Fundamental to posttranssexuality is the belief that political subjectivity for transsexuals requires not simply a revision but a refusal of sexual difference—of what has been transsexuality's very purpose: passing, belonging, attaining realness in one's gender identity. In Stone's posttranssexuality there is no space for transsexuality as a progressive narrative—for continuing to value belonging, for an ongoing desire for sexed realness and coherent embodiment: precisely the desire for a sexed place that galvanizes transsexuality's narrative in the first place. In similar vein the current campaign to remove gender identity disorder entirely from DSM does not consider that, for some transsexuals, gender identity disorder may be experienced precisely as a disorder, a physically embodied dis-ease or dysphoria that dis-locates the self from bodily home and to which sex reassignment *does* make all the difference. Stone urges transsexuals to deploy their transsexuality to refigure the binary of sexual difference, to use that position "outside the binary oppositions of gendered discourse . . . to speak from outside the boundaries of gender."[49] Yet it may be because transsexual narratives originate in an unhomely relation to sexual difference that makes publicly claiming that "outside" home such a fraught act. While "outside" may be spoken from occasionally, for those whose very purpose is sexed *assignment* its continued occupation may be intrinsically paradoxical. Even transgendered narratives such as Feinberg's elucidate how uninhabitable is sexed dislocation.

While I value the possibilities for affiliation transgender has brought (between queers, feminists, and the "gender community"), I am still skeptical about what that "post" in posttranssexuality signifies. I continue to find unrealistic—and question the political implications of—claims that somatic transitions project gender identity beyond the body in a way that reveals that sex does not matter. That transgender as much as transsexual personal accounts continue to center on sexed crossings is, in my mind, a sure sign of the ongoing centrality of sexual difference in our world: a marker of the limits of its refigurability, and as a consequence of many subjects' yearning to locate in a stable position at least at some point in relation to this difference. Recognizing this sign need not constitute an arrest of politics, however; rather, it may lay the foundation of a new one. This "politics of home" would analyze the persistence of sexual difference for organizing identity categories. It would highlight the costs to the subject of not being clearly locatable in relation to sexual difference. Above all, it would not disavow the value of belonging as the basis for livable identity. The practical applications for such a politics of home are immediate, multiple, and, indeed, transformative. They might include, for instance: enlisting the binary of sexed assignment to argue for total health insurance coverage for sex reassignment; using the state's own insistence on sexed belonging to argue for the right to it of those subjects currently denied it—the right of those who change sex to also change their birth certificates so that they may legally live, work, marry, and die in their reassigned sex. In the United Kingdom none of these latter are yet possible; in the United States, although reassigned sex is legally recognized, sexed belonging is undermined in other, subtle ways—the denial of child custody to transsexual parents for instance. In pushing past a transsexual narrative ("post"), in ceding our claims to sexed location, we relinquish what we do not yet have: the recognition of our sexed realness; acceptance as men and women; fundamentally, the right to gender homes.

That the figure emerging in debates within as much as around transgender is so often that of border-crossing reveals that the stakes of location and movement in transition (of all kinds) are high. Perhaps the ambivalence in that cliché about home may provide a productive tension for the current transgender moment, a way for us to negotiate the real differences between our trajectories at the same time as we widen transgender into a methodological field. That there is no place *like* home—home is where we long to belong; there is no place better than home—conveys the value of realness and belonging. As Odysseus's journey classically illustrates, the point of every narrative is, after all, to return home. (And if every narrative is driven by home, what would a narrative be without one?) That there is *no place* like home, however—home doesn't exist; there is no place that is home—recognizes that home is, on some level, always a place we make up, that belonging is ultimately mythic—for all of us perhaps unreachable without some act of sweet imagination. The positions of man and woman are indeed not free of fabrication, are never given facts. But, for some, acknowledgment of this fictional investment makes desire for their locations no less powerful.

I first heard Feinberg speak in the late eighties when I was presenting on a panel on butch/femme desire. At the end of our presentations Feinberg stood up from within the audience of butch and femme lesbians to offer a comment, hir flat chest, hir masculinized face, and above all hir deep voice drawing hir difference out from theirs (ours). Who is this gay man? I thought. For even in this space, surrounded by the gender difference of other butches, there seemed something both more substantial and yet unassimilable about what I thought for sure was hir maleness.

Last summer I went with another transsexual man to hear Feinberg read from hir new *Transgender Warriors*. As we squeezed ourselves into the small Bleecker Street bookstore packed with an all-women crowd, our voices thick and low as we tried to find space, I was conscious of our difference (our maleness). Before beginning Feinberg spoke of battling illness; and indeed s/he looked tired. Hir face was drawn, hir body slender—almost frail. Yet, as always, hir reading was inspiring, hir voice resonant and strong, its difference again brought into relief, now by others who asked hir questions at the end. From the other side of the mirror I became much more aware that perception of the other's location is above all a question of where you're looking from. The primary effect of an exchange of looks (and indeed a shift in homes) is to keep turning over your own freshly firmed grounds.

> In photography there are no unexplained shadows.
> —August Sander, poster advertising photography exhibition, London Underground, May 1997

epilogue

Transsexuality in Photography—Fielding the Referent

Below the final photograph in Mario Martino's autobiography the caption reads: "Emergence accomplished, at last I'm free to live as I wish and to tell my story." Showing a man with full beard and pipe writing at a desk, the photograph illustrates this "emergence" as man and autobiographer. The pipe and pen serve as evidence for the life as a man and the story, synechdoches for the body and the narrative that substantiate both aspects of Martino's "freedom." Yet the autobiography's preface reveals this freedom is circumscribed. We learn that "Mario Martino" is a pseudonym, the real authorial subject "clinging to a hope of anonymity" behind it because, as he writes, "[t]he merciless shadows of contempt and tragedy still fall on transsexuals."[1] This tension between revelation and concealment, between emerging from the shadow of a hidden gendered self to shelter under the shadow of a disguised written self, is also captured in the photograph. Shot from an awkward angle to the rear of the subject's right shoulder, the portrait masks Martino's identity as it evidences his manhood. In testimony to the truth of the posttransitioned sex

208 Epilogue: Transsexuality in Photography

Emergence accomplished, at last I'm free to live as I wish and to tell my story. FROM *EMERGENCE: A TRANSSEXUAL AUTO-BIOGRAPHY* BY MARIO MARTINO WITH HARRIET. COPYRIGHT © 1977 BY MARIO MARTINO WITH HARRIET. REPRINTED WITH PERMISSION OF CROWN PUBLISHERS, INC.

of the female-to-male transsexual that yet doesn't reveal its subject, the photograph places most of the face out of the reader's line of vision while positioning beard and pipe prominently within it.

Autobiography and photography, notes Timothy Dow Adams in an issue of *Modern Fiction Studies* devoted to their intersection, are equally haunted by the presence of the referent.[2] Both appear to represent their subject in a strikingly unmediated fashion; both appear to reveal the real. Nevertheless, as forms of representation, both are not the subject itself but its imaging, reproductions of the referent. Occupying similar ground between referentiality and representation, transsexuality might be conceived as a parallel "form." As a transformation of the material body, transsexuality is inextricably hooked into the register of the real. Yet as this corporeal reconstruction is made possible though narrative and, indeed, as the transsexual self must be represented before it is realized in the flesh, transsexuality is equally bound to representation, dependent on its symbolization to be real. Photographs of transsexuals appearing in transsexual autobiography—an overlaying of three forms of representation that yet cannot do without the referent—triple our sense of the presence of the literal. If the theoretical figuration of transgender has left out the ways in which transgender is literally embodied and lived, photographs of transsexuals in the autobiographies promise, even more than the texts themselves, to recover what has been transubstantiated.

And yet the referentiality of transsexuality proves particularly hard to capture in photography. For if the aim of transsexual reassignment is to erase the visible markers of transsexuality from the body, to erase the trace of the former sex so as to leave the body unremarkably resexed, how can transsexuality as such be represented through the medium of the photograph? Photographs of transsexuals are situated on a tension between revealing and concealing transsexuality. Their primary function is to expose the transsexual body; yet how to achieve this when transsexuality on the body is that which by definition is to be concealed? While the intersection of these forms may provide a veritable pile-up of the referent, catching transsexuality as referent itself requires some fielding.

The effect of photographs in any autobiography, transsexual autobiographies included, is immediately referential. Autobiographical photographs serve to embody the subject of the narrative. This is the real body of the autobiographer, they declare; the text you read refers to this subject you see here. Even in the most willfully anti-representational of autobiographies, *Roland Barthes by Roland Barthes,* the photographs of Barthes appearing in the text work to override Barthes's fragmenting of his self into a medley of writerly codes, underscoring instead the consubstantiality of the subject in the represented body.[3] In spite of the writing's antithetical pull, the photographs establish Barthes as a continuous, unified, and above all real (that is, existing, embodied, and not merely textual) subject.

The scene of writing in *Roland Barthes by Roland Barthes* would seem to provide an archetypal poststructuralist description of the subject: that is, not only can writing not simply refer to the subject but subjectivity itself is an effect of signification. This conception of the subject as nonreferential is encapsulated in Barthes's famous question: "Do I not know that, *in the field of the subject, there is no referent?*"[4] This question would render impossible the book's very status as autobiography. For if there is no referent in the field of the subject, then autobiography cannot—as can no form of representation—represent or refer to the self. However, by reading *Roland Barthes by Roland Barthes* alongside Barthes's next and final work, *Camera Lucida*, Paul John Eakin has shown that the last stages of Barthes's thought were very precisely a quest for the referent in the field of the subject.[5] Barthes conducted this quest through photography, begun as we have already noted with the inclusion of photographs in *Roland Barthes by Roland Barthes* and culminating in his "reflections on photography," *Camera Lucida*. Eakin summarizes the substance of *Camera Lucida*—the fact that, as an essay on photography, its subject *is* substance: "In the field of the lens, we might say, there is always a referent, and Barthes beholds in photography the truth that these referents have really existed: 'Every photograph is a certificate of presence.' "[6] Barthes presents photography as a form that overrides the equivocation around the referent in autobiography; the former book's fetishistic question ("Do I not know that," etc.) is recast into an unequivocal assertion about the existence of the referent and the capacity of photography to capture it: "It is reference," he now writes, "which is the founding order of Photography" (*CL* 77). According to *Camera Lucida* the photograph doesn't simply authenticate the referent in the most unmediated fashion; the photograph is in fact "never distinguished from its referent (from what it represents), or at least it is not *immediately or generally* distinguished from its referent" (*CL* 5). The photograph appears as the referent. Thus, Barthes writes, "the Photograph . . . has something tautological about it"; identical to the referent, in representing it, the "sign" appears to disappear (*CL* 5). In photography the medium becomes invisible, and only "the referent adheres" (*CL* 6).

With three exceptions, all of the photographs in *Camera Lucida* take their subject as the human form; they are studies of bodies and faces. And in the writing of this essay Barthes's thought repeatedly follows this same trajectory: from photograph to subject to body. In pursuing the referent Barthes consistently ends up with the body. For instance: "Photography's inimitable feature . . . is that someone has seen the referent (even if it is a matter of objects) in *flesh and blood*, or again, *in person*. Photography, moreover, began historically, as an art of the Person: of identity, of civil status, of what we might call, in all senses of the term, the body's *formal-*

ity" (*CL* 79). In the photographic "field" of the subject, we might say, the referent (what the camera seeks to evidence) is the body. And if Barthes turned to photography for "solace when the austere tenets of poststructuralist theory about the subject came into conflict with the urgent demands of private experience," as Eakin so finely argues,[7] the solace he searches for in a style less and less mediated by theory and more and more immediately personal, is his recently dead mother. Sifting through photographs of her, he looks for her flesh and blood *being*, a way to fill the absence of her body. From structuralism to poststructuralism to this signing off with the referent, the personal, and the search for his mother's presence (mater, matter): is there not something of an allegory in the final trajectory of Barthes's writings, a story for our specific theoretical time?

In the field of the transsexual subject the photograph functions as an incarnation; the photograph appears co-natural with the body, and may even begin as more referential of the self than the body. Inasmuch as the immediate purpose of transsexuality is to make real the subject's true gender on the body, the visual media are highly valued, for they promise (like transition itself) to make visible that which begins as imperceptible—there but underexposed, we might say. With less mediation than writing between signifier and soma, the visual media realize the image of the "true" self that is originally only apparitional. Katherine Cummings recounts how as a teenager beginning to crossdress, she constructs a self-timing mechanism out of cotton thread and a wind-up key for a cheap Kodak camera, allowing her to take self-portraits. The photographs serve to provide "some concrete evidence of my rare moments of femininity": "Cumbersome and slow but for the first time I could make permanent images of my stolen moments."[8] A painter, Erica Rutherford paints self-portraits based on photographs she first takes of herself dressed as a woman—also concretizations of an imperceptible self. Like Cummings's photographs these portraits begin by envisioning the woman Rutherford wishes to become and are gradually transformed as she transitions into a record of that becoming. In one photograph that appears in her autobiography, a painted self-portrait is situated behind the photographic Rutherford. In the painting the seated figure is feminized through body contour, posture, and clothing, but the face is featureless—a blank space as undetailed by the feminine as the still-masculine face of the photographic Rutherford seated before it. Yet the photographic Rutherford repeats the conven-

FROM ERICA RUTHERFORD, *NINE LIVES: THE AUTOBIOGRAPHY OF ERICA RUTHERFORD* (CHARLOTTETOWN, P.E.I., CANADA: RAGWEED, 1993). REPRINTED WITH PERMISSION OF RAGWEED PRESS

tionally feminine pose of the pictorial Rutherford (knees jammed, legs tightly crossed, hands clasped), so that the painted self-portrait appears as a model for the transsexual body to follow, this self triply textualized—a painting within a photograph within the autobiography—nevertheless reflecting more of the real transsexual self than the subject's visible body. For both Cummings and Rutherford the self-portrait is a blueprint for the transsexual subject in transition: like the photographs in the autobiographies for readers, visual means of making the transsexual's gender real.

The self-portrait (whether written or pictorial) appears to represent the subject in the present moment; this appearance is deceptive, however, for writing and painting can only ever re-present the moment in multiple moments after the fact. Nevertheless, freezing the representation at that instant (or the subsequent split second), photography is the most instantaneous medium. It is this apparent synchronization of image with the object's presence that produces the photograph's referential, tautological texture: the subject was actually there (is still there) in that instant of the photograph. As the original body for the transsexual is that which is to be changed and left behind, however, photographs of transsexuals from the past represent that which is blatantly no longer there: an absented presence. In transsexual autobiographies past photographs are arranged with present ones to form a narrative of the changing body up to the present. The effect is double: as narrative, photographs demand that we concede that transsexuality makes a thorough difference to the body and yet—part of the autobiography—that we discover consistent and continuous identity in that very place of alterity. Four shots appearing on a single page of *Katherine's Diary: The Story of a Transsexual* clearly perform this double function. The photographs convey the empirical differences between male and female personae, John and Katherine: John stalwart and squinting in the sun in crisp white naval uniform; Katherine, wide-eyed, slinky, and seductive in a black dress. And yet, in the way that these differently gendered personae are interspersed on the page (Katherine/John, John/Katherine), the photographs insist on continuity in spite of change. The chronology of dates in the captions asks us to read the photographs across the page into a narrative of transsexual transition and to pay close attention to the differences of their detail: "Katherine at seventeen dressing behind locked doors, 1952"—posing gawkily with rather heavy make-up—graduates to, simply, "Katherine, aged twenty-six, 1961"; the implication of the elision of a descriptive being that she is no longer dressing as Katherine but simply *being* her. Indeed, the low-cut top in the final photograph draws the eye to the beginnings of a breast cleavage, and later shots in *Katherine's Diary* reveal a progressively feminizing body by progressively revealing more of this body (via the backless dress to the bikini). Voluptuous in her bikini, Katherine is so "there" in a later photograph, "In the raging surf, Christchurch, New Zealand," so evident in her reassigned sex, that she no longer even requires naming.

Why *these* images? What of the self does the transsexual autobiographer consider representable? The question is especially poignant for the transsexual when s/he no longer *is* that self, when presenting the photo-

214 Epilogue: Transsexuality in Photography

(1) Katherine at seventeen, dressing behind locked doors, 1952; (2) John aged eighteen, defending the nation, 1954; (3) Sub-Lieutenant Cummings, RANR, 1960; (4) Katherine aged twenty-six, 1961. FROM KATHERINE CUMMINGS, *KATHERINE'S DIARY: THE STORY OF A TRANSSEXUAL* (PORT MELBOURNE, VICTORIA: HEINEMANN, 1992). REPRINTED WITH PERMISSION OF KATHERINE CUMMINGS

In the raging surf, Christchurch, New Zealand, 1975. FROM KATHERINE CUMMINGS, *KATHERINE'S DIARY: THE STORY OF A TRANSSEXUAL* (PORT MELBOURNE, VICTORIA: HEINEMANN, 1992). REPRINTED WITH PERMISSION OF KATHERINE CUMMINGS

graph within the autobiography is (more than the autobiography even) an act of incarnating what one is not. How to represent in the visual the body to which one's self no longer (indeed never) refers? Captions clue us in to reasons for the choice of photographs. They reveal the trace of the subject's re-vision, what s/he sees in looking back at him- or herself. In Paul Hewitt's *A Self-Made Man: The Diary of a Man Born in a Woman's Body*, the author's caption, "I was already acting the role of the protective brother," brings out as masculine the bodily posture of the ambiguous child sitting on a tree stump—one arm around twin sister, the other propped on a firmly parted knee. Martino's "My ambiguity was evident at an early age" has the same effect: again, as in the narrative but more so because photography is so evidentiary, "I was (already) there!" Challenging the evidence of the transsexual photograph (in effect: "no *he* was not!"), Bernice L. Hausman finds the caption unsubstantiated by the

Epilogue: Transsexuality in Photography

I was already acting the role of the protective brother.   PAUL HEWITT WITH JANE WARREN, *A SELF-MADE MAN: THE DIARY OF A MAN BORN IN A WOMAN'S BODY* (LONDON: HEADLINE, 1995). REPRINTED WITH PERMISSION OF PAUL HEWITT

image; she writes of this and another of Martino's photographs ("Boy's Face in Banana Curls"), "For [Martino], these pictures undeniably document her childhood masculinity (as the captions confirm), yet both merely offer the reader images of a child whose sex is largely indicated by clothing. A three-year old child with short hair is generally somewhat asexual; that is why children's, even infants', clothes are so conspicuously sex-coded. Some children maintain this sexlessness until puberty."[9] Through the minimizing force of that "merely" and the universalizing impact of that "generally" (still putting the transsexual in the dock), Hausman abrogates not only the specific evidence of the photograph for Martino but the knot of pain and contradiction entailed in representing one's transsexual past in this most unmediated of forms. If Martino's captions cope with the pain of return to the pretransition body by incorporating the photograph and smoothing over the difference, April Ashley's, for instance, perform its severing, a detachment of the unwanted past that leaves the difference starkly remarkable. Representing herself as a woman, April, Ashley's captions summarize the photographic event: "The blind leading the blind: in Rome with Sarah Churchill, 1964." But

My ambiguity was evident at an early age. FROM *EMERGENCE: A TRANSSEXUAL AUTOBIOGRAPHY* BY MARIO MARTINO WITH HARRIET. COPYRIGHT © 1977 BY MARIO MARTINO WITH HARRIET. REPRINTED WITH PERMISSION OF CROWN PUBLISHERS, INC.

when the boyhood self is pictured, invariably, he is formally and doggedly named, disowned by Ashley the autobiographer, as though his body were really another's, as though this representation were too not-me to be owned: "V.E. Day, May 1945, George Jamieson at St. Theresa's Primary School, Liverpool"; "George Jamieson, aged thirteen, with brother Ivor (nine) and sister Marjorie (seven) at home, Norris Green."

And indeed, when we turn from April to this boy, is George Jamieson not an other? For when the photograph is not a likeness, when it no longer represents the self, surely it ought to be said that then it is not a portrait. In every photograph, writes Barthes, because of the apparent presence of the referent, there is "that rather terrible thing . . . the return of the dead" (*CL* 9). Photographs of a pretransition self threaten to incarnate a "dead" self that one is not. In the case of Leslie Feinberg, as a subject whose transition doubles back, this reincarnation is twice over for hir parents:

The blind leading the blind: in Rome with Sarah Churchill, 1964. FROM DUNCAN FALLOWELL AND APRIL ASHLEY, *APRIL ASHLEY'S ODYSSEY* (LONDON: CAPE, 1982). REPRINTED WITH PERMISSION OF ERIC GLOSS LTD.

When I first entered a sex change program a decade ago, in order to avoid embarrassment my parents disposed of all pictures of me, a little girl or young woman growing up with the tenseness of puberty etched on my face. When I later took back control of my body after four years of being on the program, my parents discarded all the pictures of me living as a man.[10]

Most representational of forms, talisman of the subject, the photograph *must* be seen to represent the subject. Its spectral power is huge. The haunting feeling of at once self-recognition and self-alienation we all experience when we see ourselves in the photograph (both "So that is me!" and at the same time "That cannot be me!") is redoubled for the transsexual looking at the pretransition portrait—that doppelgänger of

Epilogue: Transsexuality in Photography 219

(1) V. E. Day, May 1945, George Jamieson at St. Theresa's Primary School, Liverpool; (2) George Jamieson, aged thirteen, with brother Ivor (nine) and sister Marjorie (seven) at home, Norris Green. FROM DUNCAN FALLOWELL AND APRIL ASHLEY, *APRIL ASHLEY'S ODYSSEY* (LONDON: CAPE, 1982). REPRINTED WITH PERMISSION OF ERIC GLASS LTD.

the subject that is yet not a double. In the "return of the dead," surely, the particular fear at work is that the image is more real than the subject; that the photograph *is* the referent. Is there not an unconscious fear that (like a legendary encounter with a self-portrait in the attic) an encounter with the image one is not might change the body back to what "nature" decrees it should have been? In the case of the theatrical Coccinelle, most famous of Paris's *travestis*, the way to avoid such an exchange is to "kill" the image—a killing that is not of just an image but of that "dead" self itself:

> When I got up, I had only one thought—to destroy Jacques Dufresnoy, who had stolen my real "ego," to get rid of this interloper who had made me assume a false outer covering. On the chest of drawers I saw a photograph of myself—myself as a boy. How revolting! I snatched up the frame, threw it down and trampled on it. Pieces of glass were scattered all over the floor. I picked up the photograph and tore it up. . . . Then I opened a drawer and took out a whole pile of photographs and negatives dealing with my childhood, my family and my life as an effeminate boy. Oh how I hated him, that creature of a sex that was not really mine! . . . I set to and destroyed them all. . . . In the end there wasn't a single photograph of me left in the house. I had burned them all.[11]

In fact, one photograph of this "false outer covering" boy remains. Interloping his way appropriately as an inset onto the cover of Coccinelle's "interview" with Mario Costa, "Jacques" appears as a melancholic pierrot-type figure, as *himself* barely substantial. Within the text, by contrast, there is a mass of photographs of the very substantial Coccinelle next to him—the true self within. This thick wad of mostly nude pictures of the Bardot-look-alike Coccinelle—Coccinelle in the bath, Coccinelle in the shower, Coccinelle stepping out of a mink at her bar ("Strictly Adult Sale": to be read only at the front desk of the British Library under the librarian's scrutinizing eye)—is in fact the text's raison d'être. The function of the photographs is to reveal all; the camera, they suggest, cannot lie: "An impromptu strip-tease, beautiful, slender, and completely feminine, Coccinelle proves in this delightful sequence . . . that she can face the camera from any angle. Proof beyond doubt of this living miracle of Man Made Woman."[12] Is this not realness? the photographs demand. And is not realness a turn-on: what everyone *desires*?

If the photograph insists on itself as documentary evidence, who is to decide if the referent is "there" or not? Hausman's reading of Martino

COVER, MARIO COSTA, *"COCCINELLE": REVERSE SEX*, TRANS. JULES J. BLOCK (LONDON, CHALLENGE, N.D.)

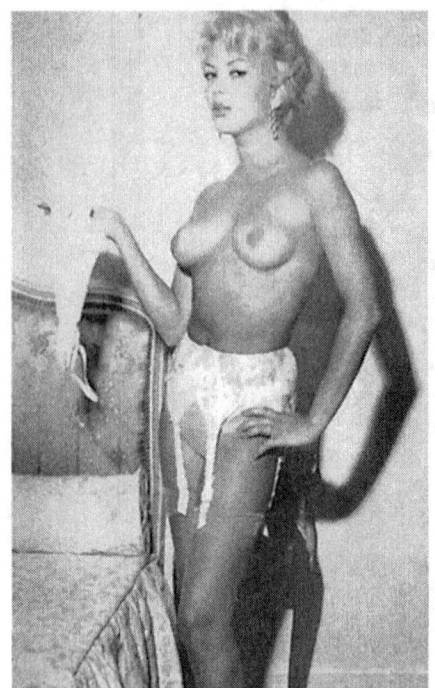 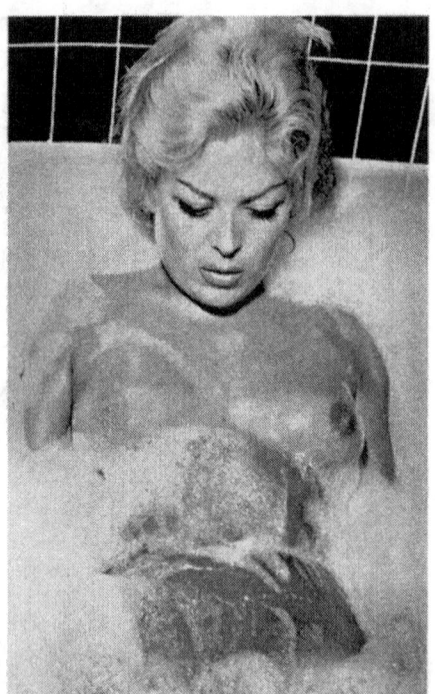

FROM MARIO COSTA, *"COCCINELLE": REVERSE SEX*, TRANS. JULES J. BLOCK (LONDON, CHALLENGE, N.D.)

brings into focus (it's a self-focusing we might say, the critic's lens turning on itself) the problematics of *reading* the transsexual in the photograph. Barthes suggests that "because of its evidential power" (*CL* 106) the photograph in fact cannot be read: "It is precisely in this *arrest* of interpretation that the Photograph's certainty resides" (*CL* 107). The more evidentiary the photograph, the less of a reading it requires—or allows: "it is in proportion to its certainty that I can say nothing about [the] photograph" (*CL* 107). Some photographs of transsexuals blatantly refuse a reading. Of two pretransition shots of Caroline Cossey as Barry, first as a child and then at sixteen (next to a posttransition shot of Cossey as "Tula" as her model self was better known, shown in the Smirnoff campaign whose slogan—once Cossey was outed as transsexual—itself was fabulously literalized); of images of Raymond Thompson, first tracing his childhood, then three years into hormone treatment at nineteen; because of the certainty in my eyes of what they evidence (the certainty that Barry is already really Caroline—the combinative effect of those eyes, those lips, and that nose; the conviction that Ray has never

As a young boy with a horrendous short-back-and-sides that did me no favours. FROM CAROLINE COSSEY, *MY STORY* (WINCHESTER, MASS.: FABER, 1992). REPRINTED WITH PERMISSION OF CAROLINE COSSEY

In London at sixteen. FROM CAROLINE COSSEY, *MY STORY* (WINCHESTER, MASS.: FABER, 1992). REPRINTED WITH PERMISSION OF CAROLINE COSSEY

been anyone else), I find I have literally nothing to say. For do they not speak the transsexual's true gender for themselves?

More than the written text of transsexual autobiographies, the photographs bring into relief the reader's gaze. Asking us to consider what nuances of gender we see in these images in looking at the transsexual, they also ask: how do *we* look?—where "look," as Teresa de Lauretis has suggested in the context of lesbian and gay film theory, should be heard as both transitive and intransitive verb.[13] That is, how do we look at the other and what look do our own bodies cast to the world? How is our reading of the transsexual invested in and produced by own gendered and sexual subject positioning, our own identifications and desires? Photographs of the transsexual, particularly of the transsexual in transition, push *us* up against the limits of gendered representation: the limits of what about gender we can consign to representation, of what we can process as identity in the visual. A series of photographs from *Second Serve* charting Dick Raskind's transformation into Renée Richards captures the subject's body in the most transitional moments of

The famous Smirnoff shot. REPRINTED WITH PERMISSION OF INTERNATIONAL DISTILLERS & VINTNERS LTD.

(1) Still pinning hopes on Father Christmas, aged 7; (2) Rebel with a cause, aged 13; (3) At 16, a precious picture of early days with Loretta (aged 21). FROM RAYMOND THOMPSON WITH KITTY SEWELL, *WHAT TOOK YOU SO LONG? A GIRL'S JOURNEY TO MANHOOD* (LONDON: PENGUIN, 1995). REPRINTED WITH PERMISSION OF RAYMOND THOMPSON

her transition, during which the subject's gender is quite indeterminate, when Richards appears, as she writes in her autobiography, as a "man-woman," "a hermaphroditic spirit."[14] There's a precarious androgyny to her body and face in these central images that makes it difficult to read her as either a man or a woman, that makes it difficult to read her alto-

Ray, aged 19. FROM RAYMOND THOMPSON WITH KITTY SEWELL, *WHAT TOOK YOU SO LONG? A GIRL'S JOURNEY TO MANHOOD* (LONDON: PENGUIN, 1995). REPRINTED WITH PERMISSION OF RAYMOND THOMPSON

gether. If the photographs before this series evidence Richards as a man and those after as a woman, do these intermediate photographs represent her at her most transsexual? What does transsexuality in fact look like? Photographs that establish gendered realness do not *reveal* transsexuality, for in them the subject passes as nontranssexual. The problem of reading the transsexual in the photograph heightens the tension around reading and passing that inhabits all transsexual representation.

Bettina Rheims's photographs of French male-to-female transsexual Kim Harlow engage exactly this problematic.[15] Rheims's photographs, together with Harlow's own autobiographical fragments, make up the brief text, *Kim*, but although Harlow is listed as the text's first author, Rheims is *Kim*'s real author. Her photographs are stylized and finished while Harlow's writings have an abbreviated quality (indeed, the note opening the text states that Harlow "was unable to finish her story" as

(1) Featured on the cover of a Long Island newspaper supplement, September 1973; (2, *inset*) With Andy in 1973. FROM RENÉE RICHARDS WITH JOHN AMES, *SECOND SERVE: THE RENÉE RICHARDS STORY* (NEW YORK: STEIN, 1983)

AIDS "cut short this work, her work" [5]). And of Kim the photographic subject, Rheims is sole author, her images producing the transsexual as model-perfect, killer-sexy. Kim is presented wearing little, but just enough: plunging-front sequined and cutaway fishnet bodysuits, lace bra, panties, stockings, and suspenders; these clothes serve to reveal perfect breasts and, in one photograph, the top of a perfect crotch.

Yet herein lies the problem for Rheims. Kim is so real, so passing, how to represent her as a transsexual? She won't reveal herself as a boy. That is, not only does her "boyness" not show on her transsexual body, Rheims notes that Kim "had always refused to show me photos taken of herself when she was still Alexandre" (24). Rheims attempts to make legible Kim's transsexuality, therefore, by restaging her transsexual history; except that, starting out with Kim's gendered realness as her representational material, Rheims can only create her as transsexual by moving back from female to male. In Harlow's description, "Bettina does tell my story but backwards. First you see me looking really feminine and sensual, going out, walking around in a big hotel, then in my room in a négligée, in my lingerie, then naked, then bit by bit you see me gradually lose my composure and cry. You see me taking off my make-up and at the end I'm dressed as a boy" (16–19). From woman to "boy"—notably, not "man": the transsexual narrative proves irreversible; in spite of the implication of the photographic sequence, it cannot "go either way." Indeed, do not the last shots of Kim cross-dressed as "male" show a still-beautiful, sexy (now boyish) *woman*?

Even so, there is something in this reversal of the narrative that sublimates transsexuality even as its purpose is to capture it. Alexandre has *passed*; he is not *there* in the photographs. As Harlow notes: "The pictures are very beautiful—they're not autobiographical, but they all have something in them that I've lived through. When I saw them I said to myself that they were a kind of sublimation of everything I'd experienced, it was really . . . I can really see myself in them. A wonderful gift from Bettina" (8; ellipses in original). Given Harlow's realness as a woman and her refusal to show past photographs of Alexandre, Rheims must resort to *her* imaginary in order to represent Kim as a transsexual, as Alexandre. Reversing the narrative and representing the somatic transitions of transsexuality as a quick change of clothes—from difficult body narrative to palatable gender performative—Rheims's imaginary sublimates the real

FROM KIM HARLOW/BETTINA RHEIMS, *KIM*, TRANS. PAUL GOULD (MUNICH: KEHAYOFF VERLAG, 1994).

experience of transsexuality: the referent of transsexuality is elided (hence, surely, Kim's ellipses) in Rheims's recreation. Even in her fictionalization of Kim as Alexandre, Rheims fails to create a passing woman—a woman who passes successfully as a man.

The middle shots in the series are particularly disturbing. They represent Kim in the stages of reverse "transition." She faces the hotel bathroom mirror, her top now off and jewelry gone, her eye make-up streaking her face; remember, she notes crying during this scene. In some images, as she scoops her hair back, she tries to conceal her breasts. These gestures look as awkward as they sound: Kim appears uncomfortable, almost gawky. These central shots represent Kim at her least posed, most naked—her most "real." Yet as the camera would appear to capture the transsexual real, the mirror serves to displace it. Only in one photograph can we see its frame; but all seven "transition" pieces are shot of the reflection in the mirror, the specular image, and not of Kim, the referential subject. There are two clues: the radiator, which remains in the bottom right corner of every shot, including the one that reveals the mirror's frame (if Rheims had shot Kim directly in any of the others, the radiator would have appeared on the bottom left); and the fact that, in two of the shots, Rheims catches the subject's nonspecular arm within the photographic frame, a blur partially concealing the reflection. Rheims must have shot all these photographs from some point to the right of (the referential) Kim, focusing on the reflected image. As well as reversing the narrative, therefore, when this body is at its least posed and most expressive—at its most "real"—the mirror serves to refract our gaze and to displace the real transsexual. While Kim's beautiful transsexual body is the object of the camera's gaze throughout the book, the double in the mirror holds at bay the real subject without blocking our view, framing the transsexual in a doubled specularity that prevents her from returning the camera/viewer's look. Like Medusa's head in Perseus's shield, this sequence before the mirror suggests, in Rheims's photographs, the "real" transsexual can only be looked at and "captured" in her reflection, in the imaginary. The specular creates Kim as the object of our look (the mirror doesn't prevent our looking via the specular image), yet it dislocates and confuses its site of production, discouraging that all-important question: how do I look?

What does it mean to consign transsexuality to the imaginary, to sublimate its narrative to reversible performance and let slip its referent in this most referential of forms? Doubtless the strength of my response to these images of Kim has everything to do with how *I* look. My "fierce protectiveness" over Kim's body, as one colleague termed it after I gave a talk on the photographs, is admittedly a product of my identification with Kim: against the odds of my narrative, my identification with the "all-woman" Kim, and my corresponding anguish over that figure of the pretransition boy.[16] As transgender studies makes its entry into the academy, however, the two questions Rheims's photographs raise—how to represent transsexuality and who is representing transsexuality—are of massive general significance. The importance of sustaining the experience of transsexuality in the midst of theory's sublimation of what's real about this experience—and the concomitant question of whether transsexuality itself can reveal the strings behind the disappearance of the referent in theory—strike me as paramount.

Photographers Loren Cameron's and Del LaGrace's recent work intersect the autobiographical, the photographic, and transsexual representation in ways that contribute important responses to these questions. Cameron's *Body Alchemy: Transsexual Portraits*, as he writes, is "the first photodocumentation of transsexual men from within our community," and as such, a work documenting female-to-males by a female-to-male, his project is groundbreaking.[17] Presenting his subjects as looking "just like men" against the backdrop of their real-life situations ("Fellas"), Cameron sustains the value of gender realness. At the same time in his "Our Bodies" series, in the close-ups of surgical reconstruction, he conveys the material differences of the female-to-male body. But while Cameron lets us look at this referential difference, he also captures how we look. In his self-portraits in the "Distortion" series near the beginning of the book, Cameron's inscriptions of address to the viewer ("You're so exotic! May I take your photograph.... Do you have a penis?") literally frame the viewer's gaze, reflecting back, here, that look of fascination, objectification and desire s/he may cast. We can only look at the transsexual, then, if we look at how we look.

Del LaGrace's photographic work-in-progress of female-to-male Zachary Nataf similarly allows an encounter with the referentiality of transsexual experience while foregrounding point of view.[18] Like Kim this is a work designed to capture the transsexual in transition; but LaGrace's set-up with Nataf couldn't be more different from Rheims's with Harlow. As Nataf initiated the project, the transsexual's representation is self-authored: as LaGrace so nicely puts it, the work is Nataf's "visual transsexual autobiography." Seen together the photographs do indeed have the quality of a document or a record. Meeting every few

Epilogue: Transsexuality in Photography 231

FROM *BODY ALCHEMY: TRANSSEXUAL PORTRAITS* (SAN FRANCISCO, CLEIS, 1996). PHOTOGRAPH © LOREN CAMERON. REPRINTED WITH PERMISSION OF CLEIS PRESS, SAN FRANCISCO

months to capture the body in the process of its changing, photographer and subject preserve the narrative structure of Nataf's transsexuality. The photographs convey with scientific precision the actual somatic progressions entailed in Nataf's becoming a man: the changes in body contours, tissue structure, skin texture; and most recently his chest's recovery from surgery. Moreover, the photographer's investment in and identification with his transsexual subject is indicated in how much we get to see of Nataf's transitioning body. Nataf appears naked in many

 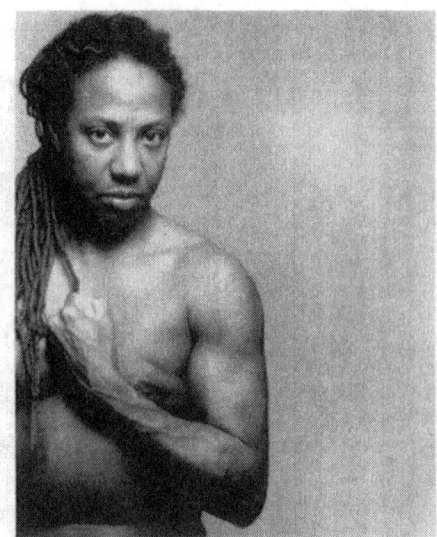

PHOTOGRAPHS BY DEL LAGRACE

images and is happy to let LaGrace in as close as he can get: a marker of the subject's absolute trust that LaGrace's regard, both as a transgendered subject himself and someone whose work over the past fifteen years has broadcast his desire for transgendered subjects, will carry how he—LaGrace—looks. (When LaGrace began taking the images, *she* was a "hermaphrodyke," now *he* identifies as an intersexual female-to-male; his analysis of the complex role played in his transition by this looking cogently suggests the essential role played in *all* transitions by representation.) Criss-crossed with his identification and desire, representing Nataf so intimately in every sense, LaGrace's photographs pass this trust on to their viewers; in their very revelation they demand that we continue its exchange.

What stands out in the series so far are the close-ups of Nataf's genitals. Nataf describes this focus as deliberately ethnographic, anthropometrical, its purpose to reveal graphically the difference of the transsexual body. And indeed, the primary effect of the startling detail of these images is to demand that the viewer take the full measure of the transsexual body—in this shot quite literally. In this regard for size, the photographs make knowing reference to a cultural tradition of phallicizing black male bodies, turning that history of racial fetishization in on itself (since Nataf's male body is evidently different, this representation interrupts that history) to challenge the fetishization of transsexual bodies. For while by no means identical or historically proportionate to the fetishization of black bodies, the fact that *trans* is simultaneously everywhere—subject of contemporary cultural projections—and nowhere—in reality absent, missing in the flesh—is the result of a similar fetishistic splitting between the subject and object of the look, a comparable dearth of self-representations in an abundance of representations of this body as other.[19] LaGrace and Nataf's project directly intervenes into that fetishization of trans by redistributing the look. The fact that Nataf's bodily revelations are his deliberate self-authoring and LaGrace's observation is participant blurs the difference between looking subject and seen object, and as a result the distinctness of the transsexual body emerges clearly into view without disavowal.

What remains of fetishism within the image—and the absolute focus on the genitals does constitute a deliberate attention to these parts apart from the rest of the body—remains in provocative affirmation of the transsexual's bodily difference. Paradoxical as this may seem, the close-up of the transsexual body works to close up the difference between

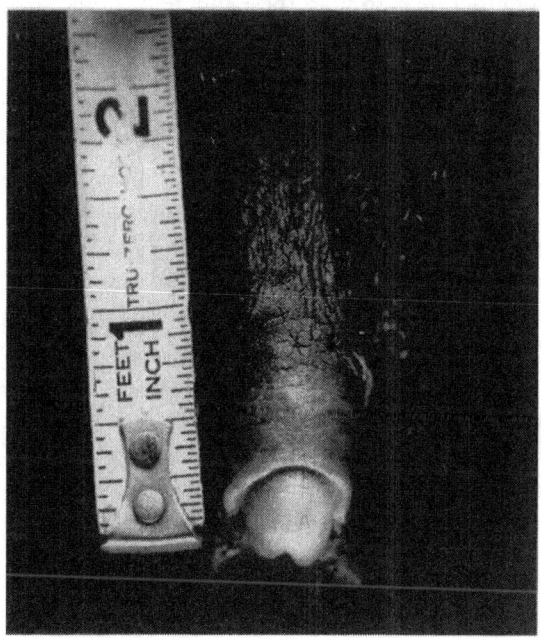

PHOTOGRAPH BY DEL LAGRACE

viewer and transsexual subject—not simply between LaGrace and Nataf but between Nataf and the viewer of the photograph. This dynamic of intimate looking is immediate and unmediated (LaGrace describes it as "physical"), almost—though not quite—beyond narrative: looking so closely at the photograph of this bodily difference, you cannot help but wonder first, surely, *what* you are looking at. You're looking at a body part, that much is clear. Yet what body part? Failing to recognize it, you must search for a reference point in the flesh you know best (your own), quickly envisioning how you look: how you look next to Nataf's body, alongside his body, even as his body. In this way, in its very representation of the adamantine difference of this flesh, the photograph draws you inexorably into its picture. Arresting your look—that is, not only holding your look but rooting it (locating it), it demands from *your* body a narrative: How do *you* look? What do you see here? And what does what you see here reveal about you?

For those unfamiliar with transsexual bodies, these shots of Nataf's clitoris-turning-penis certainly require a double-take. When I first showed these images, some in the audience not surprisingly at first thought Nataf already had a penis. And this, I think, is the ultimate achievement of these photographs: to hold these moments of its turning, to capture without sublimation and objectification the details of the transsexual's transition. Nataf's genitals reveal him as no longer female (there is no reading) but neither as a genetic male (there is no passing); rather they represent him as a transsexual man in the process of becoming. Capturing this flesh as the referent of his narrative, LaGrace's photographic field overturns the transubstantiation and, indeed, the very otherness of the transsexual body.

What needs to be sustained as we write transsexuality into theory is precisely the embodied specificity of the point of regard. Translating Adrienne Rich's politics of location into her poetics of location, Nancy K. Miller suggests that the autobiographical act, "one's own body"—what I understand as some kind of positioning of one's own body in the regarded picture—"can constitute an internal limit on discursive irresponsibility."[20] Taking her literally here, I blow my cover, and embody my narrative with this photograph.

Epilogue: Transsexuality in Photography

PHOTOGRAPH BY DEL LAGRACE

Introduction: On Transitions—Changing Bodies, Changing Narratives

1. Leslie Marmon Silko, *Ceremony* (New York: Penguin, 1992).
2. Philippe Lejeune, *On Autobiography*, ed. Paul John Eakin, trans. Katherine Leary (Minneapolis: Minnesota University Press, 1980), p. 132.
3. Lynne Segal, *Straight Sex: The Politics of Pleasure* (London: Virago, 1994), p. 228.
4. Janice Raymond, *The Transsexual Empire: The Making of the She-Male* (1979); reissued with a new introduction on transgender (New York: Teacher's College Press, 1994).
5. Dwight Billings and Thomas Urban, "The Socio-Medical Construction of Transsexualism: An Interpretation and Critique," *Social Problems* 29 (1982), reprinted in *Blending Genders: Social Aspects of Cross-Dressing and Sex-Changing*, ed. Richard Ekins and Dave King (London: Routledge, 1996), pp. 99, 112.
6. Bernice L. Hausman, *Changing Sex: Transsexualism, Technology, and the Idea of Gender* (Durham: Duke University Press, 1995).
7. Ibid., pp. 140, 110, 118.
8. Carroll Riddell, "Divided Sisterhood: A Critical Review of Janice Raymond's *The Transsexual Empire*" in *Blending Genders: Social Aspects of Cross-Dressing and Sex-Changing*, ed. Richard Ekins and Dave King, (London: Routledge, 1996), p. 189.
9. D. O. Cauldwell, "Psychopathia Transexualis," *Sexology* 16 (1949): 274–280.
10. Harry Benjamin, "Transvestism and Transsexualism," *International Journal of Sexology* 7 (1953): 12–14.
11. Harry Benjamin, *The Transsexual Phenomenon* (New York: Julian Press, 1966), p. 28.
12. Liz Hodgkinson, *Michael Née Laura* (London: Columbus, 1989).
13. Radclyffe Hall, *The Well of Loneliness* (1928; reprint, London: Virago, 1982).
14. Leslie Feinberg, *Stone Butch Blues: A Novel* (New York: Firebrand, 1993).

15. Elizabeth Grosz, *Volatile Bodies: Toward a Theory of Corporeal Feminism* (Bloomington: Indiana University Press, 1994), p. 3.

16. Cécile Lindsay, "Lyotard and the Postmodern Body," *L'Esprit Créatur* 31, no. 1 (1991): 33, cited in Julia Epstein, *Altered Conditions: Disease, Medicine, and Storytelling* (New York: Routledge, 1995), p. 180.

17. Somer Brodribb, *Nothing Mat(t)ers: A Feminist Critique of Postmodernism* (Melbourne, Australia: Spinifex, 1993), pp. 136, 143.

18. Marcia Ian, *Remembering the Phallic Mother: Psychoanalytic Modernism and the Fetish* (Ithaca: Cornell University Press, 1993), pp. 178, 185.

19. Carole-Anne Tyler, "The Supreme Sacrifice? TV, 'TV,' and the Renée Richards Story," *differences* 1, no. 3 (1989): 163; Catherine Millot, *Horsexe: An Essay on Transsexuality*, trans. Kenneth Hylton (Brooklyn: Autonomedia, 1990), p. 143; Marjorie Garber, *Vested Interests: Cross-Dressing and Cultural Anxiety* (New York: Routledge, 1992), p. 98; June L. Reich, "Genderfuck: The Law of the Dildo," *Discourse* 15, no. 1 (1992): 121.

20. Julia Epstein and Kristina Straub, eds., introduction, *BodyGuards: The Cultural Politics of Gender Ambiguity* (New York: Routledge, 1991), p. 11; Arthur and Marilouise Kroker, eds., introduction, *The Last Sex: Feminism and Outlaw Bodies* (New York: St. Martin's, 1993), p. 15; Judith Halberstam, "F2M: The Making of Female Masculinity," in *The Lesbian Postmodern*, ed. Laura Doan (New York: Columbia University Press, 1994), p. 212.

21. I owe this turn of phrase to Nancy K. Miller.

22. Eve Kosofsky Sedgwick and Adam Frank, "Shame in the Cybernetic Fold: Reading Silvan Tomkins," *Critical Inquiry* 21, no. 2 (1995): 511. Page numbers of further citations will appear directly in the text.

23. On the problematic of antiessentialist critiques, see, for instance: Teresa de Lauretis, "The Essence of the Triangle; or, Taking the Risk of Essentialism Seriously: Feminist Theory in Italy, the US, and Britain," *differences* 1, no. 2 (1989): 2–37, and Diana Fuss, *Essentially Speaking: Feminism, Nature and Difference* (New York: Routledge, 1989).

1. Judith Butler: Queer Feminism, Transgender, and the Transubstantiation of Sex

1. Eve Kosofsky Sedgwick, *Epistemology of the Closet* (Berkeley: California University Press, 1990), p. 16.

2. Eve Kosofsky Sedgwick, *Between Men: English Literature and Male Homosocial Desire* (New York: Columbia University Press, 1985).

3. Sedgwick, *Epistemology of the Closet*, pp. 37–38.

4. Eve Kosofsky Sedgwick, *Tendencies* (Durham: Duke University Press, 1993), p. 256.

5. Sedgwick, *Tendencies*, p. 9. Judith Butler emphasizes instead the contrast between Sedgwick's theoretical formulations on sexuality versus gender and her reading practice: "Although Sedgwick appears to defend this methodological separation [of gender and sexuality], her own readings often make rich and brilliant use of the problematic of cross-gendered identification and cross-sexual

identification" (Judith Butler, "Against Proper Objects," *differences* 6, nos. 2/3 [1994]: 24, n. 8).

6. Kobena Mercer, "Looking for Trouble," in *The Lesbian and Gay Studies Reader*, ed. Henry Abelove, Michèle Aina Barale, David Halperin (New York: Routledge, 1993), pp. 350–359; Kobena Mercer, "Reading Racial Fetishism: The Photographs of Robert Mapplethorpe," in *Fetishism as Cultural Discourse*, ed. Emily Apter and William Pietz (Ithaca: Cornell University Press, 1991), pp. 307–330; Kobena Mercer, "Skin Head Sex Thing: Racial Difference and the Homoerotic Imaginary," in *How Do I Look? Queer Film and Video*, ed. Bad Object-Choices (Seattle: Bay, 1991), pp. 179–210; Cherríe Moraga, *Loving in the War Years* (New York: South End, 1983); Gloria Anzaldúa, *Borderlands, La Frontera: The New Mestiza* (San Francisco: Aunt Lute, 1987).

7. Teresa de Lauretis, "Sexual Difference and Lesbian Representation," *Theatre Journal* 40, no. 2 (1988): 155–177; Sue-Ellen Case, "Toward a Butch-Femme Aesthetic," in *Making a Spectacle: Feminist Essays on Contemporary Women's Theatre*, ed. Lynda Hart (Ann Arbor: Michigan University Press, 1989), pp. 282–299; Jonathan Dollimore, *Sexual Dissidence: Augustine to Wilde, Freud to Foucault* (Oxford University Press, 1991); Marjorie Garber, *Vested Interests: Cross-Dressing and Cultural Anxiety* (New York: Routledge, 1992).

8. Judith Butler, *Gender Trouble: Feminism and the Subversion of Identity* (New York: Routledge, 1990). Page numbers of citations will appear directly in the text after *GT*.

9. Judith Butler, "Critically Queer," *glq: A Journal of Lesbian and Gay Studies* 1, no. 1 (1993): 24, 25.

10. Eve Kosofsky Sedgwick, "Queer Performativity: Henry James's *The Art of the Novel*," *glq: A Journal of Lesbian and Gay Studies* 1, no. 1 (1993): 1.

11. David Bergman, ed., introduction, *Camp Grounds: Style and Homosexuality* (Amherst: Massachusetts University Press, 1993), p. 11. See also Moe Meyer, ed., *The Politics and Poetics of Camp* (London: Routledge, 1994).

12. Scott Long, "The Loneliness of Camp," in *Camp Grounds*, ed. Bergman, p. 79.

13. Richard Ekins and Dave King, eds., *Blending Genders: Social Aspects of Cross-Dressing and Sex-Changing* (London: Routledge, 1996); see their introduction, p. 1.

14. Judith Butler, *Bodies That Matter: On the Discursive Limits of "Sex"* (New York: Routledge, 1993). Page numbers of citations will appear directly in the text after *BTM*.

15. Sedgwick, "Queer Performativity," p. 1; Sedgwick, *Tendencies*, p. 11.

16. Judith Butler, "Variations on Sex and Gender: Beauvoir, Wittig, and Foucault," in *Feminism as Critique*, ed. Seyla Benhabib and Drucilla Cornell (Minneapolis: Minnesota University Press, 1987), pp. 128–143.

17. Jacques Derrida, *Limited Inc* (Evanston: Northwestern University Press, 1988). Biddy Martin has also noted the importance of speech-act theory—although not of the Derridean deconstruction of it—to both Butler's and Sedgwick's theory of performativity (Biddy Martin, "Sexualities Without Genders and Other Queer Utopias," *Diacritics* 24, nos. 2/3 [1994]: 104–121). Butler's most recent book *Excitable*

Speech: A Politics of the Performative (London: Routledge, 1997), just out as I go to press, is a thorough exploration of the significance of speech acts (of the relation between "speech" and "act") in the contemporary cultural sphere. Since its concerns are not primarily sex or gender, I omit discussion of it here.

18. For Butler's genealogy of Beauvoir's understanding of becoming to Sartre and Hegel and a prefiguring of key arguments in *Gender Trouble*, see Judith Butler, "Sex and Gender in Simone de Beauvoir's *Second Sex*," *Yale French Studies* 72 (1986): 34–49.

19. Butler, "Critically Queer," p. 25.

20. Monique Wittig, *The Straight Mind and Other Essays* (Boston: Beacon, 1992).

21. Butler, "Critically Queer," p. 25; my emphasis.

22. Martin, "Sexualities Without Genders," p. 104.

23. Liz Kotz, "The Body You Want: Liz Kotz Interviews Judith Butler," *Artforum* 31 (November 1992): 89; Butler, "Critically Queer," p. 24.

24. Judith Butler, "Melancholy Gender/Refused Identification," *Constructing Masculinity*, ed. Maurice Berger, Brian Wallis, Simon Watson (New York, Routledge, 1995), pp. 32, 34.

25. Jacques Lacan, "The Meaning of the Phallus," in *Feminine Sexuality: Jacques Lacan and the École Freudienne*, ed. Juliet Mitchell and Jacqueline Rose (New York: Norton, 1982), pp. 74–85.

26. Joan Rivière, "Womanliness as a Masquerade,"in *Formations of Fantasy*, ed. Victor Burgin, James Donald, and Cora Kaplan (New York: Methuen, 1986), p. 38; Stephen Heath, "Joan Rivière and the Masquerade," in *Formations of Fantasy*, ed. Burgin, Donald, and Kaplan, pp. 46–61.

27. Sigmund Freud, "Mourning and Melancholia" (1917) *The Standard Edition of the Complete Psychological Works*, vol. 14, ed. James Strachey (London: Hogarth, 1968), pp. 239–258; Sigmund Freud, *The Ego and the Id* (1923), trans. Joan Rivière, ed. James Strachey (New York: Norton, 1989); Nicolas Abraham, "Notes on the Phantom: A Complement to Freud's Metapsychology," in *The Trial(s) of Psychoanalysis*, ed. Françoise Meltzer (Chicago: Chicago University Press, 1988), pp. 75–80; Nicolas Abraham and Maria Torok, "Introjection-Incorporation: Mourning or Melancholia,"in *Psychoanalysis in France*, ed. Serge Lebovici and Daniel Widlöcher (New York: International University Press, 1980), pp. 3–16; Roy Schafer, *Aspects of Internalization* (New York: International University Press, 1968); Roy Schafer, *A New Language for Psychoanalysis* (New Haven: Yale University Press, 1976).

28. Freud, *The Ego and the Id*, pp. 24, 28.

29. Freud, *The Ego and the Id*, pp. 19–20.

30. Ibid., p. 20, n. 16.

31. As I understand this influence, while Lacan's imago certainly derives from Freud's concept of the ego, its debt is not so much to the ego of *The Ego and the Id* as to Freud's second model of the ego in "On Narcissism: An Introduction": the ego as distinctly nonbiological and crucially split ("Lacan's Mirror Phase," talk given by Bice Benvenuto, Center for Freudian Psychoanalysis and Research, London, October 21, 1995). See Elizabeth Grosz, *Jacques Lacan: A Feminist*

Introduction (London: Routledge, 1990), pp. 24–49, for an account of the differences between Freud's two egos and the genealogy of only one to Lacan.

32. "The child seems to organize its earliest subjective experience around bodily sensations with their varying pleasure-pain properties. This early subjective experience is the 'bodily ego' that, according to Freud (1923a [*The Ego and the Id*]), is the first ego. Thus, from its very beginnings, the organization of experience implies physical referents such as are later subjectively defined as being inside and outside" (Schafer, *A New Language for Psychoanalysis*, p. 171). The "physical referents"—the "bodily sensations" that Freud posits as generating the ego—are in Schafer's scheme granted only retroactively and subjectively.

33. Martin, "Sexualities Without Genders," p. 106.

34. Freud, *The Ego and the Id,* 19–20.

35. "Transsexuals often claim a radical discontinuity between sexual pleasures and bodily parts. Very often what is wanted in terms of pleasure requires an imaginary participation in body parts, either appendages or orifices, that one might not actually possess, or, similarly, pleasure may require imagining an exaggerated or diminished set of parts. . . . The imaginary condition of desire always exceeds the physical body through or on which it works" (*GT* 70–71).

36. Arguing with lesbian feminism in particular, Lynne Segal makes a case for the non-normativity of heterosexual practices, their potential (for straight feminists) for putting in question gender hierarchies: "Straight sex . . . can be no less 'perverse' than its 'queer' alternatives" (Lynne Segal, *Straight Sex: The Politics of Pleasure* [London: Virago, 1994], p. 318). That straight should thus aspire to queer is a sure sign of the success of queer theory's "grounding" (of running aground) heterosexuality.

37. *Paris is Burning*, dir. Jennie Livingston, Miramax, 1990.

38. The queer/poststructuralist investment in figures of transgression might be read as a similar (unconscious?) appropriation of Catholic rhetoric.

39. bell hooks, *Black Looks: Race and Representation* (Boston: South End, 1992), p. 151.

40. Livingston's powers of representation extend beyond the cinematic. That Livingston knowingly and intentionally entered the drag ball world of Harlem as an authority is evident from the legal cautions she took before filming, including requiring all the participants in the film to sign a release. Two years after the film's success, all but two of the participants filed legal suits against Livingston, staking a claim in her profits. Their signatures on the release ensured the dismissal of their suits. For a discussion of the significance of this case to the circumscribed agency of the ball participants beyond the realm of the ball, see Philip Brian Harper, "The Subversive Edge: *Paris is Burning*, Social Critique, and the Limits of Subjective Agency," *Diacritics* 24, nos. 2/3 (1994): 90–103.

41. Although precisely for these reasons in current transgender studies, Venus (and Butler's reading of her) is proving seminal. Ki Namaste's critique of queer theory's representation of transgender—which appeared after my writing this—similarly argues that Butler "reduce[s] Extravaganza's transsexuality to an allegorical state" (" 'Tragic Misreadings': Queer Theory's Erasure of Transgender Subjectivity,"

Queer Studies: A Lesbian, Gay, Bisexual, and Transgender Anthology, ed. Brett Beemyn and Mickey Eliason [New York: New York University Press, 1996], p. 188). While I emphasize the literality of sex and the cruciality of narrative for the transsexual, Namaste's essay goes on usefully to reinstate something of the sociological context of transgender and transsexual lives in which queer's "tragic misreadings" take place.

42. Judith Butler, "Against Proper Objects," p. 2. Page numbers of further citations will appear directly in the text after "APO."

43. Gayle Rubin, "Thinking Sex: Notes for a Radical Theory of the Politics of Sexuality," *Pleasure and Danger: Exploring Female Sexuality* (1984; reprint, London: Pandora, 1989), pp. 267–319.

44. Gayle Rubin, with Judith Butler (Interview), "Sexual Traffic," *differences* 6, nos. 2–3 (1994): 88.

2. A Skin of One's Own: Toward a Theory of Transsexual Embodiment

1. Julia Epstein, *Altered Conditions: Disease, Medicine, and Storytelling* (New York: Routledge, 1995), p. 2.

2. Cited in Louise Gray, "Me, My Surgeon, and My Art," *The Guardian*, 2 April 1996, p.8.

3. Catherine Millot, *Horsexe: An Essay on Transsexuality*, trans. Kenneth Hylton (Brooklyn: Autonomedia, 1990), p. 116.

4. Ann Fausto-Sterling, "The Five Sexes: Why Male and Female Are Not Enough," *The Sciences* 33, no. 2 (1993): 20–25. See also Ann Fausto-Sterling, *Myths of Gender: Biological Theories About Women and Men* (New York: Basic, 1992).

5. Judith Butler, *Gender Trouble: Feminism and the Subversion of Identity* (New York: Routledge, 1990), p. 8.

6. Elizabeth Grosz, *Volatile Bodies: Toward a Corporeal Feminism* (Bloomington: Indiana University Press, 1994), pp. 208, 207.

7. Millot, *Horsexe*.

8. Parveen Adams, *The Emptiness of the Image: Psychoanalysis and Sexual Difference* (London: Routledge, 1996), pp. 158–159, 143–144, 159.

9. Grosz, *Volatile Bodies*, p. 208.

10. Didier Anzieu, *The Skin Ego: A Psychoanalytic Approach to the Self*, trans. Chris Turner (New Haven: Yale University Press, 1989); page numbers of further citations will appear directly in the text after *SE*. Didier Anzieu, *A Skin for Thought: Interviews with Gilbert Tarrab* (London: Karnac, 1990).

11. Sigmund Freud, *The Ego and the Id* (1923), trans. Joan Rivière, ed. James Strachey (New York: Norton, 1989), p. 20 and p. 20, n. 16; cited in Anzieu, *SE*, p. 85.

12. Anzieu, *Skin for Thought*, p. 43. Anzieu's difference with Lacan on the body, language, and the centrality of the ego is most clearly articulated in this collection of interviews: see especially pp. 33–79, and for his description of training with Lacan pp. 26–32.

13. It is in fact a measure of Lacan's role in cultural desomatization that in her most recent surgery/exhibition, Orlan's "surplus" tissues were mounted on texts from Lacan, her flesh refigured as his text. "This My Body, This My Software," Newcastle, UK, April 1996.

14. Butler, *Gender Trouble*, p. 163, n. 43.

15. Grosz, *Volatile Bodies* p. xiii.

16. Judith Butler, *Bodies That Matter: On the Discursive Limits of "Sex"* (New York: Routledge, 1993), p. 98.

17. *The Silence of the Lambs*, dir. Jonathan Demme, Orion Pictures, 1991.

18. Terming the film a "skinflick," Judith Halberstam has read the conjoining of skin, horror, and gender trouble in *Silence of the Lambs*, although she states that Gumb is not reducible to the transsexual. Judith Halberstam, *Skin Shows: Gothic Horror and the Technology of Monsters* (Duke University Press: Durham, 1995), pp. 161–177.

19. Jan Morris, *Conundrum: An Extraordinary Narrative of Transsexualism* (New York: Holt, 1986), p. 88.

20. Diane Leslie Feinberg, *Journal of a Transsexual* (New York: World View, 1980), p. 20.

21. Cited in Bryan Tully, *Accounting for Transsexuality and Transhomosexuality* (London: Whiting, 1992), p. 76.

22. Christian Hamburger, Georg K. Stürup, and E. Dahl-Iversen, "Transvestism: Hormonal, Psychiatric, and Surgical Treatment," *Journal of the American Medical Association* 52, no. 5 (1953): 391–396.

23. Raymond Thompson with Kitty Sewell, *What Took You So Long? A Girl's Journey to Manhood* (London: Penguin, 1995), p. 200. Page numbers of further citations will appear directly in the text.

24. The field of medical writings on what might be called the psychology of the skin is vast. Most current issues of the dermatology journals *Journal of the American Academy of Dermatology*, *British Journal of Dermatology*, and *International Journal of Dermatology* contain research on the psychosocial significance of skin disorders. As I intend to explore in my next project (a cultural history of skin), skin is a massively significant text: an organ that has been subject to dense and fascinating psychosocial narratives.

25. Caroline Cossey, *My Story* (Winchester, Mass.: Faber, 1992), p. 74; Renée Richards with John Ames, *Second Serve: The Renée Richards Story* (New York: Stein, 1983), pp. 81–82.

26. Oliver Sacks, *The Man Who Mistook His Wife for a Hat* (New York: Harper, 1990), p. 43.

27. Sacks, *Man Who Mistook His Wife for a Hat*. See "Hands" (pp. 59–65); "Phantoms" (pp. 66–70); "The Man Who Fell out of Bed" (pp. 55–58); and for the case of loss of total body-image ("pithing," as the patient herself so perfectly puts it), "The Disembodied Lady" (pp. 43–54).

28. Oliver Sacks, *A Leg to Stand On* (London: Picador, 1991), p. 46.

29. Sacks, *Man Who Mistook His Wife for a Hat*, pp. 48–49.

30. *SE*, p. 61. Anzieu's biological explanation for why the skin is so caught up in psychic reality, this conjunction of skin with the brain (skin and the brain are formed from the same ectodermal material, are juxtaposed in utero, and share the same double-layered organization) provides an interesting connection to the most recent biological research into transsexual etiology. Positing a transsexual brain,

this research would seem to indicate a neuroscientific genesis for transsexual body image. In one much publicized study the part of the brain considered essential for sexual behavior, the *stria terminalis*, was shown to be female-sized in male-to-female transsexuals. As the *stria terminalis* is not influenced by hormone administration in adult life, this study claims to "show a female brain structure in genetically male transsexuals and [to support] the hypothesis that gender identity develops as a result of an interaction between the developing brain and sex hormones" (Jiang-Ning Zhou, Michael A. Hofman, Louis J. G. Gooren, and Dick F. Swaab, "A Sex Difference in the Human Brain and its Relation to Transsexuality, *Nature* 378 [1995]: 68).

31. Luce Irigaray, *This Sex Which is Not One* (Ithaca: Cornell University Press, 1985).

32. Sacks, *Man Who Mistook His Wife for a Hat*, p. 52.

33. Ibid.

34. Sharon Olds, "Outside the Operating Room of the Sex-Change Doctor," *Powers of Desire: The Politics of Sexuality*, ed. Ann Snitow, Christine Stansell, and Sharon Thompson (New York: Monthly Review Press, 1983), p. 300.

35. American Psychiatric Association, "Gender Identity Disorder," in *Diagnostic and Statistical Manual of Mental Disorders IV* (Washington, D.C.: American Psychiatric Association, 1994), pp. 532–537.

36. Kathy Davis, *Reshaping the Female Body: The Dilemma Of Cosmetic Surgery* (New York: Routledge, 1995), p. 16.

37. Mario Martino with harriet, *Emergence: A Transsexual Autobiography* (New York: Crown, 1977), p. 185, my emphasis.

38. Duncan Fallowell & April Ashley, *April Ashley's Odyssey* (London: Cape, 1982), p. 89; Jan Morris, *Conundrum*, p. 141; Thompson, *What Took You So Long?*, p. 299.

39. Kim Harlow/Bettina Rheims, *Kim*, trans. Paul Gould (Munich: Kehayoff Verlag, 1994), p. 42.

40. Lucy Grealy, *In the Mind's Eye: Autobiography of a Face* (London: Arrow, 1995), p. 160.

41. Sacks, *Leg to Stand On*, p. 50.

42. Grosz, *Volatile Bodies*, p. 73.

43. Sacks, *Man Who Mistook His Wife for a Hat*, p. 69.

44. Katherine Cummings, *Katherine's Diary: The Story of a Transsexual* (Port Melbourne, Victoria: Heinemann, 1992), p. 223.

45. Ann Bolin, *In Search of Eve: Transsexual Rites of Passage* (New York: Bergin and Garvey, 1988), pp. 182, 183.

46. Dawn Langley Simmons, *Man Into Woman: A Transsexual Autobiography* (London: Icon, 1970), p. 124.

47. Julia Grant, *Just Julia: The Story of an Extraordinary Woman* (London: Boxstreet, 1994).

48. Janice Raymond, *The Transsexual Empire: The Making of the She-Male* (1979; reissued, with a new introduction on transgender, New York: Teacher's College Press, 1994), p. 31.

49. Marjorie Garber "Spare Parts," *differences* 1, no. 3 (1989); reprinted in Garber, *Vested Interests* (New York: Routledge, 1992), p. 98.

50. Arthur and Marilouise Kroker, eds., introduction, *The Last Sex: Feminism and Outlaw Bodies* (New York: St. Martin's, 1993), pp. 15, 19.

51. For an overview of the mechanics of tissue engineering by those pioneering the field, see Robert Langer and Joseph P. Vacanti, "Tissue Engineering," *Science* 260 (1993): 920–926; for a discussion of the BBC's "Tomorrow's World" special that televised the "ear-mouse" ("Test Tube Bodies, BBC1, October 24, 1995), see Sandra Goldbeck-Wood, "Brave New World of Transplant Technology," *British Medical Journal* 311 (1995): 1235–1236; for a sense of how tissue engineering might revolutionize plastic surgery, see John O. Cucan and C. Raphael Lee, "Plastic Surgery," *Journal of the American Medical Association* 275 (1996): 1844–1845.

52. Rosi Braidotti, *Nomadic Subjects: Embodiment and Sexual Difference in Contemporary Theory* (New York: Columbia University Press, 1994), p. 56.

53. Adrienne Rich, "Notes Toward a Politics of Location," *Blood, Bread, and Poetry: Selected Prose 1979–1985* (New York: Norton, 1986), p. 215.

54. Audre Lorde, *The Cancer Journals* (San Francisco: Aunt Lute, 1980). Page numbers of citations will appear directly in the text.

55. Using Frantz Fanon's *Black Skin, White Masks*, Kaja Silverman has recently explored the possibility of a "black male bodily ego." Following Anzieu (Silverman cites *The Skin Ego* in a footnote but does not read the significance of skin in Fanon), Fanon's notion of "epidermalization" would certainly seem to be the place to begin to account for the psychic and cultural materiality of racial difference (Frantz Fanon, *Black Skin, White Masks*, trans. Charles Lam Markmann [New York: Grove, 1967], p. 11). My attempt to think transsexual embodiment here runs parallel to Silverman's chapter entitled "The Bodily Ego," in which her reading of Fanon appears: Kaja Silverman, *The Threshold of the Visible World* (New York, Routledge, 1996), pp. 9–37. Beginning with Freud's definition of the ego as a bodily ego, Silverman "elaborate[s] and problematize[s]" Lacan's account of the bodily image though the work of Schilder and Wallon to produce a conception of the bodily ego as similarly sensational and "proprioceptive."

56. Eve Kosofsky Sedgwick, *Tendencies* (Durham: Duke University Press, 1993), pp. 262, 283, 262. For Sedgwick's account of how her baldness as a result of her chemotherapy treatment for the cancer made her read conversely as a lesbian (the experience was indeed apparently one of crossing identifications), see Eve Kosofsky Sedgwick, "Gosh, Boy George, You Must be Awfully Secure in Your Masculinity!" *Constructing Masculinity*, ed. Maurice Berger, Brian Wallis, Simon Watson (New York: Routledge, 1995), pp. 11–20.

3. Mirror Images: Transsexuality and Autobiography

1. Jan Morris, *Conundrum: An Extraordinary Narrative of Transsexualism* (New York: Holt, 1986), p. 140. Page numbers of further citations will appear directly in the text.

2. Morris's mirror scene is satirized in other male-to-female accounts: see Nancy Hunt, *Mirror Image: The Odyssey of a Male to Female Transsexual* (New York: Holt,

1978), p. 201, and Sandy Stone, "The 'Empire' Strikes Back: A Posttranssexual Manifesto," in *BodyGuards: The Cultural Politics of Gender Ambiguity*, ed. Julia Epstein and Kristina Straub (New York: Routledge, 1991), p. 301, n. 21.

3. Mario Martino with harriet, *Emergence: A Transsexual Autobiography* (New York: Crown, 1977), p. xi. Page numbers of further citations will appear directly in the text.

4. Jacques Lacan, "The Mirror Stage as Formative of the Function of the I," in *Écrits: A Selection*, trans. Alan Sheridan (New York: Norton, 1977), pp. 1–7.

5. Hunt, *Mirror Image*, p. 263.

6. Renée Richards with John Ames, *Second Serve: The Renée Richards Story* (New York: Stein and Day, 1983), p. 68. Page numbers of further citations will appear directly in the text.

7. American Psychiatric Association, *Diagnostic and Statistical Manual of Mental Disorders IV (DSM-IV)* (Washington, D.C.: American Psychiatric Association, 1994), p. 537.

8. Bernice L. Hausman, *Changing Sex: Transsexualism, Technology, and the Idea of Gender* (Durham: Duke University Press, 1995), p. 110. Page numbers of further citations will appear directly in the text.

9. Ira B. Pauly, "Terminology and Classification of Gender Identity Disorders," in *Gender Dysphoria: Interdisciplinary Approaches in Clinical Management*, ed. Walter O. Bockting and Eli Coleman (New York: Haworth, 1992), p. 5.

10. For transsexualism's first entry in *DSM*, see *DSM-III* (Washington, D.C.: American Psychiatric Association, 1980), pp. 261–266. For its first revision, see *DSM-III-R* (Washington, D.C.: American Psychiatric Association, 1987), pp. 71–78.

11. Paul A. Walker, Jack C. Berger, Richard Green, Donald R. Laub, Charles L. Reynolds, Leo Wollman, "Standards of Care: The Hormonal and Surgical Sex Reassignment of Gender Dysphoric Persons," appendixed in Dallas Denny, *Gender Dysphoria: A Guide to Research* (New York: Garland, 1994), p. 639.

12. Stone, "The 'Empire' Strikes Back," p. 293.

13. Harry Benjamin, *The Transsexual Phenomenon* (New York: Julian, 1966).

14. Erica Rutherford, *Nine Lives: The Autobiography of Erica Rutherford* (Charlottetown, P.E.I., Canada: Ragweed, 1993), p. 209.

15. Raymond Thompson with Kitty Sewell, *What Took You So Long? A Girl's Journey into Manhood* (London: Penguin, 1995), p. 98.

16. Ibid., p. 99.

17. Leslie Lothstein, *Female-to-Male Transsexualism: Historical, Clinical, and Theoretical Issues* (Boston: Routledge, 1983). For Lothstein's disturbing rendition of this case (he reads with the brother against the transsexual), see pp. 110–113.

18. Bryan Tully, *Accounting for Transsexuality and Transhomosexuality* (London: Whiting, 1992), p. 24.

19. Leah Cahan Schaefer, Connie Christine Wheeler, and Walter Futterweit, "Gender Identity Disorders (Transsexualism)," in *Treatments of Psychiatric Disorders*, vol. 2, ed. Glen O. Gabbard (Washington D.C.: American Psychiatric Press), p. 2027.

20. Jane Fry, *Being Different: The Autobiography of Jane Fry*, collec., comp., and ed. Robert Bogdan (New York: Wily, 1974). Page numbers of citations will appear directly in the text.

21. Georges Gusdorf, "Conditions and Limits of Autobiography," in *Autobiography: Essays Theoretical and Critical*, ed. James Olney (Princeton: Princeton University Press, 1980), p. 41.

22. Hunt, *Mirror Image: The Odyssey of a Male-to-Female Transsexual*; Duncan Fallowell and April Ashley, *April Ashley's Odyssey* (London: Cape, 1982).

23. Claudine Griggs, *Passage Through Trinidad: Journal of a Surgical Sex Change* (Jefferson, N.C.: McFarland, 1996).

24. Gusdorf, "Conditions and Limits of Autobiography," p. 40.

25. Stephanie Castle, *Feelings: A Transsexual's Explanation of a Baffling Condition* (Vancouver BC: Persephone, 1992), p. 38.

26. Paul Hewitt with Jane Warren, *A Self-Made Man: The Diary of a Man Born in a Woman's Body* (London: Headline, 1995); Jerry/Jerri McClain, *To Be a Woman* (Provincetown, Mass.: Different Path, 1992).

27. Mark Rees, *Dear Sir or Madam: The Autobiography of a Female-to-Male Transsexual* (London: Cassell, 1996).

28. Kitty Sewell, "Introduction," in *What Took You So Long?*, by Raymond Thompson with Kitty Sewell, p. viii.

29. Canary Conn, "A Little Boy Discovers Herself," in *Canary: The Story of a Transsexual* (Los Angeles: Nash, 1974), p. 29; Thompson, *What Took You So Long? A Girl's Journey to Manhood*.

30. Christine Jorgensen, *Christine Jorgensen: A Personal Autobiography* (New York: Eriksson, 1967). For reference to Jorgensen see, for instance, Hunt, *Mirror Image*, pp. 74–75; Martino, *Emergence*, pp. 40, 51, 163; Dawn Langley Simmons, *Man Into Woman: A Transsexual Autobiography* (London: Icon, 1970), p. 94. Lili Elbe's biography is recounted in Neils Hoyer, ed., *Man Into Woman: An Authentic Record of a Change of Sex—The True Story of the Miraculous Transformation of the Danish Painter, Einar Wegener*, trans. H. J. Stenning (New York: Popular Library, 1953), a book cited in Castle, *Feelings*, p. 44; Morris, *Conundrum*, p. 45; Richards, *Second Serve*, p. 55.

31. Hunt, *Mirror Image*, pp. 139–140.

32. Stone, "The 'Empire' Strikes Back," p. 285.

33. See for instance Julia Grant, *Just Julia: The Story of an Extraordinary Woman* (London: Boxstreet, 1994); Rees, *Dear Sir or Madam*.

34. Gusdorf, "Conditions and Limits of Autobiography," p. 32.

35. Harry Benjamin, introduction, in *Christine Jorgensen*, pp. xi–xii, p. xii, p. ix, my emphasis.

36. Conn, *Canary*.

37. If Richard's narrative comes close to reading as a critique of Robert Stoller's psychoanalytic account of male-to-female transsexuality as the product of a masculine mother and an absent father, Martino's comes close to Lothstein's of female-to-male transsexuality as—mirror image—engendered by the little girl taking the

place of the father (an unsurprising parallel between the clinical texts considering that Lothstein cites Stoller as his mentor). See Robert Stoller, *Sex and Gender: The Transsexual Experiment* (New York: Aronson, 1976) and *Sex and Gender: The Development of Masculinity and Femininity* (London: Karnac, 1974); Lothstein, *Female-to-Male Transsexualism*.

38. Robert Allen, *But for the Grace* (London: Allen, 1954), p. 77.

39. Roberta Cowell, *Roberta Cowell's Story* (London: Heinemann, 1954), p. 154.

4. "Some Primitive Thing Conceived in a Turbulent Age of Transition": The Invert, *The Well of Loneliness*, and the Narrative Origins of Transsexuality

1. Radclyffe Hall, *The Well of Loneliness* (1928; reprint, London: Virago, 1982). Page numbers of citations will appear directly in the text.

2. Transcript of the appeal, cited in Michael Baker, *Our Three Selves: The Life of Radclyffe Hall* (New York: William Morrow, 1985), p. 243.

3. *Time and Tide*, 23 November, 1928, cited in Baker, *Our Three Selves*, p. 246.

4. Jane Rule, *Lesbian Images* (London: Davies, 1976), p. 50.

5. Blanche Wiesen-Cook, " 'Women Alone Stir My Imagination': Lesbianism and the Cultural Tradition," *Signs* 4, no. 4 (1979): 718–739; Lillian Faderman, *Surpassing the Love of Men: Romantic Friendship and Love Between Women from the Renaissance to the Present* (1981; reprint, London: The Women's Press, 1991), pp. 317–323; Catharine Stimpson, *Where the Meanings Are: Feminism and Cultural Spaces* (New York: Routledge, 1984), pp. 97–110; Caroll Smith-Rosenberg, *Disorderly Conduct: Visions of Gender in Victorian America* (New York: Oxford University Press, 1985), pp. 245–296 passim; Esther Newton, "The Mythic Mannish Lesbian: Radclyffe Hall and the New Woman," *The Lesbian Issue: Essays from* Signs, ed. Estelle B. Freedman, Barbara C. Gelpi, Susan L. Johnson, Kathleen M. Weston (Chicago: Chicago University Press, 1985), pp. 7–26; Sonja Ruehl, "Inverts and Experts: Radclyffe Hall and the Lesbian Identity," in *Feminism, Culture, and Politics*, ed. Rosalind Brunt and Caroline Rowan (London: Lawrence, 1982), pp. 15–36; Jean Radford, "An Inverted Romance: *The Well of Loneliness* and Sexual Ideology," in *The Progress of Romance: The Politics of Popular Fiction*, ed. Jean Radford (London: Routledge 1986), pp. 97–111; Gillian Whitlock, " 'Everything is Out of Place': Radclyffe Hall and the Lesbian Literary Tradition," *Feminist Studies* 13, no. 3 (1987): 555–582; Teresa de Lauretis, *The Practice of Love: Lesbian Sexuality and Perverse Desire* (Bloomington: Indiana University Press, 1994), pp. 203–256. Claudia Stillman Franks alone produces a nonlesbian-centered reading of the novel as about a woman coming to writing. Claudia Stillman Franks, *Beyond* The Well of Loneliness: *The Fiction of Radclyffe Hall* (Avebury, England: Avebury, 1982), pp. 97–114.

6. Sandra M. Gilbert and Susan Gubar, *Sexchanges*, vol. 2, *No Man's Land: The Place of the Woman Writer in the Twentieth Century* (New Haven: Yale University Press, 1989), p. 220.

7. Newton, "The Mythic Mannish Lesbian," pp. 21, 23.

8. George Chauncey, "From Sexual Inversion to Homosexuality: Medicine and the Changing Conceptualization of Female Deviance," *Salmagundi* 58/59

(1982/1983): 117–118. For other significant renditions of sexology as about homosexuality, see Faderman, *Surpassing the Love of Men*, pp. 239–253; Smith-Rosenberg, *Disorderly Conduct*, pp. 245–296; David F. Greenberg, *The Construction of Homosexuality* (Chicago: Chicago University Press, 1988) pp. 397–435; and Gert Hekma, " 'A Female Soul in a Male Body': Sexual Inversion as Gender Inversion in Nineteenth-Century Sexology," in *Third Sex, Third Gender: Beyond Sexual Dimorphism in Culture and History*, ed. Gilbert Herdt (New York: Zone, 1994), pp. 213–240. Even though its stated purpose is to elucidate sexual inversion as a discourse of gender inversion, Hekma's essay nevertheless follows its precursors in reading gender inversion as the sexologists' conceptual frame for homosexuality rather than a specifically transgendered paradigm.

9. Michel Foucault, *The History of Sexuality*, vol. 1, *An Introduction*, trans. Robert Hurley (New York: Vintage, 1990), p. 43.

10. Stephen's inversion has been read successively as the projection of "homosexuality as a sickness" (Stimpson, *Where the Meanings Are*, p. 101); a "congenitalist trap" for conceiving love between women (Faderman, *Surpassing the Love of Men*, p. 322); lesbian "self-hating" (Wiesen-Cook, " 'Women Alone Stir My Imagination,' " p. 721); an attempt to transform sexological object into self-designating lesbian subject (Ruehl, "Inverts and Experts"); "the New Woman['s] lay[ing] claim to her full sexuality" (Newton "The Mythic Mannish Lesbian," p. 23); a lesbian feminist strategy for insisting on the "homosexual's right to existence" (Radford, "An Inverted Romance," p. 97); a bid to create "space for lesbians to speak for themselves" (Whitlock, " 'Everything is Out of Place,' " p. 560) and a "fetish, the signifier of [lesbian] desire" (de Lauretis, *The Practice of Love*, p. 242). None of these readings doubts that the female invert is lesbian, even if some of them criticize her roundly as a bad or outmoded one.

We might see the sublimation of inversion into sexuality at work in the very publication of *The Well*. Hall's publisher, Jonathan Cape, clearly mindful of the obscenity trial that in 1898 had beset the sexologist's own *Sexual Inversion*, modified Havelock Ellis's original praise for the novel that appeared as the preface to the first edition as realistically presenting "various aspects of sexual inversion," to "one particular aspect of sexual life." Ellis's remarks on the novel's specific contribution to sexual inversion were thereby transmuted into a vague assertion about sexuality. Original commentary cited in Baker, *Our Three Selves*, p. 205; published version in Havelock Ellis, Commentary, *The Well of Loneliness*, Radclyffe Hall (Paris: Pegasus, 1928) n. p.

11. Chauncey, "From Sexual Inversion to Homosexuality," p. 116.

12. Carl Westphal, "Die Konträre Sexualempfindung," *Archiv für Psychiatrie und Nervenkrankheiten* 2 (1869): 73–108, cited in Leslie Lothstein, *Female-to-Male Transsexualism: Historical, Clinical, and Theoretical Issues* (Boston: Routledge, 1983), pp. 21–22. (Thanks to James Hall for help with translation.) For its citation in the context of inversion, see Richard von Krafft-Ebing, *Psychopathia Sexualis: With Especial Reference to the Antipathic Sexual Instinct*, trans. from the 10th German edition by F. J. Rebman (London: Rebman Ltd., 1901), p. 326; and Havelock Ellis,

Studies in the Psychology of Sex, vol. 2, *Sexual Inversion* (New York: Random, 1936), p. 65; and, in the context of transsexuality, Ira Pauly, "Adult Manifestations of Female Transsexualism," in *Transsexualism and Sex Reassignment*, ed. Richard Green and John Money, (Baltimore: Johns Hopkins University Press, 1969) p. 59, and Lothstein, *Female-to-Male Transsexualism*, pp. 21–22.

13. Nelly Oudshoorn (*Beyond the Natural Body: An Archaeology of Sex Hormones* [London: Routledge, 1994]) dates the beginning of endocrinology to the 1900s but describes how the isolation and the manufacture of sex hormones took the best part of the next three decades.

14. Hirschfeld's case, originally published in *Sexual Pathologie: Ein Lehrbuch Für Artze und Studierende* (1922), is cited in Lothstein, *Female-to-Male Transsexualism*, p. 22 and Pauly, "Adult Manifestations of Female Transsexualism," p. 59. The genital masculinization of Herman Karl (born Sophia Hedwig) is mentioned in Hans Houstein, "Transvestism and the State at the End of the Eighteenth and Nineteenth Centuries," *Zeitschrift für Sexual Wissenschaft* 15 (1928–29): 353, and is cited by Vern Bullough and Bonnie Bullough as "[t]he earliest known case of modern surgical intervention" (although the Bulloughs add that it is not clear whether the surgery entailed sex change or corrective treatment for pseudohermaphroditism) (Vern Bullough and Bonnie Bullough, *Cross-Dressing, Sex, and Gender* [Philadelphia: Pennsylvania University Press, 1993], p. 255).

15. Krafft-Ebing, *Psychopathia Sexualis*, p. 410; Ellis, *Sexual Inversion*, pp. 255, 251. Page numbers of further citations to both works will appear directly in the text. According to Ellis, most female inverts are marked by transgender: "It appears to me that the great majority of inverted women possess some masculine or boyish traits, even though only as slight as those which may occasionally be revealed by a normal woman" (251).

16. Vern Bullough, "A Nineteenth-Century Transsexual," *Archives of Sexual Behavior* 16 (1987): 81.

17. Ulrichs writing as Numa Numantius, "Inclusa," *Anthropologische Studien über mannmännliche Geschlechtsliebe* (Leipzig: Matthes, 1898), cited and translated in Hubert Kennedy, *Ulrichs: The Life and Works of Karl Heinrich Ulrichs, Pioneer of the Modern Gay Movement* (Boston: Alyson, 1988), p. 56.

18. Karl Heinrich Ulrichs, *Forshungen über das Rätsel der mannmänlichen Liebe*, vol. 2, p. 4, cited in Hugh C. Kennedy, "The 'Third Sex' Theory of Karl Heinrich Ulrichs," in *Historical Perspectives on Homosexuality*, ed. Salvatore J. Licata and Robert P. Petersen (New York: Haworth, 1981), p. 106.

19. Numa Numantius, "Formatrix," *Anthropologische Studien über urnische Liebe* (Leipzig: Matthes, 1898), cited in Kennedy, *Ulrichs*, p. 73. In spite of recounting incidents in Ulrichs's life that if not indicators of the desire to be differently sexed are at least evidence of a transgendered identification ("he recalled that as a child of three and four years old he wore girls' clothes and found it painful when he first had to put on boys' clothes. He protested, 'No, I want to be a girl' " [15]), Ulrichs's main commentator, Kennedy, reads him unproblematically as "the first self-proclaimed homosexual" (*Ulrichs*, p. 9).

20. Julia Epstein, *Altered Conditions: Disease, Medicine, and Storytelling* (New York: Routledge, 1995), p. 53.

21. Early on in modern transsexual research, psychiatrist Richard Green also reads this case as precursory transsexual: Richard Green, "Transsexualism: Mythological, Historical, and Cross-Cultural Aspects," in *The Transsexual Phenomenon*, Harry Benjamin (New York: Julian Press, 1966), p. 178.

22. The case does not appear in the tenth edition. Citations are taken from the English translation of the twelfth edition, trans. Franklin S. Klaf (New York: Stein, 1965), p. 282.

23. Pauly "Adult Manifestations of Female Transsexualism," p. 83.

24. Krafft-Ebing's case of Sandor/Sarolta is cited by Ellis, *Sexual Inversion,* p. 195, n. 1, and Lothstein, *Female-to-Male Transsexualism*, p. 52. Lothstein makes a similar argument (though through psychoanalysis) about the transsexuality of Krafft-Ebing's transgendered female inverts, including Sandor: "While it may [seem] compelling to explain these patients' 'male identity and role' disorders as stemming from a stigmatized homosexual condition, it [is] also clear that, for some of the women, their 'sexual inversion' was ego syntonic and acceptable" (51).

25. Sigmund Freud, "Psychogenesis of a Case of Homosexuality in a Woman" (1920); reprinted in *Sexuality and the Psychology of Love*, ed. Philip Rieff (New York: MacMillan, 1963), pp. 157–158.

26. Ibid., p. 145, my emphasis.

27. Sigmund Freud, "Psychoanalytic Notes Upon an Autobiographical Account of a Case of Paranoia (Dementia Paranoides)" (1911); reprinted in *Three Case Histories*, ed. Philip Rieff (New York: MacMillan, 1963), pp. 103–186.

28. Mary Jacobus, *Reading Women: Essays in Feminist Criticism* (Bristol: Methuen, 1985), p. 217.

29. The category "transvestism" was coined in Magnus Hirschfeld, *Transvestites: The Erotic Drive to Cross Dress* (1910), trans. Michael Lombardi-Nash (Buffalo, N.Y.: Prometheus, 1991).

30. Liz Hodgkinson, *Michael, Née Laura* (London: Columbus, 1989).

31. Michael Dillon, *Self: A Study in Endocrinology and Ethics*, (London: Heinemann, 1946), pp. 39–56. Page numbers of citations will appear directly in the text.

32. See, for instance. Ellis, "Sexual Inversion," p. 316.

33. Ruehl, "Inverts and Experts," p. 21.

34. Martha Vicinus, " 'They Wonder to Which Sex I Belong': The Historical Roots of the Modern Lesbian Identity," *The Lesbian and Gay Studies Reader*, ed. Henry Abelove, Michèle Aina Barale, David M. Halperin (New York: Routledge, 1993), p. 445.

35. Radclyffe Hall, letter to Havelock Ellis, April 18, 1928; cited in Baker, *Our Three Selves*, p. 203.

36. That Krafft-Ebing has the same function for Renée Richards in her mother's study, highlights the remarkable continuity and stability of what, for transsexuals, has constituted a recognizable transsexual narrative: Renée Richards

with John Ames, *Second Serve: The Renée Richards Story* (New York: Stein and Day, 1983), p. 54.

37. Newton, "The Mythic Mannish Lesbian," p. 24, n. 41.
38. De Lauretis, *The Practice of Love*, p. 216.
39. Ibid., p. 213.
40. Ibid., p. 211. De Lauretis herself acknowledges the contrariness of her reading in the context of the novel: "a word of warning: my reading of a crucial passage in the text—crucial because it inscribes a fantasy of the female body that works against the grain of the novel's explicit message—is likely to appear far-fetched. This is so, I suggest, because my reading also works against the heterosexual coding of sexual difference (masculinity and femininity) which the novel itself employs *and in which it demands to be read*" (*The Practice of Love*, p. 209, my emphasis). While de Lauretis appears to take her lead from Newton in reading Stephen as butch, my interpretation of this scene is actually much closer to Newton's at this point. Newton writes, "In one of Hall's most moving passages Stephen expresses this hatred [for herself] as alienation from her body" ("The Mythic Mannish Lesbian," p. 20).
41. Adam Parkes's recent attempt to read these Nelson passages as illustrating a Butlerian "theatricality of social roles" thus strikes me as absolutely wrong for it fails to consider the contextual significance of the gender performance, to address Stephen's relentless desire to be real: Adam Parkes, "Lesbianism, History, and Censorship: *The Well of Loneliness* and the 'Suppressed Randiness' of Virginia Woolf's *Orlando*," *Twentieth-Century Literature: A Scholarly and Critical Journal* 40, no. 4 (1994): 443.
42. And thus even according to a psychoanalytic reading, Stephen's dream returns her to an identification with men. Of the rescue fantasy in a female subject, Freud wrote in "Psychogenesis of a Case of Homosexuality in a Woman" that it resembled those of the heterosexual men he had described ten years earlier in "A Special Type of Object Choice Made by Men." Although Freud names his case homosexual therefore, *her* fantasy returns *her* (like Stephen) to an original identification with heterosexual masculinity. Freud, "Psychogenesis of a Case of Homosexuality in a Woman," and "A Special Type of Object Choice Made by Men" (1910); reprinted in *Sexuality and the Psychology of Love*, ed. Rieff, pp. 49–57.
43. Peter Stallybrass and Allon White have shown the significance of the kneeling maid to the development of bourgeois childhood sexuality at the beginning of the century. See Peter Stallybrass and Allon White, *The Politics and Poetics of Transgression* (Ithaca: Cornell University Press, 1986), pp. 125–140.
44. Newton, "The Mythic Mannish Lesbian," p. 24, n. 1.
45. Stimpson, *Where the Meanings Are*, pp. 102, 98.
46. De Lauretis, *The Practice of Love*, p. 211.
47. Gayle Rubin, "Of Catamites and Kings: Reflections on Butch, Gender, and Boundaries," in *The Persistent Desire: A Femme-Butch Reader*, ed. Joan Nestle (New York: Alyson, 1992), p. 474.
48. Terry Castle, *The Apparational Lesbian: Female Homosexuality and Modern Culture* (New York: Columbia University Press, 1993), p. 10.

49. Virginia Woolf, *The Diary of Virginia Woolf*, vol. 3 (1925–1930), ed. Anne Olivier Bell with Andrew McNellie (New York: Harcourt, 1980), p. 207.

50. Virginia Woolf, *Orlando* (1928; reprint, London: Vintage, 1992).

51. Parkes, "Lesbianism, History, and Censorship," p. 434.

52. Other critics have compared the novels similarly but have failed to conclude from their difference a distinction between the novel's subjects: "[T]hroughout *Orlando*, clothes, not genitals or personality, symbolize gender change. The body remains amorphous, Orlando's character beyond gender. . . . Tying gender to dress rather than dress to gender, Woolf inverts Krafft-Ebing's dark vision of the 'Mannish Lesbian' " (Smith-Rosenberg, *Disorderly Conduct*, p. 289); "Unlike Orlando, Stephen is trapped in history; she cannot declare gender an irrelevant game" (Newton, "The Mythic Mannish Lesbian," p. 20).

53. *Orlando*, dir. Sally Potter, Adventure Pictures, 1993.

54. Leslie Feinberg, *Stone Butch Blues: A Novel* (New York: Firebrand, 1993).

5. No Place Like Home: Transgender and Trans-Genre in Leslie Feinberg's *Stone Butch Blues*

1. Gayle Rubin, "Of Catamites and Kings: Reflections on Butch, Gender, and Boundaries," in *The Persistent Desire: A Femme-Butch Reader*, ed. Joan Nestle (Boston: Alyson, 1992), p. 474.

2. Janice Raymond, *The Transsexual Empire: The Making of the She Male* (1979; reissued with a new introduction on transgender, New York: Teacher's College Press, 1994).

3. Ibid., pp. xi–xxxv.

4. Sandy Stone, "The 'Empire' Strikes Back: A Posttranssexual Manifesto," in *BodyGuards: The Cultural Politics of Gender Ambiguity*, ed. Julia Epstein and Kristina Straub (New York: Routledge, 1991), p. 295.

5. Ibid., p. 296.

6. Cited in James Green, "Camp Trans," *FTM Newsletter* 29 (January 1995): 7.

7. Beth Elliot, "AND? AND? AND? A Stonewall for the Rest of Us," *Transsexual News Telegraph* 3 (1994): 10–13, 28.

8. Barbara Warren cited in Carey Goldberg, "Shunning 'He' and 'She,' They Fight for Respect," *New York Times*, September 8, 1996, p. 24. Prominent writers in the transgender movement all emphasize passing as politically incapacitating: "Passing becomes silence. Passing becomes invisibility. Passing becomes lies" (Kate Bornstein, *Gender Outlaw: On Men, Women, and the Rest of Us* [New York: Routledge, 1994], p. 125); "It is *passing* that is a product of oppression" (Leslie Feinberg, *Transgender Warriors: Making History From Joan of Arc to Ru Paul* [Boston: Beacon, 1996], p. 89); "Being out and proud versus passing has become the measure of the political consciousness and commitment of transgendered people" (Zachary I. Nataf, *Lesbians Talk Transgender* [London: Scarlett, 1996], p. 29).

9. Dallas Denny, "APA Target of 2nd Demonstration by Transactivists," *Aegis News*, 2 August, 1996, Online, Internet.

10. The key research that brought about the closure of the pioneering Johns Hopkins University Gender Identity Clinic and others following is presented in J.

K. Meyer and D. Reter, "Sex Reassignment: Follow-Up," *Archives of General Psychiatry* 36, no. 9 (1979): 1010–1015.

11. Leah C. Schaefer and Connie Christine Wheeler, "The Non-Surgery True Transsexual: A Theoretical Rationale" (paper presented at the Eighth International Symposium on Gender Dysphoria, Harry Benjamin Gender Dysphoria Association, Bordeaux, France, October 1983).

12. Bornstein, *Gender Outlaw*, p. 3.

13. Donna Minkowitz, "Love Hurts. Brandon Teena Was a Woman Who Lived and Loved as a Man. She Was Killed For Carrying It Off," *Village Voice*, April, 1994, pp. 24–30. For transsexual criticism of the representation of Teena as lesbian see *FTM Newsletter* 26 (February 1994): 3 and *TNT* (Winter 1994): 6. For the popular rendition of Teena's story that also describes how the transgender movement emerged from it, see Aphrodite Jones, *All She Wanted* (New York: Simon and Schuster, 1996).

14. Virginia Prince, founder of *Tranvestia* magazine and prominent figure in the cross-dressing community, has been credited with the coining of "transgender": see Feinberg, *Transgender Warriors*, p. x.

15. Feinberg, *Transgender Warriors*, p. 67; Minnie Bruce Pratt, *S/he* (New York: Firebrand, 1995). In referring to Feinberg I follow the author's practice.

16. Leslie Feinberg, *Stone Butch Blues: A Novel* (New York: Firebrand, 1993). Page numbers of citations will appear directly in the text.

17. Bryan Tully, *Accounting for Transsexuality and Transhomosexuality* (London: Whiting, 1992), p. 254. The following section is a rewriting of my essay "No Place Like Home: The Transgendered Narrative of Leslie Feinberg's *Stone Butch Blues*," *Modern Fiction Studies* 41, nos. 3/4 (1995): 483–514. I am grateful to Judith Halberstam who, in dialogue with this essay's critique of her work on female-to-male transsexuality, has in turn urged me to pay more attention to the transgendered specificity of the stone butch.

18. Rubin, "Of Catamites and Kings," p. 473. For a review of modern stone butch identity that addresses this permeation with transsexuality, see Heather Findlay's "Modern Stone: What is Stone Butch Now?" *Girlfriends* (March/April 1995): 20, 21–22, 44–45. Halberstam's concept of the "transgendered butch" in her exploration of female masculinity promises to further our thinking of this intersection dramatically. Judith Halberstam, *Female Masculinity* (forthcoming, Durham, N.C.: Duke University Press, 1998); see especially her chapter "Transgender Butch: Butch/FTM Border Wars and the Masculine Continuum," also forthcoming in 1998 in *glq: A Journal of Lesbian and Gay Studies*.

19. Gershen Kaufman, *The Psychology of Shame: Theory and Treatment of Shame-Based Syndromes* (London: Routledge, 1993), p. 5.

20. Leah Cahan Schaefer and Connie Christine Wheeler have written eloquently on the etiology of "existential" shame in gender identity disorder in their "Guilt and Gender Identity Disorders and Condition: Understanding, Recognizing, Diagnosing and its Treatment," *Journal of the International Society for the Study of Personal Relationships* (forthcoming).

21. Freud locates shame at the moment at which man stood upright and "made his genitals, which were previously concealed, visible and in need of protection" (Sigmund Freud, *Civilization and Its Discontents*, trans. and ed. James Strachey [New York: Norton, 1962], p. 46, n. 1), and psychologist Donald L. Nathanson has connected adult shame to infantile genital shame (Donald L. Nathanson, "A Timetable for Shame," in *The Many Faces of Shame*, ed. Donald Nathanson [London: Guildford, 1987] p. 27), cited in Eve Kosofsky Sedgwick, "Queer Performativity: Henry James's *The Art of the Novel*," glq: *A Journal of Lesbian and Gay Studies* 1, no. 1 [1993]: 12). For a thorough account of shame that bridges psychoanalysis and biological theory, see Donald L. Nathanson, *Shame and Pride: Affect, Sex, and the Birth of the Self* (New York: Norton 1992). Sedgwick's own work has recently explored the productive possibilities of shame in theory. In addition to *Queer Performativity*, see her essay on Silvan Tomkins (to whom most of this psychological work on shame—Kaufman's and Nathanson's included—is openly indebted), Eve Kosofsky Sedgwick and Adam Frank, "Shame in the Cybernetic Fold: Reading Silvan Tomkins," *Critical Inquiry* 21, no. 2 (1995): 496–522.

22. Feinberg similarly naturalizes hir own childhood gender difference through the other's question: "My own gender expression felt quite natural. I liked my hair short and I felt most relaxed in sneakers, jeans and a t-shirt. However, when I was most at home with how I looked, adults did a double-take or stopped short when they saw me. The question 'Is that a boy or a girl?' hounded me throughout my childhood. The answer didn't matter much. *The very fact that the strangers had to ask the question already marked me as a gender outlaw*" (Feinberg, *Transgender Warriors*, p. 4, my emphasis).

23. Feinberg, *Transgender Warriors*, p. 85.

24. From *The Souls of Black Folks* given Jess by her friend Edwin, an African-American butch who also takes hormones to pass. When Edwin kills herself she leaves Jess this page marked in Du Bois to speak for her: "It is a peculiar sensation, this double-consciousness, this sense of always looking at one's self through the eyes of others, of measuring one's soul by the tape of a world that looks on in amused contempt and pity. One ever feels his twoness—an American, a Negro; two souls, two thoughts, two unreconciled strivings; two warring ideals in one dark body, whose dogged strength alone keeps it from being torn asunder" (178). Through Edwin's parallel—and abbreviated—plot, Feinberg grapples with the complex intersection of race and gender passing (Edwin can only pass along one axis). On racial passsings and their intersection with those of gender and sexuality (but not of transsexuality and with no mention of *Stone Butch Blues*), see Elaine K. Ginsberg, ed., *Passing and the Fictions of Identity* (Durham: Duke University Press, 1996). The essays in this volume suggest that that mirror scenes are also paradigmatic in narratives of racial passing. Compare, for instance, the remarkable coincidence of textual tropes and concerns (mirror scenes, the question of home, even the undecidability of genre) between Samira Kawash's essay on James Weldon Johnson ("*The Autobiography of an Ex-Colored Man:* [Passing for] Black Passing for White," pp. 59–74) with my reading of Feinberg here. Perhaps this striking cross-

over of critical concerns hints at a literary influence of narratives of racial passing on *Stone Butch Blues*.

25. As in *The Well of Loneliness* the dreams constitute the dis-placed body narrative of the text: the kernel that is the narrative's signifying "home."

26. Leslie Feinberg, *Transgender Liberation: A Movement Whose Time Has Come* (New York: World View, 1992), p. 6. Biddy Martin and Chandra Talpade Mohanty suggest that home is a prominent trope particularly in lesbian autobiographies by women of color because such writers "cannot easily assume 'home' within feminist communities as they have been constituted" ("Feminist Politics: What's Home Got to Do with It?" in *Feminist Studies/Critical Studies*, ed. Teresa de Lauretis [Bloomington: Indiana University Press, 1986], p. 192). The significance of home for transgendered subjects who come from within the lesbian and gay community may be powerfully parallel. For other discussions of home and departure in autobiographies by lesbians and/or women of color, see Leigh Gilmore and Marcia Aldrich, "Writing Home: 'Home' and Lesbian Representation in Minnie Bruce Pratt," *Genre* 25 (1992): 25–46; Julia Watson, "The Politics of Gender in Lesbian and Heterosexual Women's Autobiographies," in *De/Colonizing the Subject: The Politics of Gender in Women's Autobiography*, ed. Sidonie Smith and Julia Watson (Minneapolis: Minnesota University Press, 1992), pp. 139–168; Caren Kaplan, "Resisting Autobiography: Out-Law Genres and Transnational Feminist Subjects," in *De/Colonizing the Subject*, ed. Smith and Watson, pp. 115–137.

27. Feinberg's life can be gleaned both from her nonfictional writings—the pamphlet, *Journal of a Transsexual* (New York: World View, 1980), the autobiographical frame of *Transgender Warriors*—and from various reviews and interviews. See in particular: Victoria A. Brownworth, "Stone Butch But Not Blue: Leslie Feinberg and Transgender Liberation," *Deneuve* (July/August 1993): 24–26, and the excellent, revealing, three-part interview by Kevin Horwitz, "Politics & Gender: An Interview with Leslie Feinberg," *FTM Newsletter* 23 (May 1993): 1–3, *FTM Newsletter* 24 (July 1993): 10–11, *FTM Newsletter* 26 (February 1994): 13–14.

28. Leslie Feinberg, E-mail to the author, 15 September, 1996. I am grateful to Feinberg for hir generous engagement with my writings on hir work, for hir permission to reprint hir comments here, and above all for hir indulgence toward my reading *Stone Butch Blues* on the subject of genre.

29. Horwitz, "Politics & Gender," *FTM Newsletter* 26, p. 13; my emphasis.

30. Leigh Gilmore, *Autobiographics: A Feminist Theory of Women's Self-Representation* (Ithaca: Cornell University Press, 1994), p. 96. For other work on this generic border, see Janice Morgan and Colette T. Hall, eds., *Redefining Autobiography in Twentieth-Century Women's Fiction: An Essay Collection* (New York: Garland, 1991).

31. If early feminist autobiography criticism emphasized the differences between women's and men's autobiographies (see, for instance, Estelle Jelinek, ed., *Women's Autobiography: Essays in Criticism* [Bloomington: Indiana University Press, 1980]), and later work examined how these differences had constructed the very canon of autobiography (Domna C. Stanton, "Autogynography: Is the Subject Different?" in

Domna C. Stanton, ed., *The Female Autograph: Theory and Practice of Autobiography from the Tenth to the Twentieth Century* [Chicago: Chicago University Press, 1987], pp. 3–20), more recent work has questioned the costs of continuing to polarize genre according to gender. In this last category Nancy K. Miller's call for the development of "a way of thinking flexible enough to accommodate styles of self-production that cross the lines of the models we have established" resonates in the context of the double-leveled crossings of *Stone Butch Blues* (Nancy K. Miller, "Representing Others: Gender and the Subjects of Autobiography," *differences* 6, no. 1 [1994]: 17).

32. Horwitz, "Politics & Gender," *FTM Newsletter* 26, p. 13. In the preface to her *Trash* (London: Penguin, 1990), Dorothy Allison describes how she came to produce about her comparably painful life a kind of writing that is "not biography and yet not lies" (6).

33. Raymond, *The Transsexual Empire*, pp. xxx, xxxii, xxx.

34. Leslie Feinberg, E-mail to the author, 24 September, 1996.

35. Philippe Lejeune, "The Autobiographical Pact," in *On Autobiography*, ed. Paul John Eakin, trans. Katherine Leary (Minneapolis University Press, 1989), p. 13.

36. Lejeune, "The Autobiographical Pact (bis)," in *On Autobiography*, p. 125.

37. In a wonderful illustration of the alternative autobiographic fictional pact Feinberg draws up with hir readers, undergraduate students at Hunter College, CUNY, found in this front-cover photograph justification for reading *Stone Butch Blues* as autobiographical even while acknowledging its fictional surround. They discovered a scar above Feinberg's eyebrow, correlating this with a scar in the same place that the fictional Jess acquires (see *Stone Butch Blues*, p. 57). In the absence of identity between authorial and protagonist's names, the apparent identity of the scar (the photograph as mug shot) functioned as their "proof" that the text *must have been* (in spite of its fictionality) the "true story" of Feinberg's life. Thanks to Lorna Smedman for inviting me to visit her dazzling class.

38. Paul de Man, *The Rhetoric of Romanticism* (New York: Columbia University Press, 1984), p. 70.

39. Ibid., p. 76.

40. See Jacques Derrida's "The Law of Genre," *Critical Inquiry* 7 (1980): 55–81: " 'Genres are not to be mixed' . . . 'Do,' 'Do not' says 'genre,' the word 'genre,' the figure, the voice, or the law of genre" (56). Turning the law in on itself, Derrida's essay isolates a moment of mixing in Maurice Blanchot's *La Folie du Jour* in which the masculine "I" apparently shifts into or passes for a feminine subject: a display of grammatical, genderic, and generic translation to which Derrida refers significantly as "transsexuality" (76). Derrida's critique of the interdiction on mixture will become key to Stone's vision of posttranssexuality.

41. Leslie Feinberg, E-mail to the author, 24 September, 1996.

42. Ibid.

43. Feinberg, *Journal of a Transsexual*, p. 6.

44. Rita Felski, "Fin de Siècle, Fin de Sexe: Transsexuality, Postmodernism, and the Death of History," *New Literary History* 27 (1996): 341–342.

45. Ibid., p. 347

46. On this subject see Rosi Braidotti's conception of sexual difference feminism versus the recent "turn to gender" symptomized by Judith Butler's work (Rosi Braidotti with Judith Butler [interview], "Feminism by any Other Name," *differences* 6, nos. 2/3 [1994]: 27–61). On what would seem to be the most obvious split between these two projects, Braidotti remarks: "The starting point for the project of sexual difference is the political will to assert the specificity of the lived, female experience. This involves the refusal to disembody sexual difference through the valorization of a new allegedly 'postmodern' and 'antiessentialist' subject; in other words, the project of sexual difference engages a will to reconnect the whole debate on difference to the bodily existence and experience of women" (40). Braidotti's denotation "female feminist" appearing throughout her *Nomadic Subjects: Embodiment and Sexual Difference in Contemporary Theory* (New York: Columbia University Press, 1994) (not therefore a tautology in the current theoretical figuration of gender-crossing) should be understood as an example of the "political will" of the sexual difference project to reembody the feminist subject.

47. Raymond, The Transsexual Empire, p. xxix.

48. Ann Bolin, "Transcending and Transgendering: Male-to-Female Transsexuals, Dichotomy, and Diversity," in *Third Sex, Third Gender: Beyond Sexual Dimorphism in Culture and History* ed. Gilbert Herdt (New York: Zone, 1994), pp. 482, 485.

49. Stone, "The 'Empire' Strikes Back," p. 295.

Epilogue: Transsexuality in Photography—Fielding the Referent

1. Mario Martino with harriet, *Emergence: A Transsexual Autobiography* (New York: Crown, 1977), p. xii.

2. Timothy Dow Adams, "Introduction: Life Writing and Light Writing; Autobiography and Photography," *Modern Fiction Studies* 40, no. 3 (Fall 1994): 459–492.

3. Roland Barthes, *Roland Barthes by Roland Barthes* (1975), trans. Richard Howard (New York: Farrar, 1977).

4. Ibid., p. 56.

5. Paul John Eakin, *Touching the World: Reference in Autobiography* (Princeton: Princeton University Press, 1985), pp. 3–23.

6. Eakin, *Touching the World*, pp. 18–19; Roland Barthes, *Camera Lucida* (1980), trans. Richard Howard, (London: Vintage, 1993), p. 87. Page numbers of further citations to *Camera Lucida* will appear directly in the text after *CL*.

7. Eakin, *Touching the World*, p. 4.

8. Katherine Cummings, *Katherine's Diary: The Story of a Transsexual* (Port Melbourne, Victoria: Heinemann, 1992), pp. 13, 14.

9. Bernice L. Hausman, *Changing Sex: Transsexualism, Technology, and the Idea of Gender* (Durham: Duke University Press, 1995), p. 154.

10. Leslie Feinberg, *Journal of a Transsexual* (New York: World View, 1980), p. 10.

11. Mario Costa, *"Coccinelle": Reverse Sex*, trans. Jules J. Block (London: Challenge, n. d.), pp. 47–48.

12. Ibid., p. 38.

13. Teresa de Lauretis, "Film and the Visible," in *How Do I Look? Queer Film and Video*, ed. Bad Object-Choices (Seattle: Bay Press, 1991), pp. 223–263.

14. Renée Richards with John Ames, *Second Serve: The Renée Richards Story* (New York: Stein and Day, 1983), pp. 189, 228.

15. Kim Harlow/Bettina Rheims, *Kim*, trans. Paul Gould (Munich: Kehayoff Verlag, 1994). Page numbers of citations will appear directly in the text.

16. Clare Hemmings, E-mail to the author, 20 March, 1996.

17. Loren Cameron, *Body Alchemy: Transsexual Portraits* (Pittsburgh, Cleis, 1996), p. 12.

18. I am indebted to LaGrace and Nataf for sharing and discussing their work with me.

19. If Robert Mapplethorpe's investment in the black penis is the obvious artistic intertext for this genital focus of LaGrace and Nataf, Kobena Mercer's layered reading of Mapplethorpe's photographs—his complication of the antitheses between subject and object, black body and white auteur in his brilliant revision of his critique of fetishism—is the critical precedent for my reading here. Kobena Mercer, "Reading Racial Fetishism: The Photographs of Robert Mapplethorpe," in *Fetishism as Cultural Discourse*, ed. Emily Apter and William Pietz (Ithaca: Cornell University Press, 1991), pp. 307–330.

20. Nancy K. Miller, *Getting Personal: Feminist Occasions and Other Autobiographical Acts*, (New York: Routledge, 1991), p. xiii; Adrienne Rich, " Notes Toward a Politics of Location," *Blood, Bread, and Poetry: Selected Prose 1979–1985* (New York: Norton, 1986), pp. 210–231.

index

Abraham, Nicolas, and Maria Torok, 36–38
Adams, Parveen, 64
Adams, Timothy Dow, 208
Allen, Robert, 130
Allison, Dorothy, 192, 257*n*32
Anzaldúa, Gloria, 23
Anzieu, Didier: *The Skin Ego*, 61, 65–67, 72–74, 76, 79–80, 243*n*30; *A Skin for Thought*, 242*n*12
Ashley, April, 216–19; cited, 83 (244*n*38), 116 (247*n*22)
Autobiography: conversion and identity in, 119; feminist criticism of, 256*n*31; and fiction, 191–92, 196–98; by lesbians of color, 256*n*26; narrative coherence of, 115–17, 121; parallels with photography, 208–10; retrospectiveness of, 103, 117; in sexual inversion, 142, 144; split subject in, 100–2, 125–26; as transsexual symptom, 9, 101, 103–7; *see also* Transsexual autobiographies

Barney, Natalie, in *The Well of Loneliness*, 156

Barthes, Roland, 209–11, 222
Beauvoir, Simone de, 29–30, 32–33
Benjamin, Harry, 9; in Nancy Hunt's *Mirror Image*, 124; preface to Christine Jorgensen's *A Personal Autobiography*, 126–27; in Renée Richards's *Second Serve*, 107–8
Bergman, David, 25
Billings, Dwight, and Thomas Urban, 7–8
Body: agnosia, 78, 84–85, 88, 109, 146; as constructed, 7, 62; ego/image, 41–44, 65, 78–80, 83–84, 94–96; materiality of 6–7, 62, 66, 86, 89; phantom limb, 84–85, 88; in poststructuralist theory, 7, 12–13, 66, 92–93, 96; and proprioception, 78, 245*n*55; *see also* Fetishism; Sex; Transsexuality
Body narrative: hysteria as, 152; and photography, 234; sexual inversion as, 142; and *Stone Butch Blues*, 194, 256*n*25; transsexual autobiography as, 120; transsexuality as, 12, 16, 103–5; in *The Well of Loneliness*, 165, 256*n*25

Bogdan, Robert, 112–13
Bolin, Ann, 88–89, 202
Bornstein, Kate, 174–75, 253n8
Braidotti, Rosi, 92, 258n46
Brodribb, Somer, 13
Bullough, Vern, 142
Bullough, Vern, and Bonnie, 250n14
Burkholder, Nancy, 171
Butler, Judith: on feminism and lesbian and gay studies, 55–60; on sex, 28–29, 33–45, 67, 258n46; theory of gender performativity, 27–33, 153; and transgender, 5–6, 24–27, 43, 56–57; and transsexuality, 6, 27, 33, 43, 45–57, 241n35, 241n41
——Works: "Against Proper Objects," 55–60, 238n5; *Bodies That Matter*, 27–29, 32, 41–42, 44–55, 67; "Contingent Foundations," quoted, 34; "Critically Queer," 24, 26, 30–32, 34; *Excitable Speech*, 239n17; *Gender Trouble*, 24–36, 38–45, 59, 65, 66, 173, 240n18; *Gender Trouble*, quoted, 64 (242n5); "Melancholy Gender/Refused Identification," 34 (240n24); *Subjects of Desire*, quoted, 21

Cameron, Loren, 230–31
Camp, 25–26, 32, 44
Camp Trans, 171–73, 175–77
Case, Sue-Ellen, 23
Castle, Stephanie, 117, 247n30
Castle, Terry, 167
Cauldwell, David, 9
Cavafy, C. P., quoted, 171
Chauncey, George, 138
Coccinelle, 220–22
Conn, Canary, 126–27; quoted, 121 (247n29)
Cossey, Caroline, 77, 89, 222–24
Cowell, Roberta, 131
Cummings, Katherine, 86–88, 99, 211–15

Davis, Kathy, 81–82
De Lauretis, Teresa, 23, 223; on *The Well of Loneliness*, 136, 160–61, 166, 249n10, 252n40
De Man, Paul, 197–98
Derrida, Jacques, 13, 28, 257n40
Dillon, Michael, 10, 165, 167; *Self: A Study in Endocrinology and Ethics*, 152–55
Dollimore, Jonathan, 23
Drag, 24, 26, 28, 30, 34; and transsexuality, 48, 57–58, 176; *see also* Butler, Judith; Camp
Du Bois, W. E. B., in *Stone Butch Blues*, 186, 255n24

Eakin, Paul John, 210
Eighner, Lars, quoted, 171
Ekins, Richard, and Dave King, 26–27 (239n13)
Elbe, Lili, 124
Elliot, Beth, quoted, 173 (253n7)
Ellis, Havelock: "Commentary" in *The Well of Loneliness*, 157, 249n10; *Sexual Inversion*, 141, 147–51, 155
Epstein, Julia, 61, 144
Epstein, Julia, and Kristina Straub, 14

Faderman, Lillian, 136, 249n10
Fallowell, Duncan, and April Ashley, *see* Ashley, April
Fanon, Frantz, 245n55
Fausto-Sterling, Ann, 63
Feinberg, Leslie; 177, 190, 202–3; *Journal of a Transsexual*, 68, 200, 217–18; *Transgender Liberation*, quoted, 189–90 (256n26); *Transgender Warriors*, 199, 253n8, 255n22; *Transgender Warriors*, quoted, 177 (254n15), 183 (255n23)
——*Stone Butch Blues*: genre of, 190–99; transgender in, 11, 171, 177–90; and *The Well of Loneliness*, 169

Felski, Rita, 200–2
Ferenczi, Sandor, in *The Well of Loneliness*, 156
Fetishism: and medicine, 92–93; and poststructuralist theory, 13; and race, 23, 232–33, 259n20; and transsexuality, 90, 232–34
Foucault, Michel, 13, 35, 138, 145
Franks, Claudia Stillman, 248n5
Freud, Sigmund, 13, 35; *Civilization and Its Discontents*, 255n21; *The Ego and the Id*, 36–37, 40–43, 65, 79, 240n31, 241n32; "Mourning and Melancholia," 36; "On Narcissism," 240n31; "Psychoanalytic Notes Upon an Autobiographical Account of a Case of Paranoia," 151; "Psychogenesis of a Case of Homosexuality in a Woman," 150, 252n42; "A Special Type of Object Choice Made by Men," 252n42
Fry, Jane, 112–13

Garber, Marjorie, 14, 23, 90, 92
Gilbert, Sandra, and Susan Gubar, 137
Gilmore, Leigh, 191
Grant, Julia, 89
Grealy, Lucy, 83–84, 88
Green, Richard, 251n21
Griggs, Claudine, 116
Grosz, Elizabeth, 12, 64–66, 84
Gusdorf, Georges, 99, 116–17, 121, 125

Halberstam, Judith, 14, 243n18, 254nn17, 18
Hall, Radclyffe, *The Well of Loneliness*, 10; lesbian criticism on, 135–37, 249n10; and *Orlando*, 168–69, 253n52; role in emergence of transsexuality of, 140, 155; sexology in, 155–58; and *Stone Butch Blues*, 169; as a transsexual narrative, 155–68; trial of, 135–36, 168

Hamburger, Christian, Georg K Stürup, and E. Dahl-Iversen, quoted, 69 (243n22)
Harlow, Kim, 83, 226–30
Hausman, Bernice L.: constructionist theory of transsexuality, 7–8; relation to transsexuality, 112, 132–33; on transsexual autobiographies, 114–15, 118–19, 130–31; on transsexual diagnosis, 104–5; on transsexual photographs, 215–16, 220–22
Heath, Stephen, 35
Hekma, Gert, 249n8
Heterosexuality, 30–31, 39–40, 44, 241n36; and transsexuality, 48
Hewitt, Paul, 118, 215–16
Hirschfeld, Magnus, 141, 152 (251n29)
Homosexuality: medicalization of, 10, 137–38; and transgender, 11, 22, 24, 31, 137–38; and transsexuality, 9, 106, 146–47, 153–54
hooks, bell, 50–51, 54, 55
Hunt, Nancy, *Mirror Image*: and Jan Morris, 124, 245n2; mirror images in, 101–2; as an odyssey, 116 (247n22); opening of, 127

Ian, Marcia, 13
Irigaray, Luce, 79

Jacobus, Mary, 152
Jelinek, Estelle, 256n31
Jorgensen, Christine: diagnosed as transvestite, 69, 152; introduction and preface in *A Personal Autobiography*, 126–27; narrative model for transsexuals, 124, 247n30

Kaufman, Gershen, 179
Kawash, Samira, 255n24
Kennedy, Hubert, 250n19
Krafft-Ebing, Richard von, *Psychopathia Sexualis*, 141, 142, 144–47, 150; in Renée Richards's *Second*

Serve, 125, 251*n*36; in *The Well of Loneliness*, 157
Kristeva, Julia, 39
Kroker, Arthur, and Marilouise, 14, 90–91

Lacan, Jacques, 13, 35, 42, 79, 80, 100, 105, 240*n*31, 242*n*13; and Didier Anzieu, 66, 242*n*12
LaGrace, Del, 230–35
Lejeune, Philippe, 196; quoted, 4 (237*n*2)
Lindsay, Cécile, 12
Livingston, Jennie, 50–55, 241*n*40; *see also Paris is Burning*
Long, Scott, 25
Lorde, Audre, 93–95
Lothstein, Leslie, 111, 246*n*17, 247*n*37, 251*n*24

McClain, Jerry/Jerri, 118
Mapplethorpe, Robert, 23, 259*n*20
Martin, Biddy, 31, 42, 239*n*17
Martin, Biddy, and Chandra Talpade Mohanty, 256*n*26
Martino, Mario, *Emergence*: clinical narrative in, 128–29, 247*n*37; mirror images in, 100, 102; photographs in, 207–8, 215–17; sex reassignment in, 82, 89
Mercer, Kobena, 23, 259*n*20
Michigan Womyn's Music Festival, *see* Camp Trans
Miller, Nancy K., 234, 257*n*31; quoted, 15 (238*n*21)
Millot, Catherine, 13–14, 64; quoted, 63 (242*n*3)
Minkowitz, Donna, 175, 176
Mishima, Yukio, quoted, 61
Moraga, Cherríe, 23
Morris, Jan, *Conundrum*: body image in, 68, 83 (244*n*38); cited in other transsexual texts, 124, 245*n*12; mirror image in, 99–100; retro-activity in, 117–18; transition as a journey in, 116; and transsexual history, 130–31

Namaste, Ki, 241*n*41
Narrative: and diagnosis of transsexuality, 9, 113; role in emergence of transsexuality of, 10, 158; and transition, 5, 102, 116–17; *see also* Autobiography; Body Narrative
Nataf, Zachary I., 230–34, 253*n*8
Nathanson, Donald, 255*n*21
Newton, Esther, on *The Well of Loneliness*: and history, 136, 249*n*10; and lesbian butch in, 137; and mirror scene in, 252*n*40; and *Orlando*, 253*n*52; as not transsexual, 158, 166

Olds, Sharon, 80–81
Orlan, 61–64, 242*n*13
Orlando (Virginia Woolf and Sally Potter), 168–69
O'Rourke, Rebecca, citation from, 135
Oudshoorn, Nelly, 250*n*13

Paris is Burning (Jennie Livingston), 44–55
Parkes, Adam, 252*n*41; quoted, 168 (253*n*51)
Passing: and coming out, 11; and the loss of the past, 130–31, 187–88; preoperative, 75; reconstructive surgery as the ultimate, 89, 92; reevaluation of, in transgender, 172–74, 184–87, 253*n*8; and Venus Xtravaganza, 46, 49; *see also* Reading
Pauly, Ira, 105–6, 109, 146–47
Photography: and the body, 210–11; as evidence, 220, 222; as referential, 12, 209–10, 213, 218, 220; *see also* Transsexual autobiographies
Poststructuralist theory: antiessentialism in, 16; the body in,

12–13, 66; and referentiality, 15, 209–11; transsexuality in, 13–14
Pratt, Minnie Bruce, 177; quoted, 171
Prince, Virginia, 254n14

Queer theory: and camp, 25; and transgender, 5–6, 21–24, 26, 29, 57, 241n41; and transsexuality, 6, 56–57; *see also* Butler, Judith; Sedgwick, Eve Kosofsky

Radford, Jean, 136, 166, 249n10
Raymond, Janice: on *Stone Butch Blues*, 194–95; on transgender, 202; on transsexuality, 7–9, 90, 92, 171–72
Reading: photography's resistance to, 222–23, 226; Sandy Stone on, 172–74; and transgender, 187; during transition, 2; and transsexual autobiographies, 129–31; and transsexual diagnosis, 108, 152
Rees, Mark, 120
Reich, June L., 14
Rheims, Bettina, 226–29
Rich, Adrienne, 92–93, 234
Richards, Renée, *Second Serve*: body image in, 77; clinical narrative in, 125, 127–28, 247n37; diagnosis in, 107–8; mirror images in, 99, 102–3; photographs in, 223, 225–27; surgery in, 89; transition in, 121–24
Riddell, Carroll, 9
Rivière, Joan, 35
Rubin, Gayle, 57, 58, 166–67, 171, 179
Ruehl, Sonja, 136, 156, 166, 249n10
Rule, Jane, 136
Rutherford, Erica, 108–9, 211–12

Sacks, Oliver, 78–80, 84–85
St. Laurent, Octavia, 51–54
Sander, August, quoted, 207
Schaefer, Leah Cahan, and Connie Christine Wheeler, 111, 174 (254n11), 254n20

Schafer, Roy, 36, 42, 241n32
Sedgwick, Eve Kosofsky, 31, 57; *Between Men,* 22, 25; *Epistemology of the Closet,* 22; Judith Butler on, 238n5; "Queer Performativity," 24, 27, 255n21; *Tendencies,* 21, 23, 27–28, 96
Sedgwick, Eve Kosofsky, and Adam Frank, 15–17, 255n21
Segal, Lynne, 7, 241n36
Sex: deliteralization of, 38–40, 43, 63–65; materiality of, 43–44
Sex reassignment surgery, 63–64, 66–67, 80–92; earliest forms of, 10, 141; male-to-female, 80–81, 86; mastectomy, 82, 89; phalloplasty, 10, 74–75, 86–89, 92, 102, 128–29, 165
Sexology, *see* Ellis, Havelock; Hirschfeld, Magnus; Krafft-Ebing, Richard von; Sexual inversion; Ulrichs, Karl Heinrich
Sexual inversion: in Freud, 150–51; in lesbian and gay history, 10, 137–38; transgendered paradigms of, 138–50; in transsexual history, 10, 140–41
Silence of the Lambs (Jonathan Demme), 67–68
Silko, Leslie Marmon, 2–3; quoted, 1
Silverman, Kaja, 245n55
Simmons, Dawn Langley, 89
Skin; as interface, 65, 71–73, 75, 243n24; and race, 95–96, 245n55; second, 75, 112; and vision, 78–79; *see also* Anzieu, Didier; Sex reassignment surgery; Surgery
Smith-Rosenberg, 136, 253n52
Stallybrass, Peter, and Allon White, 252n43
"Standards of Care," 106
Stanton, Domna C., 256n31
Stimpson, Catharine, 136, 156, 166, 249n10
Stoller, Robert, 247n37

Stone, Sandy, 107, 125, 172–73, 203, 245*n*2
Surgery: cosmetic, 81–82; mastectomy, 93–95; plastic, 81–82; reconstructive, 83–84; and tissue engineering, 91–92; *see also* Sex reassignment surgery

Teena, Brandon, 175
Thompson, Raymond, *What Took You So Long?* body image in, 61, 69–77; diagnosis in, 109–10; photographs in, 222, 225–26; sex reassignment in, 82, 83 (244*n*38), 85–90; and therapy, 121
Transexual Menace, 174, 175
Transgender: etymology of, 176; as figure, 21–24, 26, 32, 44, 137–38, 150–51, 152, 200–2; and homosexuality, 11, 146–48; medicalization of, 10, 139–40; movement, 11, 171–76; and race, 23, 255*n*24; relation to queer, 31–32, 56, 173–77, 179, 189–90, 201; and shame of gender dysphoria, 179–81; studies, 26–27, 56, 60, 201–2, 205; *see also* Feinberg, Leslie; Queer theory; Transsexuality
Transphobia, 8, 47, 67
Transsexual autobiographies (published), 8, 9; body in, 67–77, 82–83, 85–90, 92–93; and clinical narrative, 114–15, 125–29; conformity of, 101–3, 115–17, 120–21; in journal form, 118; mirror scenes in, 99–103; photographs in, 12, 207–9, 211–29; readership, 129, 194; and retroaction, 117–20; transition in, 121–24
Transsexuality: and body image, 7, 43–44, 67–79, 82–83, 100, 142–43, 146, 163, 243*n*30; and case history, 113, 127–29, 139–52; and constructionism, 7–9, 133, 145, 149, 167; and cross-dressing, 102–3, 211; in cultural theory, 7–8, 13–14, 63–64, 90–92; in *Diagnostic and Statistical Manual of Mental Disorders*, 81 (244*n*35), 104–7, 134, 174, 203, 246*n*10; distinct from queer, 59; emergence of, 9–10, 133–34, 139–52, 167; and feminism, 201; and homosexuality, 9, 153–54, 166, 167; and hormones, 66, 75, 141; importance of autobiography for, 9, 101–14, 120–21, 124–25, 142, 144; materiality of, 6, 12, 17, 66–67, 79, 89; and narrative, 5, 9–11, 46, 120, 124–25, 174; nonperformativity of, 27, 32–33, 153–54, 161–62, 252*n*41; popular conceptions of, 62–63, 67–68, 81; and race, 3, 46, 47, 50–54, 232–33; and realness, 11–12, 47–49, 162, 227; and transgender, 11–12, 173–77, 202–4; and transition, 1–5, 75, 99–91; transubstantiation of, 49–50, 52, 54–55, 62–63, 227–30, 234; and transvestism, 9, 69, 152 (251*n*29); *see also* Passing; Reading; Sex reassignment surgery; Sexual inversion; Transsexual autobiographies
Transvestism, *see under* Transsexuality
Tully, Bryan, 111, 177; citation from, 68 (243*n*21)
Tyler, Carole-Anne, 13

Ulrichs, Karl Heinrich, 143; in *The Well of Loneliness*, 157

Vicinus, Martha, 156

Warren, Barbara, quoted, 174 (253*n*8)
Wegener, Einar, *see* Elbe, Lili
Westphal, Carl, 140, 142
Whitlock, Gillian, 136, 166, 249*n*10

Wiesen-Cook, Blanche, 136, 249n10
Wittig, Monique, 30
Woolf, Virginia, 168–69; quoted, 135

Xtravaganza, Angie, 46, 55
Xtravaganza, Venus, 32, 33, 45–50, 53–55, 56, 57, 58, 241n41; *see also* *Paris is Burning*

Zhou, Jiang-Ning, Michael A. Hofman, Louis J. G. Gooren, and Dick F. Swaab, 243n30

GENDER AND CULTURE
A SERIES OF COLUMBIA UNIVERSITY PRESS
Edited by Nancy K. Miller

In Dora's Case: Freud, Hysteria, Feminism
Edited by Charles Bernheimer and Claire Kahane

Breaking the Chain: Women, Theory, and French Realist Fiction
Naomi Schor

Between Men: English Literature and Male Homosocial Desire
Eve Kosofsky Sedgwick

Romantic Imprisonment: Women and Other Glorified Outcasts
Nina Auerbach

The Poetics of Gender
Edited by Nancy K. Miller

Reading Woman: Essays in Feminist Criticism
Mary Jacobus

Honey-Mad Women: Emancipatory Strategies in Women's Writing
Patricia Yaeger

Subject to Change: Reading Feminist Writing
Nancy K. Miller

Thinking Through the Body
Jane Gallop

Gender and the Politics of History
Joan Wallach Scott

*The Dialogic and Difference:
"AnOther Woman" in Virginia Woolf and Christa Wolf*
Anne Herrmann

Plotting Women: Gender and Representation in Mexico
Jean Franco

Inspiriting Influences: Tradition, Revision, and Afro-American Women's Novels
Michael Awkward

Hamlet's Mother and Other Women
Carolyn G. Heilbrun

Rape and Representation
Edited by Lynn A. Higgins and Brenda R. Silver

Shifting Scenes: Interviews on Women, Writing, and Politics in Post-68 France
Edited by Alice A. Jardine and Anne M. Menke

Tender Geographies: Women and the Origins of the Novel in France
Joan DeJean

Modern Feminisms: Political, Literary, Cultural
Maggie Humm

Unbecoming Women: British Women Writers and the Novel of Development
Susan Fraiman

The Apparitional Lesbian: Female Homosexuality and Modern Culture
Terry Castle

George Sand and Idealism
Naomi Schor

Becoming a Heroine: Reading About Women in Novels
Rachel M. Brownstein

Nomadic Subjects: Embodiment and Sexual Difference in Contemporary Feminist Theory
Rosi Braidotti

Engaging with Irigaray: Feminist Philosophy and Modern European Thought
Edited by Carolyn Burke, Naomi Schor, and Margaret Whitford

A Certain Age: Reflecting on Menopause
Edited by Joanna Goldsworthy

Mothers in Law: Feminist Theory and the Legal Regulation of Motherhood
Edited by Martha Albertson Fineman and Isabelle Karpin

Critical Condition: Feminism at the Turn of the Century
Susan Gubar

Feminist Consequences: Theory for the New Century
Edited by Elisabeth Bronfen and Misha Kavka

Simone de Beauvoir, Philosophy, and Feminism
Nancy Bauer

Pursuing Privacy in Cold War America
Deborah Nelson

But Enough About Me: Why We Read Other People's Lives
Nancy K. Miller

Palatable Poison: Critical Perspectives on The Well of Loneliness
Edited by Laura Doan and Jay Prosser

Cool Men and the Second Sex
Susan Fraiman

Modernism and the Architecture of Private Life
Victoria Rosner

GENDER AND CULTURE READERS

Feminism and Sexuality: A Reader
Edited by Stevi Jackson and Sue Scott

Writing on the Body: Female Embodiment and Feminist Theory
Edited by Katie Conboy, Nadia Medina, and Sarah Stanbury

GPSR Authorized Representative: Easy Access System Europe, Mustamäe tee 50, 10621 Tallinn, Estonia, gpsr.requests@easproject.com

www.ingramcontent.com/pod-product-compliance
Lightning Source LLC
Chambersburg PA
CBHW070827300426
44111CB00014B/2474